POISON

Also by Jon Wells

Heat: A Firefighter's Story (James Lorimer & Company)
Sniper (John Wiley & Sons)

POISON

FROM STEELTOWN TO THE PUNJAB, THE TRUE STORY OF A SERIAL KILLER

JON WELLS

John Wiley & Sons Canada, Ltd.

Library and Archives Canada Cataloguing in Publication Data

Wells, Jon
    Poison : from Steeltown to the Punjab, the true story of a serial killer / JonWells.

ISBN 978-0-470-15548-6

    1. Dhillon, Sukhwinder. 2. Dhillon, Parvesh. 3. Khela, Ranjit. 4. Murder—Ontario—Hamilton. 5. Murder—India—Punjab. 6. Serial murderers—Ontario—Hamilton. 7. Serial murderers—India—Punjab. I. Title.

HV6248.D49W44 2008   364.152'30971352   C2008-902161-4

Production Credits
Cover: Ian Koo
Interior text design: Mike Chan
Typesetting: Tegan Wallace
Cover photo: Digital Vision/Getty Images
Printer: Quebecor World—Fairfield

John Wiley & Sons Canada, Ltd.
6045 Freemont Blvd.
Mississauga, Ontario
L5R 4J3

Printed in the United States

1 2 3 4 5 QW 12 11 10 09 08

This one is for Scott Petepiece. Even on my best writing day, I could never string words together that would adequately express the infinite value of your friendship over the years, in all of life's arenas.

TABLE OF CONTENTS

Preface

In the fall of 2001 I was asked to write a series on the crimes of a serial poisoner for *The Hamilton Spectator*. To that point, I had enjoyed the variety of writing at the newspaper. Highlights included covering the U.S. presidential race in Washington, L.A., New York and Miami, Pierre Trudeau's funeral in Montreal, the crash of United Airlines Flight 93 in rural Pennsylvania on 9/11, and following Tiger Woods over four days at the Canadian Open. When approached with this new task, I wasn't sure I even wanted to focus on a single story over the long haul. Soon enough I understood the expectations. Editor-in-Chief Dana Robbins told me to craft a series that, long down the road in my career, I'd look back on as "the best thing I ever wrote." Seven years later, the *Poison* story might just qualify; without question I could never have imagined a more exhilarating creative experience.

I worked on the piece almost exclusively for over a year. For inspiration, early on I posted a color photo of Parvesh Dhillon, the killer's first victim, at my desk. Her beautiful face and haunting green-blue eyes looked at me every day. I quickly discovered the story had everything: a greedy and lecherous killer; dashing detectives driven to hunt him down across the globe; dynamic prosecutors and defenders battling through a protracted trial full of twists and turns. The question was, how to do it all justice given the confines of daily newspaper journalism?

I had dreamed of writing a book since I was a teenager, had even penned a couple of spy "novels" in my English journal at A. B. Lucas high school in London, Ontario. With Dana establishing the sky as the limit, from the start I wanted to write it long, taking as my inspiration both mystery fiction and the novelistic journalism of my hero, Tom Wolfe. I told few colleagues of my ambition, and half expected that at some point an editor would see a draft then tell me to scrap it and write a conventional five-part report. Instead, they let me write my book.

All of the detail in *Poison* is true, based entirely on reportage. Research took me through piles of court transcripts and police

investigative documents. I conducted more than 70 interviews
—including detectives, lawyers, and the presiding judge—and
hired a Punjabi interpreter so I could talk with the families of
victims in Canada and India. I also spent two blazing hot weeks in
the Punjab with photographer Scott Gardner, where we retraced
the steps of the killer and those of Canadian and Indian investigators who chased his shadow there, from chaotic cities to dusty
villages. Documenting what we saw, heard, smelled, and felt was
a writer's nirvana.

In the end the story came out as I had hoped. *Poison* broke
new ground in print journalism, running in the *Spec* every day
over five weeks. It won a National Newspaper Award (Canada's
Pulitzer's) and I have now edited, polished, and updated it for this
book—the book I set out to write from the start.

As it happened, *Poison* was a beginning for me, not an end.
I have written six more book-length narratives, but the original
experience remains a part of me that never fades—and neither
does the face of Parvesh, who still looks at me across my desk each
time my fingers touch the keyboard.

Jon Wells
Hamilton, Ontario

ACKNOWLEDGMENTS

I want to express gratitude to Don Loney, Executive Editor at John Wiley & Sons, for making this book possible, and to Andrew Borkowski for his assistance editing the manuscript. I thank Dana Robbins for giving me the opportunity to tackle the original *Poison* story for *The Hamilton Spectator*, and both Dana and Roger Gillespie for their encouragement and guidance. Also for their contributions to the original story in the *Spectator*, thanks to Dan Kislenko, Douglas Haggo, and Bob Hutton; Dan for his support and editing of the project, Doug for his impeccable copy editing, and Bob for his design.

The research journey to India was the trip of a lifetime, and I was fortunate to experience it with the brilliant photographer Scott Gardner, who is also quite simply a great road trip partner. Kevin Dhinsa, Crown prosecutors Brent Bentham and Tony Leitch, defense lawyer Russell Silverstein, and Justice Stephen Glithero were invaluable sources. I thank Punjabi interpreter Neeta Johar, and, in India, the indispensable Inspector Subhash Kundu, who, among other things, helped us find villages that do not exist on maps. As always I thank Pete Reintjes for his assistance. And I reserve special thanks for Warren Korol, the lead detective on the case with Hamilton Police, for investing his trust in me when his initial instincts surely urged otherwise.

POISON

CHAPTER 1 ~ DEATH GRIN

"Kuchila."

The Punjabi shopkeeper cocked his head, feigning puzzlement. The customer repeated the word, more phonetically this time—"koo-chi-la." The wide, dark eyes seemed to convey both anger and confusion. In India, those meeting him for the first time noticed a peculiar light in them—the literal English translation of the word describing it would be "too sharp," but what they meant was the dark side of clever. Wicked.

An aromatic cocktail filled the hot air in claustrophobic Sarafa Bazaar, in a city called Ludhiana, in the northern Indian province of Punjab—samosas frying in oil, warm bananas, roasting corn, incense, the sweet pungency of burning garbage, and the shaving cream lathered on perspiring faces of Hindu men on the sidewalk, ready to be scraped by rust-stained blades. Sikhs in colorful turbans rode scooters through teeming crowds, weaving around rumbling rickshaws that spewed diesel exhaust into the soupy haze, announcing their passage with the dominant sound of India's cities—the horn. The turban, worn atop bundled hair, is a sacred cloth for Sikh men, a symbol of their violent history of survival. At nearly 10 meters when unwound, it is long enough to cover a Sikh man's body if he dies in righteous battle.

The customer was a Sikh. But he did not wear the turban. Thick in the chest and shoulders, full stomach straining against the shirt, his size loomed like an insult among the smaller Indian men. Ink-black hair styled longer in the back, beard trimmed, he looked like a foreigner next to orthodox Sikh men who let their hair and beards grow as a sign of humbleness before God.

Raw *kuchila* was available in the market to those who were persistent. The seeds are brown, rough textured and round, the size of a walnut but flat. The trees that bear them grow along the Coromandel coast on India's southeastern tip. The botanical name is *Strychnos nux-vomica*. In India's homeopathic lore, a refined version of *kuchila* (the English word is strychnine) taken in precise, highly diluted quantities is said to stimulate the senses, invigorate muscles, even enhance sexual satisfaction. Consumed incorrectly, the result is something entirely different.

On the trip back to Canada, he cleared customs at Pearson International Airport in Toronto. He spoke quickly in a nasal voice pitched higher than his burly physique suggested. He was an excellent liar, the unblinking eyes conveying a guileless innocence. He returned to his home in Hamilton, the steel town on the western tip of Lake Ontario, southwest of Toronto.

Grind the seeds in the mortar and pestle into a white paste. Squeeze the tiny headache medicine capsule, pull apart the fragile casing. Dump some of the existing powder, dip a knife in the paste. Gingerly now, on the knife, into the capsule. It only takes a fraction of what you could fit on your fingernail. Slide the two halves of the capsule back together. Death is God's will.

* * *

Hamilton, Ontario
January 30, 1995

Sikh tradition dictated that Parvesh must not cut her hair, ever, and so she tied it back, trapping it. But after a shower, her hair, black as

Courtesy of the author

a moonless night, hung free, long and wet. Both girls in school, husband away, for the moment. She basked in the quiet, her migraines and back pain magically absent.

Parvesh Dhillon was a beautiful woman. Fragile smile, a gentle, regal aura, and skin that was a pale tan, like wood leached of its color by storms. Her teardrop-shaped eyes looked pale blue at first. No, they were more a drained aqua. The color seemed in the eye of

Parvesh Dhillon

the beholder, as though framed by the setting, the way water captures a sky's dark ceiling, golden dawn or dying blue, red and gray at sunset.

The odds were very much against Parvesh living at all. She grew up on the other side of the world in the Punjab, a male-dominated, son-revering culture. She was the first girl born and kept in her family in generations. Sikhs believe God wills everyone's life story. What would Parvesh's story be?

The brush gently tugged at the scalp, kneading her neck, a hypnotic massage. She savored the moment, sighed deeply, eyes shut, muscles loose. Her hair dry and ready to be tied, the rest of her day, and life, beckoned.

* * *

Teeth and fists clenched, it felt like every muscle flexed without pause, as though a bolt of lightning ripped through her spinal cord, igniting every fiber, raping the nervous system. Worst of all, Parvesh Dhillon had horrifying clarity of mind, intensified with a sense of dread. She saw her fate rush toward her like a train's light in a black tunnel.

"I am—dying," she moaned.

Senses on fire, eyes stung by blinding white light, ears ringing with the voices of gathered family members shouting her name. It was Monday, dinnertime. Parvesh lay on the living room rug but only her heels and back of her head touched the floor. Her back arched, every muscle contracting violently, teeth pressed together as though in a vise, freezing her face in a grotesque mask. *Risus sardonicus* was the Latin name the old forensic pathologists gave it: The sardonic smile. The death grin.

The Dhillons lived in Hamilton's east end, a suburb called Stoney Creek. Next door, Olga Vidal spread tomato sauce on homemade dough, added cheese, olives, and pepperoni. A panicked knock at the door. Olga's teenage daughter answered. It was Aman, Parvesh Dhillon's seven-year-old daughter. Her eyes were red and wet.

"My mom is dying!" Aman screamed. The teenager laughed, thinking Aman was joking. Aman ran past her to the kitchen.

"Don't say that, dear," Olga said.

Aman ran back out of the house, and Olga followed her next door. Inside the Dhillons' home, she saw her friend convulsing on the floor, spine bent, as though possessed by an evil spirit. The husband, Sukhwinder, called to his wife. "Parvesh! Parvesh!"

In Parvesh's state, sounds exploded in her ears, every sensation knifing sensors in the brain. Sukhwinder lowered a glass of water to her mouth, the water singeing her lips like molten steel. Olga dropped to her knees, gently taking Parvesh's foot in her hand, rubbing it, trying to bring comfort, but it only encouraged spasms.

Her stomach swelled like a balloon, then deflated. The aqua eyes focused on Olga, a light of recognition flashed. Parvesh tried to tell her something, tried so hard to process a signal from her oxygen-starved brain. A deep moan came from the back of her throat.

Soon she was, mercifully, nearly unconscious, her breathing labored, pale eyes flickering. The firefighters were there first, then a paramedic named Stephen Bell. A young woman, fingers clenched like talons; arched back, lips peeled back over gums in a sick grimace. En route to Hamilton General Hospital downtown, tight straps on trembling arms. Chest compressions. Two electric shocks from the life pack. Her eyelids quivered.

There was a chance, perhaps, to save her, but neither paramedics nor hospital staff had ever seen symptoms like this before. An immediate, strong dose of Valium or an anticonvulsant would help. A neuromuscular blocking agent could induce temporary paralysis by halting the extreme signals sent to muscles by her brain.

At the General she was placed on life support.

For the next four days she lay unconscious, displaying occasional muscle seizures and twitching. Perhaps Parvesh could still dream, her soul sweeping back home to the Punjab and the place called Kiratpur Sahib, ripples dancing in the Sutlej River, the water a green-gold in dying sunlight, surrounded by fields of elephant grass and sugar cane leaning with the wind. A verdant, tropical place invoking life—and death. It is the holy place where Sikhs sprinkle the ashes of their dead into water that is still and soft, warm to the touch. Then she glimpses the end of her golden dream, sees the orange inferno behind the iron door just as it slams shut, hears her brother weeping in the thick hot air at the river's edge.

Sikhs sprinkle ashes in the Sutlej River.

In the hospital, Parvesh's husband, Sukhwinder, gave his approval to remove her from life support on February 3. The four-day time lag from her collapse to death was unusual. Victims of that particularly exotic terror usually die within minutes, a few hours at most. But she wouldn't let go. Parvesh is a Punjabi name that means "entry." Parvesh had not been ready to exit this world, whatever the will of God. Or her killer.

* * *

Hamilton General Hospital
Forensic Pathology Department

The body lay on the cold metal table, the thick antiseptic odor of formaldehyde filling the air. Forensic pathologist Dr. David King began the autopsy. There was little blood; corpses don't bleed. It is protocol for a homicide detective investigating a murder to attend the autopsy, answer the forensic pathologist's questions, take notes. For a young or green cop, it can be difficult to stomach.

Years ago, when lax rules allowed for such things, detectives lit up
cigars in the autopsy room to mask the scent of death. But there
was no police officer in the room at Parvesh Dhillon's autopsy.
Police had not been called to investigate. The case belonged to
David King alone.

King, a slight, silver-haired man with round eyes, took the
electric saw in his hand, the circular blade rotating into a blur. To
the unschooled eye, an autopsy strips the human body of all mystery. The autopsy may seem an open book thanks to Hollywood;
the camera cutting in and out, flashing glimpses of tissue here,
a bullet hole there. In the real world the autopsy exists behind
a curtain. Forensic pathologists prefer it that way. It is science
they are engaged in, science of the most important kind: science
in pursuit of a killer's fingerprints. But they know that, to the
untrained eye, the autopsy flashes a rude fluorescent light on our
own mortality. The cadaver is made hollow, the internal wiring
exposed, handled, prodded, diced. Tissues, valves, membranes,
skin, bone. If there is a soul, a self, it is not here, not anymore.
To pull back that curtain for the public, they fear, would put the
practice itself at risk.

John Rennison

At 65 years old, David
King was retired. Techni-
cally he was, anyway, but
forensic pathologists with his
experience and professional
memory were rare. He had
a national reputation. Until
a replacement was found, he
agreed to stay on the job at
Hamilton General. Why had
this young woman died so
suddenly, violently, without
explanation? King examined
Parvesh's heart. There appeared
to be no disease, no scarring.
With a large knife he carved
off pieces of organs, including

Dr. David King, forensic pathologist

the liver, the organ that holds poison and drugs the longest. As he cut, he deposited bits of tissue into small plastic containers of fixing formula, so the samples would later harden, allowing him to slice thin layers for microscopic examination. He noticed that on Parvesh's hospital chart, staff had, as a matter of protocol, screened her blood for drugs and found nothing. But he also knew the hospital screen was limited in scope, unlike a detailed toxicology screen that can detect more than 100 drugs, poisons, and other compounds.

Poisoning is the most difficult homicide to detect and prosecute, which is the reason poisoners get away with murder more than other killers. And they are among the most difficult cases a forensic pathologist encounters. There are those rare occasions, certainly, when a quick glance at a victim can tell the tale: hair loss points to the presence of thallium and other heavy metals; constricted pupils to opiates and pesticides; garlic odor to arsenic; almond odor to cyanide; shoe polish odor to nitrobenzene; blue skin color to nitrates. The most common tip-off is a dark pink or cherry color in the skin or tissue suggesting carbon monoxide poisoning. Carbon monoxide is attracted to hemoglobin, the oxygen-carrying substance in red blood cells. The poison lowers the oxygen-carrying capacity of blood and saturates the hemoglobin, causing that dark hue in the skin. But it's a tricky game—redness can also suggest cyanide, or arsenic when it appears on intestinal tissue.

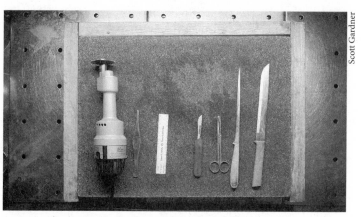

Scott Gardner

Autopsy tools: electric saw, knives, scalpels

King saw on the chart that Parvesh's medical history included severe headaches, visits to a Hamilton neurologist. But the CT scan had showed nothing irregular. After King removed the skull cap, he severed connections and lifted out the brain. It weighed just over a kilogram. There was no bruising, no abrasions. He placed the brain in fixing solution. He wanted to retain it for closer examination, even after the body had been returned to the family for cremation. It was an unusual step, as the brain isn't usually kept after the autopsy. But he was reaching for an answer now. Even with Parvesh Dhillon's body open before him, he had none.

* * *

A forensic pathologist is the death sleuth. It is the coroner, however, who is the public's representative for questionable or sudden deaths, deciding how to proceed in the early hours of an investigation. But the coroner is not necessarily an expert in death. In Ontario, he is typically a family doctor doing coroner work on the side, one of 400 or so in the province paid a flat $250 per case. Dr. Bashir Khambalia, a family physician in Hamilton's east end, was the reporting coroner when Parvesh Dhillon died. He was born in Zanzibar, an island off the coast of East Africa. In 1963, the year the island gained independence as a British protectorate, he left for medical school in Ireland. Khambalia, 50, was fluent in Gujarati, a western Indian dialect. Starting in 1995, he had handled about 200 coroner's cases a year as an Ontario coroner over a period of three years.

It is up to the attending hospital doctor to decide if a death should be referred to the coroner. Dr. Mary Devlin had treated Parvesh in hospital, was mystified by her death, and asked the chief neurologist for his opinion. His best guess was a massive seizure leading to cardiac arrest. But the constant muscle spasms and rigidity were unusual. Devlin called Khambalia soon after she was pronounced dead. He visited the morgue to view the body and decide what to do next. Hospital charts documented her final moments, included notes from residents, doctors, and nurses who logged in comments at specific times during her stay.

A coroner is not required to examine the notes, but it is normal practice to do so.

* * *

Monday, January 30
Nurse notes: Family reports Parvesh Dhillon ingested two capsules of
Fiorinal C1/4 given by a family member. Soon after, body observed
to exhibit rigidity, including an opisthotonic position lying on the
floor. Family reports clenched teeth. Loss of consciousness, fell to
the floor. Ambulance at scene at 16:20, approx. 20 minutes after
the episode, found her lying in the rec room. No pulse, skin warm,
cyanotic. No respiration, no blood pressure. Patient resuscitated and
transported to Hamilton General.

In E.R.: dilated fixed pupils, jerky movements in both arms.
Treatment: midazolam, dextrose in water, naloxone.

In ICU: subsequent to resuscitation, frequent myoclonic jerk-
ing, increased muscle tone and reflexes. Treatment: midazolam,
vecuronium. Lab report: severe acidosis, elevated blood lactate level.
Difficult to ventilate due to seizures. Tox screen: absence of barbi-
turates, acetone, ethanol, ethylene glycol, isopropanol, methanol,
phenobarbital, and salicylate. 21:00: myoglobinuria.

* * *

Tuesday, January 31
07:00: patient has spontaneous twitching. 08:00 body spontaneously
jerking. Neurological assessment at 11:30: increased muscle tone
but has myocloni–spasmatic –response to facial stimulation. 19:40
patient has brisk flexion of all limbs in response to stimuli.

* * *

Wednesday, February 1
CT scan 18:30. Normal.

* * *

Thursday, February 2
Neurology note: second CT scan of head shows subarachnoid hem-
orrhage, edema, transtentorial herniation.

* * *

Friday, February 3
Ms. Dhillon pronounced dead at 10:30.

* * *

Hospital staff had never seen anything like it, a woman so horribly sick for no apparent reason, and they'd never seen seizures
like that. Parvesh was "cyanotic" in her home, meaning her skin
turned blue. The reference in the notes to "myoglobinuria" meant
that Parvesh had spasmed so violently, and continually, that cells
from her overworked, shredded muscle fiber were found in her
urine, which became the color of tea. "Acidosis" referred to high
acidity in the muscles from overuse, a pH level of 6.75, the worst
doctors had seen in a patient who was still alive. Her muscles
produced so much lactic acid that her blood lactate level hit 10.6,
when the upper limit in most patients is 2. It was the highest the
ER doctors had ever seen.

There were two critical bits of information in the notes.
The first was the description of Parvesh's severe rigidity and
"opisthotonic" state. The word was scribbled messily on one
of the notes. It meant that her back was severely arched—an
unusual condition. The second was the hospital's own limited
drug screen, given to Parvesh upon her arrival, which showed no
barbiturates in her blood, even though an earlier note said her
husband reported that she had taken two prescription Fiorinal
headache capsules, which are barbiturates. Those facts were
contradictory. The staff report concluded that Parvesh died of
natural but unexplainable causes.

Khambalia ordered an autopsy. It was a routine decision. Going
that far was accepted protocol in 1995 for the sudden death of a
young adult. If a coroner does not report a death to police, they do

not get involved. There is an office in the Hamilton Police Service that liaises with the coroner, but it is up to the coroner to make the call. Khambalia ordered no further testing of Parvesh's blood or body tissue. He ordered nothing sent to the Centre of Forensic Sciences in Toronto for a more detailed toxicology screen. One day, coroners would be required to phone police and order blood screens for any questionable sudden death. Khambalia, trained as a family doctor, was following accepted procedure in 1995 and there were no alarm bells going off anywhere. Even seasoned specialists did not make the connections in Parvesh's death.

* * *

The Sikh woman bathed the body then rubbed white yogurt over the pale, cool skin of Parvesh Dhillon. Later the woman dressed her in Parvesh's finest clothes, a rose-colored dress, the head and hair covered. The funeral was February 8. The morning broke bitterly cold, winds whipping off Lake Ontario, the water charcoal beneath the ashen sky. Inside the Donald Brown Funeral Home on Lake Avenue in east Hamilton, Parvesh lay in an open casket. Even in death her face was radiant. The sobs of Parvesh's daughters, Aman, seven, and Harpreet, nine, accompanied the priest's Sikh readings.

Courtesy of the author

Parvesh and her daughters, Aman (left) and Harpreet

God is only One, He is obtained by the Grace of the True Guru/In whatever house meditation on God is practiced and His praises are sung.

Sing His praises and meditate upon Him in that house/You, please, sing the praises of my God, the Fearless/I am a sacrifice to the Song which gives perpetual peace.

Sikhs cremate their dead; the body is just a vessel of water and air. There is earthly reincarnation of the soul—but only for sinners. The goal for the just soul is to return to God at death, as one began at birth, to avoid the toil of hell on earth. The priest prays for the soul of the dead: forgive the deceased of sin; keep the soul with God always.

On the other side of Hamilton Harbor, across the Skyway bridge, past billowing smoke and lapping flames of steel mills, sat Bayview Crematorium. The casket arrived that afternoon, was carried into the chapel room. More prayers. The oven—what crematory officials call the "crematory retort"—was heard humming across the hall. The burner incinerates the casket and all contents. Afterward, brass fixtures and screws are separated, and surviving bones pulverized in a blender-like machine, then added to the ashes.

In Indian culture, sons are revered. And so, at a cremation, it is the eldest son of the deceased who pushes the burner switch. But Parvesh never had a boy. That meant it was up to her husband to do it. Sukhwinder Dhillon. His middle name was Singh, like most Sikh men, a symbol of the fundamental Sikh belief opposing the Hindu caste system, so that all should carry the same name to illustrate equality. Singh, in English, means lion. Another tenet of Sikhism is respect for women, especially your wife.

Dhillon and the other Sikh men carried the casket holding Parvesh from the chapel area to the brass door with the cross inscribed on it, then into the burner room. A wall of dry heat hit their faces, as though in a boiler room, the burner droning loudly. They lifted the casket, slid it into the burner. The black iron door shut. There was a tiny round window through which the orange flame was visible. The button on the wall was labeled "primary burner." Dhillon placed his thick finger on it and pushed, igniting 2,000 degrees of heat to swallow Parvesh's body. Dhillon left his wife's ashes at the crematory in a plain box with instructions that they be mailed to her brother, Seva, in India. His treatment of the ashes was, in Sikh culture, blasphemous, equivalent to a Christian urinating on a loved one's grave. A few days later Dhillon heard the voice on the phone from overseas shake with rage.

"Dhillon, if you have done anything to my sister, anything, I swear—" Seva, usually a warm, quiet man, was yelling now. The normally serene green eyes he shared with his sister burned. He knew Dhillon. Did not trust him.

"Veerji!" Dhillon interrupted, using a Punjabi term of affection that means brother. "I didn't do anything!"

Scott Gardner

"If you have, I will get you. I will see to that, I promise you."

With time, Seva's anger would fade, but sorrow never left him—sorrow and confusion. "Why, God?" Seva asked in prayer the day he took his sister's ashes to the holy Sutlej River at Kiratpur Sahib. "Why did you take her?"

Seva Singh Grewal, Parvesh's brother, at home in Ludhiana, India

CHAPTER 2 ~ CHASING DEMONS

Hamilton, Ontario
1967

The little boy's liquid-blue eyes stared out the car window. His dad, Maurice Korol, had parked his white Ford Meteor on the street in front of Mike and Sally's house on West 1st in Hamilton. Warren was six years old. Something was wrong. A pile of lumber, dumped right in the middle of Uncle Mike and Aunt Sally's driveway. What was that all about? And why did Aunt Sally look so upset? When Warren got a bit older he learned the truth. The unsolicited delivery was mob harassment. Big Uncle Mike Pauloski was a Hamilton cop, and the delivery was courtesy of one of Johnny "Pops" Papalia's goons.

Aunt Sally would receive crank phone calls late at night when Mike was on the clock. "I'm sorry to inform you, miss," the rough-edged voice began, "that Mike Pauloski's body is in the morgue." And then the next day, funereal flower arrangements arrived at the house, the card reading, "In Memory of Mike Pauloski." Black humor from Papalia, The Enforcer, Steeltown's most notorious Mafia chief. Or perhaps a chilling prophecy.

One time, Mike was actually home and answered the phone. "It's Pauloski," he growled. "I swear I won't rest until your balls are hanging on display."

He wasn't just any cop, but a famous cop in a time when cops were famous, founder of the Hamilton Police "morality squad." Big Mike, six-foot-four, 265 pounds, drove around Hamilton in a bread truck with spy holes cut out. He helped nail Papalia on the French Connection deal. Pauloski and his partner, Albert Welsh, showed up in New York City for the godfather's trial, and the sight of the pair in court enraged Pops.

Each year at the annual Hamilton Shriners parade, Mike led the way, holding aloft a sword. Standing in the crowd, front row, wide-eyed, worshipping Big Mike, was little Warren, his nephew, the glory of being a cop branded on his soul. In 1972, when Warren was 11, his uncle died young, killed by a drunk driver on Upper

James Street. Mobsters crashed the funeral. Could it be that their arch-enemy was really dead? No, the mob didn't kill Uncle Mike, but Warren never forgot, nor forgave, that bastard Papalia, who, years later, much to his chagrin, survived into old age, attaining a kind of grandfatherly celebrity aura in Hamilton.

Scott Gardner

Warren Korol

Twenty-four years later, in September 1996, the broad-shouldered homicide detective stared at the glowing screen of his computer with eyes that had a metallic core outlined by a ring of propane-flame blue. Warren Korol. On his office wall hung a framed old newspaper photo, black and white, just like the morality of the time. The photo showed Johnny Papalia, in flowing trench coat and dark glasses, holding a handkerchief over his mouth to hide from cameras, escorted along downtown King Street by plainclothes detectives and a couple of jacket-and-tie-wearing reporters. The tall cop at the far right side of the frame was Mike Pauloski. The photo inspired Warren Korol—big Mike and, in a different way, Pops himself, two symbols forever joined. The good and the bad. One to emulate, the other to pursue.

Hard to believe, but in 1996, at 35, Korol had already been a cop for nearly half his life. He started on the force in the cadet program at 18 when he was still playing football for the Hamilton Hurricanes. He graduated to officer status at 21. And now, as a plainclothes detective in the homicide branch, called Major Crimes, he had yet to tackle a high-profile case. That would all soon change. The cursor hopped across the computer screen as his fingers tapped at the keys:

I, Warren Korol, of the City of Hamilton, in the Province of Ontario am a Peace Officer employed by the Hamilton Police Service, working out of the Major Crime unit and I hold the rank of Detective.

Hamilton Spectator archives

Mike Pauloski (far right) escorts Johnny Papalia (handkerchief over face) downtown.

His late father Maurice was a hard-working, driven man who moved the family out west, toiled in the fishery and as a lumberjack before heading back east to Hamilton where jobs seemed more plentiful. Warren had not faced similar odds, so sought other challenges. Nobody in his family had a university degree. He would make that happen, one day. Korol, while still physically imposing, had carried 255 pounds on a six-foot-two frame until he decided change was in order and sheared 40 pounds.

Policing ran in his blood and, from the start, he wanted to work in homicide. Could there be a bigger challenge than chasing murder cases, serving as emissary for the living and the dead? Korol's ice cool was made for detective work. He emanated an easy, "hey-how-ya-doin'?" manner that put others at ease, with an omnipresent smirk and smiling eyes. Those around him reveled in sharing his confident glow. Korol seemed the type that, even after a day following death and chasing demons, would sleep soundly at night, comfortable in his own skin.

But working homicide carries a price: witnessing, up close, gaping bullet holes in skulls; finding a woman still wearing a white satin nightie in a ditch, body so decomposed identification seems impossible. Worst of all were the kids. They are the pure victims. Korol struggled with these experiences the most: a child shaken to death by a parent; meeting the three-year-old boy who spent a night in his house with the bloodied corpses of his dead mother and her boyfriend; Korol's first child autopsy, seeing a kid similar to his own three little ones split open on a metal table in the morgue. Then another, and another, five, ten, maybe 20 child postmortems by now. He didn't like to think of the numbers.

In a sense, by the fall of 1996, Warren Korol's best days on the job were behind him—the early smashmouth days as a raw, brash uniformed cop. Korol, barely out of his teens and still playing defensive line in football part time, gleefully drove around downtown in the paddy wagon. Hell, that was when you could still call the paddy wagon a paddy wagon and have no fear of offending politically correct sensibilities. Great days. On patrol Korol could enter a downtown bar at closing time, confront an unruly drunk, take a punch in the face, feel his cheekbones sink, eyes losing focus, pain flowing down the spine to the ankles. In those days he could reply in kind, and then some, with no fear that some gang punk would pull a gun or bury a machete blade in his skull, or that Korol himself would be convicted of assault.

Korol's philosophy was, what would the public expect of him? He was certain they would expect him to hit back when warranted. That's what happened one night at Hanrahan's when he worked vice and drugs. Korol split the curtain of cigaret smoke in the cave-like gloom of the Barton Street strip club, women on stage named Kenya and Montana gyrating before the vacant stares of the regular patrons. He approached a group of hard-faced dancers, their skin darkened and lingerie-themed costumes glowing under black light. He read a dancer her rights on a drug arrest. Suddenly his vision went black as a woman's fingernails gouged his eyes, attacking him from behind, he tasted blood as the nails slipped lower into his mouth, tearing at his gums. He wheeled and punched her in the face, dropping her instantly.

"We don't expect our police officers to pick fights," intoned a judge weeks later in court, addressing the stripper's defense lawyer, who had—with the kind of chutzpah that keeps the lawyer joke industry humming—tried to bring the police brutality book down on Korol. "But when our police officers do get in a fight, we don't expect them to lose." Korol sat there, unsuccessfully stopping his smirk from breaking into a full grin. Not guilty.

The keyboard clicked as Detective Warren Korol continued typing:

I have personal knowledge of the facts hereinafter reported except where same are stated to be based upon information and belief.

In a high school life of forgotten quadratic equations and African river names, Grade 9 touch-typing was the best course he ever took. Sixty-four words a minute by summertime, and he could still hear the distinctive sound: clack-clack-clack. fff-jjj-fff-jjj. All the laborious drills on the old manual typewriters where you slammed ink-stained keys into paper.

I make oath and say as follows: On 11 Sept. 1996, I was assigned a suspicious death investigation.

That's when everything changed, when the days of football and the paddy wagon rapidly receded in life's rear-view mirror. The new assignment would consume Warren Korol, take him across the world, his ambition and the Byzantine case of the serial killer pushing him deeper and deeper into a stew of violence and lies, testing his will, his professional and his personal life, drawing hate out of him like never before.

* * *

Hamilton, Ont.
February 1995

Sukhwinder Dhillon drew stares as usual when he emerged from
the gym locker room. He wore a garish yellow track suit, matching top and pants. It was 7:30 a.m. at Family Fitness Center on
Barton Street in east Hamilton. He liked working out in the morning when his friends were there. He did not stretch, wandered
to the bench press, loaded two 25-pound plates, lay on his back,
wrapped each hand around the bar, and lifted. One. Two. Three.
Four. Five. The bar clinked back into place. He stood and moved
on. A spotty workout, as usual. But so what? He was already a big
man, a strong man. Everyone knew it. He did a few situps, couple
of pushups. Then the treadmill, barely breaking a sweat. Back to
the locker room.

Dhillon was average height, perhaps five-foot-ten, and over
200 pounds, his shoulders broad, arms thick, but the stomach was
soft and round. The dark eyes stared back at him in the mirror.
Alarmingly, the ink-black color in his beard was marred by specks
of gray. Dhillon was almost 36 years old, and he couldn't stand
it. He showered, returned to his locker, retrieved the toothbrush
and bottle. Back at the mirror, inches from his reflection, he
dipped the brush in black liquid and colored the bristles. Across
the room, two Indian men smiled. They had seen him paint his
beard, and even his hair, before in the locker room. It got them
every time. Dhillon. That guy. The vanity. He was like a woman.
They shook their heads.

"You know, Dhillon, if you're going to do that you should
do it at home," one of them said. He shrugged, said nothing and
continued. He always heard the chuckles. He didn't care. After he
dressed, it was off to work. He sold used cars. Loved to wheel and
deal. And there were other deals in the works, too. Deals? Was
that the word for it? Well, he had recently received the $2,850
insurance payout on the fender-bender. And five months before,
for $2,325. Same car. A nice deal, auto insurance. You pay a little
money and make a lot more. Accidents happen. Sometimes you
can make them happen.

Sukhwinder Dhillon's passport photo

* * *

Sunday, March 7, 1995
Ludhiana, India

Four weeks after Parvesh died, Dhillon landed in New Delhi, India, after the 14-hour flight from Toronto. He had a long trip planned, two months. Business and pleasure. His destination was his hometown, Ludhiana, an eight-hour drive north of the Indian capital. He bounced along the ragged Indian roads in his compact, white, Indian-made Maruti, one of the relatively privileged Indians to own a car, a bottle of Aristocrat whisky under the seat. The Maruti was like a toy, too small for Dhillon's thick frame. Imagine if he had his Lincoln here! In India he proudly showed friends the home movie of himself in his driveway in Hamilton, leaning against the massive car, wearing cowboy boots and duster trench coat, holding a cellphone.

On the road out of New Delhi, traffic cops in tan uniforms occasionally pulled a motorist over, in some cases offering the driver a chance to pay his way out of a ticket. "Give me 50 rupees and I'll forget about the ticket for 100 I'm about to give you." Trucks and scooters, rickshaws and horse-drawn carts and goat herders jockey for position on the two-lane highway. Coca-Cola signs dot roads running through villages where sidewalk commerce spills nearly into the path of the traffic. "*Life ho to aisi*," one sign declares, meaning, literally, in English, "If life is there, it has to be this." Dhillon zipped past fields of sugar cane and rice, women walking along the road carrying crops on their heads and wearing purple and green dresses that flowed in the warm wind.

Who was the young woman Dhillon would soon meet? What would she look like? He would be having sex before long. Who should he take as his bride?

* * *

Hamilton General Hospital
Forensic Pathology Department

Through February and into March, Dr. David King continued working on the postmortem report. He studied samples of hardened, sliced brain tissue under a microscope. There were no scars. But there had been swelling of the brain, a sign of oxygen debt. Lack of oxygen, but why? Parvesh Dhillon: a young woman, relatively healthy. She does have a history of headaches. A tumor could possibly have gone undetected. But it would be unlikely that an undetected, microscopic tumor could have caused a seizure powerful enough to kill her. An epileptic seizure could be the cause of death. It certainly had earmarks of it. Except Parvesh wasn't epileptic. Murder? A forensic pathologist, King liked to say, has an unusually low threshold of suspicion. Medical students sitting before him were told the basic rule of forensic pathology—suspect the worst. "Not that we're paranoid," he said in his British accent, "but it's our job."

It was part of King's wiring to consider foul play and criminal poisoning from the start. The professional memory unwound in his mind, 30 years on the job, his vast library of cases, back to his education at St. Bartholomew's Hospital in London, England. Poisoning cases? There was the cyanide case he worked 15 years earlier. Police were stumped over a man's sudden death. King examined the body, noticed something on the tissue, and asked a cop, had the deceased ever been involved in photography? Well, yes, he had. King knew that cyanide was once used as a chemical component in developing processes. The man had access to it. Suicide. Case closed. No cyanide in the case of Parvesh Dhillon, though.

Tetanus? It causes prolonged, painful death, stiffness in its victims. But there would be a puncture wound of some kind. Her skin was unmarked. Other poisoning cases? Actually, that was precisely the title of one chapter in the classic 1950 biography of the Englishman Bernard Spilsbury, a pioneer in forensic pathology. At 18 years old, King gave his father, a family doctor, the Spilsbury biography for his birthday. The son also hungrily devoured the forensic bible himself. Spilsbury specialized in discovering poison in corpses, often long after burial. Spilsbury, the gentleman pathologist, King's hero. The legend once showed up at a graveside, dressed immaculately in a dark top hat. The coffin raised, Spilsbury ran his nose along it, straightened himself, cleared his throat and said, simply, "Arsenic, gentlemen." Arsenic? No, gentlemen, not in the Parvesh Dhillon case. So what, exactly, was the damned answer? King had none.

Parvesh suffered from anoxic brain damage, or a lack of oxygen to the brain. He didn't know why. Years later, King would lament this case. In forensic pathology you spend a lifetime learning from your mistakes and those of others. He would never make the same mistake again. Except King was nearly retired. The harsh lesson would help another forensic pathologist, someday. What bothered him most was that, in hindsight, the clues were there. Not obvious, not at all. Making the connection would have been difficult for any forensic pathologist, regardless of experience.

For one thing, he didn't notice the contradiction between the claim in the hospital staff notes that the husband had given Parvesh a Fiorinal capsule, a barbiturate, and the drug screen just a few hours later showed no presence of the substance. At the time, the discrepancy didn't ring a bell with King. But it should have. There was something else. He missed the key word in a note describing Parvesh's "opisthotonic" position. The word was both misspelled and scrawled messily, and King's eye had skipped right over it during his initial review of the charts. Had he deciphered the word, it would have been an instant tip-off. Opisthotonos refers to a rigid body and bowed back. It was a classic sign of a kind of poisoning. How could King miss it?

Perhaps Spilsbury, the great man, would have figured it out. But then Spilsbury was not without weakness. After being knighted, the aging master left a Bunsen burner running in his lab, knocking himself unconscious. No pathologist would miss the clues. Official cause of death: coronary thrombosis brought on by carbon monoxide poisoning. Suicide.

It was four months from the time of Parvesh's death before Dr. David King completed the final lines of his autopsy report, reaching for answers to the end, his conclusion left dangling like a question mark. He wrote, in part:

Summary of abnormal findings:
Postmortem examination revealed the body of a young-appearing, East Indian female showing no significant external abnormality. Internal examination showed oedema of the brain with evidence of herniation, but no subarachnoid or subdural hemorrhage and no other external evidence of the cause of the brain pathology....

Changes of very early acute bronchitis noted in the right lung. The heart was normal. No pulmonary emboli were present, microscopic examination revealed changes in the brain of early but established anoxic ischaemic encephalopathy but an underlying pathology was not identified. It is quite possible the collapse could have been due to some cerebral pathology but this could not be identified.

Cause of death:
1a) anoxic ischaemic encephalopathy due to
b) collapse of unknown cause.

Parvesh Dhillon's brain was sent off for incineration, meeting the same fate as her body already had. As a matter of protocol, King had tiny tissue samples from the brain and other organs sealed in paraffin wax, then packed in a series of thumbnail-sized blue-gray plastic cartridges and placed in a cardboard container the size of a box of chocolates. The case closed, a technician carried the box to a cramped storage room in the bowels of the hospital and put it on a shelf, squeezed between hundreds of other containers of tissue samples from other dead. That's where the final traces of Parvesh Dhillon remained, in darkness, her secret, and her killer, still safe.

CHAPTER 3 ~ "YOU KILLED MY DAUGHTER"

April 5, 1995
Ludhiana, India

Sarabjit Kaur Brar had tanned, smooth skin; her voice was soft and hesitant. She usually managed to keep her smile at bay, but it would occasionally crack and briefly light up a room. In English her name meant "the universe." She sat on the edge of the bed, the moment nearing when her new husband, a man she neither knew nor loved, would arrive and expect intercourse from her. His name was Sukhwinder Dhillon. He was 36 years old, had two young daughters. She was 20, and had never even kissed a man before. Sarabjit waited to hear him mount the stairs and enter the room. She sat there, her small hands clasped on her lap as though in prayer, head bowed, staring at her bare feet, wearing a magenta lehnga—a formal silk blouse and skirt—and sheer chunni wrapped regally around her neck. Traditional bridal bracelets colored ivory, maroon, and gold lined the new bride's thin wrists and forearms. The ritual red dye that covered the palms of her hands in an intricate pattern looked like dried blood.

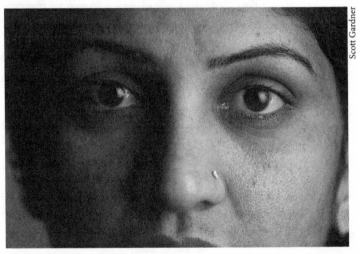

Sarabjit Kaur Brar

Scott Gardner

She lived in a farm village called Panj Grain, two hours southwest of Ludhiana, where 2,000 people lived in a collection of bungalows made of a combination of concrete and sun-hardened mud and cow dung. The road to her arranged marriage had begun two weeks earlier when Sarabjit had first been presented to Dhillon. She had sat in the living room of her uncle Iqbal's home along with her parents. Sarabjit wore a blouse known as a salwar kameez, rose-colored pants, and her head was covered in a scarf.

Scott Gardner

Panj Grain, the village Sarabjit called home.

Iqbal had suggested his niece to Dhillon as a prospective bride. And now, to her uncle and others, the bride-to-be seemed happy. Why wouldn't she be? Marrying a Canadian citizen like Dhillon meant she could move to Canada, a new life, new opportunity. It was the dream of many Punjabis. Not all young women like Sarabjit held such an arrangement as their life mission, but what did the wishes of an Indian girl matter? To even hope to marry a man of your choice would mean exercising an independence that in the arranged-marriage culture was unacceptable. Sarabjit would marry whomever her parents deemed appropriate. "Love" marriages, as Indians called them, were more common in liberal circles in the big cities, but arranged marriages were still the overwhelming major-ity. Even in Canada, Sikh girls who left India as toddlers felt the pressure of their culture. Rebelling against an arranged marriage in Punjab, for a girl like Sarabjit from a traditional village family, was not even a remote possibility. It would mean disgracing the entire family in the eyes of the community, perhaps even bringing death upon herself.

Sarabjit averted her brown eyes from Dhillon's stare. Everyone seemed to call Dhillon by his nickname, *Jodha*, which means brave warrior. Sarabjit heard him speak in his rough Punjabi. The man was clearly uneducated, she could tell immediately.

"I'm bringing a hundred friends to the wedding," Dhillon declared in his rapid-fire cadence. "Look after them properly." He said not one word to Sarabjit. She felt angry, claustrophobic. It was all closing in on her, out of her control. She locked her mother's eyes in a cold stare. At the wedding, she saw the looks on the faces of her friends. They felt sorry for her, even though they knew their number would be up one day, too. Hopefully their parents would arrange marriages to more appealing men. Sarabjit's closest friend, Pinky, leaned over and whispered, "Sarabey, what have you gotten yourself into? It's all right. Everything's going to be fine."

Scott Gardner

Dhillon on his wedding video

Wedding guests paraded past Dhillon as he sat with Sarabjit. They handed him cash and jewels. Dhillon had told Sarabjit's family to sweeten the dowry, and handed her parents, Gurjant and Ranjit, a wish list. He requested rings for his brother and father—even though Dhillon's father had long been dead. Dowry is a serious business in India. When the dowry is found wanting by the groom or in-laws, the new bride is on occasion burned alive. "Dowry deaths" the local newspapers call them. The dowry paid to Dhillon included the rings, three bracelets, including a gold one for his mother, a neck chain, clothes. Dhillon told the parents he didn't want stuff like a TV, fridge, or the family's prized motorcycle. He could get those things in Canada. He preferred cash. The dowry he received totaled two Indian lakhs, or

200,000 rupees—about $9,000 Canadian. To Dhillon, the amount
was modest; he could earn that much in Canada selling one used
car. But for Sarabjit's family, who owned a house and a patch of
farmland, it was a massive expense; two lakhs is a small fortune
in India. They borrowed money and, to help pay Dhillon, Sarabjit's grandfather sold half of his farm and the family tractor. The
family considered it an investment. They mortgage their lives to
Dhillon, give him their daughter, and the payoff would be a move
to Canada for all of them in the future through family reunification. The golden dream.

* * *

Dhillon had taken his two young daughters, Aman and Harpreet—
still grieving the loss of their mother—out of school in Hamilton
to India for the wedding. At the wedding he was also accompanied
by his friend, a man named Manjit Singh Sidhu, a hulking inspector with the Punjab state police who went by the nickname *Dulla*
(pronounced doo-la), which meant "the groom" in English. Dulla
always carried a revolver sticking out of his waistband for all to
see. After the wedding, the families returned to the bride's home
in Panj Grain to pick up Sarabjit's belongings. As Sarabjit got into
the car with Dhillon to drive the two hours to his family home
in Ludhiana, Dulla pulled the gun and fired several celebratory
shots into the air.

Scott Gardner

Dhillon and friend "Dulla" in wedding video

In the middle of
Ludhiana was Dhillon's
neighborhood, called
Birk Barsal. The
change for Sarabjit was
like a slap in the face.
Panj Grain consisted
of taupe bungalows
surrounded by green
fields, a farm village
where at midday the
loudest sound was a

water pump filling the rice paddies. Birk Barsal buzzed within the city's overheated old industrial core, a mess of impossibly narrow streets and wires overhead, gray-walled textile factories clacking and shucking, horns and bells from rickshaws, scooters, bicycles, trucks and cars squeezing past one another loaded with wool, and other goods. Shops and markets spilled onto the street, diesel exhaust filling the air along with the smell of sweat and fruit and vegetables decaying in the heat.

Ludhiana at night

The white Maruti turned left off the main street, up a narrow alley, past a woolen goods store and a noisy textile shop, and stopped in front of Dhillon's walk-up apartment. Sarabjit's bracelets jangled as she scaled the steps. That night, her wedding night, sitting on Dhillon's bed, Sarabjit had never felt more alone, afraid or trapped. She tried to block out her fear. What was the point of letting doubts creep in? Do not resist. It is pointless, only brings more pain. But subversive thoughts danced in and out of her mind anyway. She knew the entire concept was so Western, but what of her dreams? She grew up in a village called Mairu, even smaller than Panj Grain, with three younger brothers. She completed high school then moved to Panj Grain at 19. She was still in the first year of college, studying Punjabi and history, trying not to dream of a future of her own design, but somewhere inside, in a perfect world, she had wanted to be a teacher. She always knew it would never come true.

* * *

Heavy footsteps up the stairs. Sukhwinder Dhillon entered the bed-room. Even at the best of times, the first night is an awkward moment for a young Indian woman in an arranged marriage. Sometimes new brides are able to put off sex until getting to know the groom better. Sometimes there is no option. Sarabjit knew there would be none with Dhillon. She was afraid. He sat down on the bed, the mattress straining underneath him. He was quiet at first, the only sound horns coming from cars and scooters in the darkened alleys below. They had barely even talked before, not even at the wedding, where the ceremony requires no speaking from the couple, or at the reception, where Dhillon drank copious amounts of whisky with his male friends and danced with them in a circle.

"I am happy, you know, that you are my wife," Dhillon said. Sarabjit murmured quietly, inaudibly, staring at her bare feet. She was unaccustomed to a man even having the familiarity to look her square in the eye. She wanted to cry.

Dhillon continued. "We will get to know each other much better, and it will make it much easier." Sarabjit nodded. "And now that we are husband and wife, we can spend the night. Why don't you take off your clothes?"

Sarabjit said nothing. She expected this bluntness, but it still shocked her. "It would make me happy," he said, "if you would undress for bed."

It went on like this, Dhillon asking her to disrobe: *Kaprey laah dey*. The thought of running out on him did not cross her mind, it was beyond the pale. It would humiliate her family, her parents would be ostracized in the community, likely asked to leave their village. Her in-laws would probably burn her for it. All she could do was stall. *Kaprey laah dey*.

Finally, she slid off the lehnga, the thin scarf, then her blouse, pants. Dhillon removed his shirt and undershirt, and pants. Un-prepared both mentally and physically for what was happening, Sarabjit felt the weight of the large body on top of her, then a painful burning sensation as he entered her. Later, they lay on the bed. It was all very odd, she thought. She felt nothing.

Dhillon, his mind now freed, began to chatter. Sikh men are often considered chauvinistic by Western standards, not inclined toward expressions of affection for their wives in either word or deed. Indians joke that men feel no shame urinating in public, but it's taboo to kiss a woman in front of others.

"I am a very experienced man, you know," Dhillon said. "I was married for many years."

Sarabjit knew he was married before. Why was he talking like this? He lamented his lot in the world. "The Punjabis see me visit, and all they see is Canada. They don't see me as a person. The fact is, I could bring 10 girls back just like you. They were offering me even younger girls, 16, 17 years old."

Sarabjit felt the muscles in her face tighten in anger. She had decided at the wedding that no matter how bad it all seemed, she was strong. She would will herself to make her life work, no matter what. But now, in the darkness, with her virginity—in Indian culture, her most precious possession—painfully torn away by a man she was rapidly growing to hate, she knew the story was not going to end well. She closed her eyes, tuned out Dhillon's rambling words and the clanging and hooting of the streets below, thought of quiet Panj Grain, and forced herself to sleep.

* * *

Dhillon and Sarbjit signed marriage papers in Ludhiana—he had the choice of declaring his status as unmarried, widower, or divorced; he lied and checked off unmarried. And then, five days after their wedding, Dhillon drove the Maruti along the ragged roads, Sarabjit beside him, and his niece, Sarvjit, and his two daughters in the back. This was a day Dhillon had tried to put off as long as possible—visiting Parvesh's parents. His young daughters yearned to see their grandparents. Soon they arrived in Parvesh's old village, called Sahkewal, a half hour through heavy traffic from Birk Barsal. Dhillon's only contact with Parvesh's parents since her death was when he had, insultingly, mailed Hardial and Hardev Grewal their daughter's ashes.

Hardial, Parvesh's mother, wasn't surprised by anything Dhillon did, not anymore. She and Hardev had lived with Dhillon and Parvesh while visiting Canada for long stretches. His behavior after her daughter's death only confirmed in her mind the evil that defined her son-in-law. It was not uncommon for a Sikh man to treat his in-laws with just enough indifference to show who wielded the power, but Dhillon took it to an ugly extreme. Hardial knew, long before she saw it herself, that Dhillon beat Parvesh. Harpreet, the older child, once told her grandmother so. The girl saw her father hit her mother with an object but she never told anyone about it because her dad said he would kill her if she repeated the story. Was that just a child's imagination? No, Hardial saw it for herself. She had cringed in fear at the house on Berkindale Drive in Hamilton when Dhillon turned on Parvesh, screaming at her, threatening to kill her. She waited in horror for the blows that followed, for Dhillon to seize Parvesh by the throat. There were times she stood in front of Parvesh, trying to protect her, but Dhillon had merely swatted her out of the way.

In the car with Sarabjit, Dhillon drove in silence, then finally spoke. "Hardial may say some bad things about me," he warned. "Whatever she says, don't believe her."

Why does he say things like that? Sarabjit wondered. She was suspicious, to say the least, and fearful. The Maruti pulled up to the house. Dhillon got out and saw Hardev, Parvesh's father. "You never visited us when our daughter was alive. So why now?" he asked. Inside, Hardev took Dhillon's niece and his granddaughters to a different room, and now it was just Hardial, Dhillon, and Sarabjit together in the living room. Dhillon tried to make small talk. Parvesh's mother could barely look at him, the very sight disgusted her. She looked at Sarabjit.

"Be careful," she said. "He killed my daughter. He'll do the same thing to you. He'll take you over there and do the same thing." Sarabjit stood there as Dhillon and Hardial went at it, arguing. Dhillon tried to turn the tables. What about you, Hardial? You were never a good grandmother. Never! How come you never came to Canada to visit Harpreet when she was sick? Well?

Hardial was livid. She called Dhillon *kanjra*, Punjabi for bastard.

"My granddaughters!" she shouted. "You might as well kill both of them, too. You killed my daughter, why not my granddaughters?" Dhillon motioned to Sarabjit. We're leaving. Did he not predict the crazy old woman would lie about him? Dhillon herded the girls, his niece, and Sarabjit back in the car. As they drove away, Sarabjit didn't want to believe Hardial, but she had already seen enough of Dhillon to assume the worst. She reflected on the nickname Dhillon's friends called him: Jodha. Brave warrior. Right.

Sarabjit satisfied his appetite for sex as she was expected. Dhillon received it on demand nearly every day. On Thursday, April 27, he left Sarabjit in Birk Barsal. He had to drive two hours to Chandigarh, the capital of Punjab. "Business to take care of." He did not go to Chandigarh. Instead he picked up his friend Dulla and they drove to a farm village called Tibba. It was surrounded by fields of rice, corn, and sugar cane. Brick and clay homes clustered tightly together on cobblestone streets and, at the end of a long dirt path, was a funeral pyre beside the Gudwara temple. Elderly women sat on the ground washing pots, ignoring flies buzzing around their faces, in a courtyard that blocked out wind and trapped heat like an oven. Dhillon and Dulla entered the home of a man named Rai Singh Toor.

Rai Singh had heard that Dhillon was in the area and interested in remarrying following the death of Parvesh in Canada. Both Rai Singh and his wife desperately wanted to marry one of their two daughters to an Indo-Canadian, and then ultimately join her overseas. Nearly everyone in Tibba wanted to get to Canada. Those with a relative overseas erected proud displays on their homes to show it, elaborate gates or family crests that stood out like flashing neon in the dusty village. These were called "dollar homes," meaning the family received money from abroad—foreign currency, not mere Indian rupees. Dhillon and Dulla looked over Rai Singh's daughters. The youngest was named Sukie. She stood off to one side in the courtyard. Dhillon moved closer.

"You're pretty," he said. "I should marry you." Sukie wouldn't turn 19 for another two weeks. Her sister, Kushpreet, was slightly older. Tradition says the father must marry off his daughters in descending order of age. Shown Kushpreet, Dhillon looked her

Kushpreet Kaur Toor, Dhillon's third wife

over, said nothing, and nodded in agreement.

"The marriage will be held in 12 days," Rai Singh announced. Dhillon agreed, then saw Dulla's glare, the ever-present revolver handle sticking out of his pants. That wouldn't work. Dhillon remembered he had a flight back to Canada that left in 12 days.

"Let's get this over with," Dulla said. Rai Singh agreed to speed up arrangements with the temple. They could be married in three days, on April 30, then Dhillon could return to Canada, finalize immigration papers for Kushpreet, and bring her to the promised land.

Dhillon and Dulla left the village and returned to Ludhiana, where Sarabjit waited. Three days later, Dhillon told Sarabjit he had to leave again, this time for New Delhi. He always had some place to go. This time he was signing deals to import used cars from Canada to sell in India.

Dhillon and Dulla instead drove an hour to his next wedding, at the Manjal Hotel in a village called Sahnewal. Dhillon made sure his marriage to Kushpreet was registered in a neighboring district called Moga, to disguise his marriage to Sarabjit. There were 150 guests, Dhillon collected his dowry, got drunk on whisky. The wedding reception over, Kushpreet returned to Tibba, festooned with the ceremonial maroon and ivory-colored bracelets, her palms painted red. Dhillon was anxious to consummate the nuptials, but Rai Singh would not allow his daughter to live with Dhillon until immigration papers were finalized—to ensure that Kushpreet's, and the family's, ticket to Canada was secure. If Dhillon slept with his daughter, and then left her, she would lose her value in the eyes of the community and he would never get to Canada. Dhillon still had Sarabjit waiting in Birk Barsal to provide sex over the remaining nine days.

On May 9, three months after Parvesh died, 33 days after marrying Sarabjit, and nine days since exchanging vows with Kushpreet, Dhillon's flight took off from New Delhi. When he was preparing to leave, Dhillon told Sarabjit to be patient. It wouldn't be long now, he would bring her to Canada. He phoned Kushpreet and told her the same thing. Everything would work out. Sarabjit stayed at Dhillon's home in Ludhiana; Kushpreet remained with her parents in Tibba. When Dhillon arrived back in Hamilton with his daughters, rumors of his exploits in India spread in the local Sikh community. Marrying a woman so soon after Parvesh's death was scandalous. Dhillon lamented that he had no choice but to remarry quickly. He needed a wife to look after the girls. The rumors persisted. Was there a *third* wife? On May 23, Dhillon phoned an immigration lawyer in Etobicoke, near Toronto. He was interested in bringing his new wife, Kushpreet Kaur Toor, to Canada. He said nothing about Sarabjit.

Dhillon had received $1,100 a month widower's pension since Parvesh's death. He was collecting about $5,000 a year in revenue from his family's farm in Ludhiana. He was buying and selling used cars in Hamilton, grossing $38,500 between October 1994 and September 1995. He received compensation from a 1991 workplace "accident," now worth about $9,000 a year.

There was a stack of mail on the table in Dhillon's house. A friend of his in Hamilton, a man named Ranjit Khela, had collected it for him while he was away. Near the top was a worker's compensation form. It was dated May 2. It asked if Sukhwinder Dhillon was working again. He checked off the "no" box. He dated the form May 10 and mailed it in. It was all small change.

The biggest windfall was to come—Parvesh's life insurance money. A cool $200,000.

Dhillon had some other deals in mind, too. He planned a return trip to India. Perhaps he should find another wife. Was there any reason not to? In the spring of 1995, Dhillon was invincible. His dreams were coming true. And it was just the beginning.

CHAPTER 4 ~ A PATHOLOGICAL GREED

New Delhi, India
1981

Gobind Kaur Dhillon and the youngest of her three sons, Sukhwinder, boarded a flight at Indira Gandhi Airport in New Delhi for the trip to Canada. It was 1981 and Sukhwinder was 22 years old.

Punjab is India's wealthiest state; many who live there see themselves as separate from the rest of the country. Relative to Indians in the south living in dire poverty, Punjabis have wealth, entertain the possibility of increasing that wealth, and Canada has long been the place to do it. For years there has been a sea of colorful turbans outside the Canadian High Commission in New Delhi, more than 100 of them at any time, seeking visas. Helping Punjabis get to Canada is big business. The posters are everywhere in the state—"World's Largest Canadian Immigration Service"—on poles in the cities or painted in Maple Leaf red and white on pump houses amid the cane fields in the countryside: "Your passport to Canada!" The easiest way to accomplish it is family reunification.

Scott Gardner

A billboard in Ludhiana advertises immigration consultants

In 1981, the parents of a pretty young woman named Parvesh Kaur Grewal shared that yearning for Canada. There was a man her age named Sukhwinder Singh Dhillon who was moving to Canada with his mother. An arranged marriage with him was the ticket for their family to also make it. Dhillon was engaged to Parvesh before he left with Gobind for Canada. The plan was that after planting roots overseas, he would return to marry Parvesh and bring her back. The jet took off from New Delhi, a stop in London, then the parabolic flight over Greenland, the descent over northern Quebec, the St. Lawrence River snaking through green hinterland below. Neither mother nor son had ever been outside India before.

* * *

Sukhwinder Singh Dhillon was the third and last son of Fagun and Gobind Dhillon. He was born May 9, 1959. His arrival in the world surely came as a surprise, for his mother had last given birth to her son Sukhbir 11 years earlier. Their eldest son was Darshan. Rambunctious Sukhwinder rolled around the living room of their walk-up apartment, a ball of mischief even before he could walk. His father, tongue in cheek, tagged the infant Jodha —brave warrior—and Dhillon proudly carried the name with him into his adult life.

His father owned a farm, wealth his three sons would one day inherit. Fagun Singh Dhillon had started with a handful of buffalo on his dairy farm, a few calves. Later the herd expanded to 40 head with four servants to care for the livestock. How Fagun came into his wealth was not entirely clear. He had been a career police officer for years but, not long after Sukhwinder was born, he abruptly left the police force. Why? The explanation became murky in family accounts. Gobind said it was because corruption on the force turned Fagun's stomach, so he got out despite pleas to stay from the chief. Others in the family had a different interpretation than Gobind's. Corruption has long been endemic in Indian law enforcement—beatings, forced confessions, bribery, confiscated property. Modern reforms reflect the ugly past. For example, any witness statements taken by police are inadmissible in court. Fagun was in fact quite a player himself. He didn't leave the force—he was fired.

It may have been the defining moment in Sukhwinder Dhillon's life. One day in 1964, when he was just five, he heard the news that his father had died suddenly, and young. Practically speaking, it meant Sukhwinder, little Jodha, already spoiled as the baby and center of attention in a family with means, had no father to discipline him and inject reality into his fantasy world. He was young enough to feel little pain at Fagun's death, having been told that there was no need to grieve. Fagun had led a successful life. And death is God's will. Do not grieve. You needn't feel—anything. More ominously, something peculiar may have taken root, right then, in his soul, internalizing a pathological belief in the power of fate. Taken to a twisted extreme, could such fatalism justify murder? If God wills all, permits—no, guides—death, then even a murder is a natural event; the killer's hands merely execute that which is predestined to occur.

The family story went that a heart attack felled Fagun. But he hadn't been sick, had no history of heart problems. "Heart attack" is a euphemism in Punjab for murder. Some in the family were convinced he was killed by enemies. As a police officer, there was no shortage of people whom Fagun may have upset over the years. And payback is an old Indian tradition, especially in the villages. Grievances last generations, revenge is patient. Sometimes it comes in the form of powder slipped into a drink, causing the victim to double over and die in a manner that, in fact, resembles a heart attack. Physicians were known to take bribes in order to declare a murder was in fact death by natural causes.

With Fagun gone, young Sukhwinder, well-fed and mischievous, continued on happily, living on magically inherited wealth. Fagun's death also killed whatever chance there was that Dhillon would grow up as an orthodox Sikh. Sikhism as a religion is in one sense a rebellion against the old ways of the Hindus, with their hundreds of gods, lavish temples, and rigid caste system that orders people according to their social class. The founding Sikh gurus disdained religious symbols, but ultimately, in order to survive, the "five Ks" were introduced to distinguish Sikh men from others: *Kesh* (the hair must be uncut), *Khanga* (a small comb worn in the hair), *Karra* (steel bracelet), *Kachha* (underwear similar to breeches), *Kirpan* (a small sword, or dagger, about six to nine inches in length, to be used only in self-defense). Sikhism, in its purest form, promotes one God, as well as equality, respect, dignity, courage. Treat your fellow men, and women, with respect. It is a noble calling, for those who honor the precepts.

Scott Gardner

A Sikh man bathes at the Golden Temple in Amritsar.

Sukhwinder had been raised as a believing Sikh, just like his brothers Sukhbir and Darshan had, following Fagun, who had worn the turban. As a boy, Sukhwinder wore the thin nylon wrap that fitted the head like a bathing cap. Orthodox Sikh boys wear them, with their uncut hair tied in a small ball underneath. One day, they are permitted to wear the turban, the essential, powerful symbol of a Sikh man's belief, a sign that he is a warrior of faith. Darshan, the eldest brother, kept the tradition, and his turban. But with Fagun gone, Sukhwinder rebelled, wanted to cut his hair. Gobind gave in to her youngest son.

When it was time for young Sukhwinder to go to school in Ludhiana, his twisted logic hardened like concrete. "Let's see. We own land, have servants. Why should I have to go to school?" he asked his mother. Her answer was not persuasive. He was the only one of the three brothers who didn't complete at least an elementary school education. Early on, he discovered the folly of attending school sporadically. Miss a day, then show up the next, and the teacher would give him a spanking. The solution was not to go to school at all—and lie effectively about it. He left his mother in the kitchen in the morning, lunch in hand, then disappeared into the bustle of the street below. He would return at the end of the school day, up the steps, his lunch eaten. How was school? Fine. He was not in class. He was out in the markets, in a yard, playing, dreaming. The phone rang on many afternoons in the house. Gobind answered.

"Mrs. Dhillon? Where is Sukhwinder today?"

"He's in school."

"No, he's not. He's not in class. Again."

Gobind fretted over his behavior, but was unable to change it. She hired a tutor to come to the house and connect with the boy. It didn't work. The same tutor taught a pretty, pale-faced girl who was one year younger than Sukhwinder. The girl never actually crossed paths with Dhillon back then. Her family lived in the north end of the city as well, where she walked to school five minutes away. Her name was Parvesh Kaur Grewal.

Nothing worked with Sukhwinder. He learned to read and write only a few basic Punjabi words. "Why get so upset at him, Mom?" Sukhbir said. "He's not going to study anyway. We are *jats* [farmers], we have our land, servants. What is the point of making him go to school?"

This was the Sukhwinder Dhillon who left India for Canada in 1981: a young, poorly educated man with inherited wealth who had done no work of his own, had no grounding in the morality and honor of Sikh orthodoxy, and who possessed a dreamy sense of himself and a natural affinity for lying in order to create the life he felt he deserved. It was as though Dhillon's sense of entitlement to easy wealth was fuelled by a peculiar, childish vanity, under which lay a bedrock of insecurity and rage at his shortcomings. He hungered for attention, any attention, from others. Most tragic of all was his greed. It grew inside Dhillon like a mutating bacteria, fuelling an instinctive, morally vacuous conviction that the end, when it comes to money, justifies the means.

* * *

Darshan remained in India. Sukhbir, Gobind's middle son, had already made it to Canada, and met Sukhwinder and their mother at Pearson Airport in Toronto. They climbed into a car and merged onto the 401, Canada's busiest highway. It was their first time on a Western road, and it was a different world.

In India, most highways are two-way but narrow affairs with no lane markings, braided with holes and bumps. Cars are a luxury item, almost all of them made domestically. Most are the tiny Marutis or white Ambassadors produced in old British factories now owned and run by Indians, all of them looking like roundish 1960s-era diplomatic vehicles. In addition, trucks, buses, bicycles, auto rickshaws, manual rickshaws, horse-drawn carts, goat herders, pedestrians, women carrying crops and pots on their heads, scooters, and motorcycles pack the roads. Many of the vehicles are overloaded with passengers and goods, as if people were racing for the hills to avoid a looming flood, bringing every possession they have. Driving is based on constant split-second reactions. Signaling is rare. Drivers pass at every opportunity, and when confronted with a bus looming straight ahead, you lean on your horn, forcing the other vehicle to slow down or take a wider berth onto the shoulder, where heat-scorched crumbling asphalt morphs into hardpan dirt. Often the vehicles run three or four abreast. The overwhelming sound is that of horns, which all drivers use constantly, employing them as the eyes and ears of the road.

Somehow it works, this free flow where the fast and the large get priority and no one takes umbrage at this fact of life. Indian traffic is a communal, cooperative activity. Yet it balances on the head of a pin, for if just one person disregards a horn or fails to use their own or loses trust in another driver, it can mean death.

Now, leaving Toronto for Hamilton, Sukhwinder and his mother were on this superhighway, and it was staggering. The surface was like driving on marble, the car glided along as though on air, silently, no car horns; the road was black and clean, white lines shining in the dark as though lit by electricity, magically keeping traffic in different lanes, a spartan orderly progression. And there was no traffic coming at you the other way. You drove in one of your four or five lanes, and were separated from the on-coming traffic by a wall. There were no villages to wind through, no railway crossings where a corrupt official lowered the wooden arm, blocking everybody for an hour in order to accommodate the roadside merchants who paid him off. In the moonlight and the fluorescence of the street lamps, the cars looked so new, clean:

deep blues and greens, red, black, yellow, even, all of them reflecting light like diamonds. It was not just a few fancy cars like the ones that carried local political figures in Punjab, with their cherry-top sirens announcing a representative's journey through town. No, in Canada, they were all fancy. So much money. Back in Ludhiana, the Dhillon family was relatively wealthy. Canada, for Sukhwinder and his mother, offered not economic survival, but gold at the end of the rainbow, a promised land of riches.

At Hamilton they crossed the Skyway bridge, swells on the lake turned silver by moonlight. They saw Canada's Big Steel, smokestacks billowing, flames grasping at the blackness. The Dhillons—Sukhwinder, Gobind, brother Sukhbir, and his wife, Ravinder—all lived in a narrow two-storey brick house on Rosslyn Avenue North, in an earnest, working-class neighborhood not far from Gage Park. The Canadian dream was here, but in 1981 the path for Indians—"East Indians" they were called by Canadians—was not a glamorous one. Dhillon saw his older brother go to work every day as a chipper at Brown Boggs Foundry. It wasn't far from the house where they all lived, in the shadow of Hamilton's industrial heart. To Indians accustomed to Ludhiana's gritty pollution and chaos, Hamilton was quiet and clean. Sukhbir eventually left the foundry, became a bus driver. What would young Sukhwinder do?

* * *

In 1983 Dhillon returned to Ludhiana to wed Parvesh Grewal, the young woman his parents had arranged for him to marry. Dhillon and Parvesh lived in the house on Rosslyn Avenue North with Sukhbir and his wife, Ravinder. He worked briefly at a mushroom farm, earn-

Industrial skyline of Hamilton, Ontario

Scott Gardner

ing $4 an hour, then later got a job in a cheese factory. Then, like Sukhbir, he landed at the Brown Boggs Foundry. He was now making $14 an hour. His resumé was an earnest one, on paper. Reality was something else. He often didn't show up for work at Boggs but had a co-worker punch his time card. For a short time Dhillon drove a cab, but his scatter-brained nature didn't serve him well trying to navigate the city. He and Parvesh briefly moved to an apartment of their own on Queen Street North, then into a two-storey brown brick house on Rosslyn, a little north of where Sukhbir lived.

Scott Gardner

Dhillon at a used car sales lot in Hamilton

Dhillon—*Jodha* —earned a clownish reputation in the local Indian community. He spoke Punjabi in broken sentences, quickly, peppered with vulgarity, talked nonsense in a nasal tone. The tell-tale sign of his poor education, everyone knew, was his English. All educated Sikhs new to the city spoke decent English. That included Parvesh. But Dhillon spoke no English, at first. He picked it up later, not from the classroom like the others, but from the street, friends, television. When he spoke English it was often gibberish, the words strung together incorrectly, quickly repeated over and over. His behavior made him an easy target. Dhillon was always anxious to please, was easily swayed by any suggestion, and was comically boastful, with an instinct for lying, and lying big. He would meet someone for the first time and brag that he was a champion wrestler back in Ludhiana. In truth his wrestling had never extended beyond horseplay with other kids. He portrayed his life in India as a tableau of sensational adventures and feats of strength. Listeners couldn't tell if Dhillon was joking or delusional, or if he was really the tough guy he described. His friends learned to tune him out.

Dhillon said people feared him back home, and even claimed to possess, literally, a black tongue—the *Kallijeeb* that Indian lore said was the sign of an evil man. (One friend swore that Dhillon's tongue was, in fact, black. Saw it with his own eyes.) Dhillon had a bearish physique, with round, thick shoulders. His protruding belly, however, betrayed softness below the surface. Still, he delighted in boasting of his strength, the weight he could lift. He told the stories and others listened in amazement. Was he for real?

In September 1986, Dhillon started a job at J.I. Case, a sprawling factory on Sherman Avenue North that manufactured farm machinery. The steady pay, along with Parvesh's earnings, ultimately allowed them to move to a house in Stoney Creek, a suburb east of Hamilton, on Berkindale Drive. It was near the Riverdale neighborhood, a place where Indians new to Hamilton had congregated since the late 1970s. Eventually the community grew enough to require a temple; the new *gurdwara* was a nice enough building, red brick with domed shapes etched into the walls. It sat like a lone healthy tooth on Covington Street, a dusty gray stretch of industrial road wedged between Barton Street and the QEW highway.

Dhillon worked at several stations at the plant, on the assembly line hanging small pieces on a line for painting, then removing them afterwards. The work was not heavy labor, but it was boringly repetitive. He also did what the guys called "bull work" in the heat of the forger, loading steel into a furnace, picking up the glowing red piece with tongs and holding it for a hammer man to crush. It was hot, heavy, dangerous work. Dhillon hated bull work because it required effort, but it did allow him to indulge in his fantasy of being the strong man. A man named Cliff Hewer supervised him. Dhillon seemed to be off work quite a bit. On occasion, Hewer phoned his house to check on him. Invariably, he would speak to Harpreet, Dhillon's five-year-old daughter. Her dad was not there, she would say.

Hewer had some excellent workers of Indian origin. One of them was a man named Gurmej Khattra. Gurmej grew up on a prosperous farm in a village called Chahalkalan, in the Ludhiana area. He had always worked hard. When he turned five he helped his father in the fields in the morning, attended school during the day, then worked on the farm at night. A tall man with thick hands and broad smile, Gurmej possessed an independent, adventurous spirit. He worked for a time on a Greek cargo ship and sailed for three years on routes between England, the Great Lakes, and Africa. One day, the ship docked at Hamilton Harbor and he deboarded for the last time. He was alone, starting from scratch. He eventually married a Canadian girl from Sudbury, had two children, was hired at J.I. Case as a punch press operator the same year as Sukhwinder Dhillon.

One day in the fall of 1986, Dhillon was sitting in his usual spot in the huge Case lunchroom. There was a table of about a dozen Indian men among the 80 or so in the entire room. Dhillon, the new guy, took center stage. I'm strong, stronger than all of you, he boasted. Back home, I was the strongest in the village. The other men egged him on. "Oh, Dhillon," one of his Indian co-workers said with a grin. "You are a big man. No question about it, you are the biggest man." Sarcasm didn't appear to register in Dhillon's mind. Maybe he understood it completely, but reveled in his role as the clown, the only role he felt he could play. Suddenly, Dhillon was on the lunchroom floor, the others looking on with broad grins. One. Two. Three. Pushups—he was doing pushups for them, weighed down in his workpants and boots.

"That's pretty impressive. But what about situps?"

Dhillon moved outside now, through an adjacent door into a courtyard. One. Two. Three. He curled his body for the situps, folding his belly over and over. The others laughed. Dhillon, they thought, the guy's nuts, brain-dead. Dhillon's performance complete, he stood, walked back inside, forehead flecked with sweat.

At a table sat Gurmej Khattra. He was one of Dhillon's first friends in Hamilton, but the pair hadn't spent much time together in recent months. A couple of the other guys saw a new opportunity to push Dhillon's buttons. They knew Gurmej was married to a white Canadian woman. "Hey, Dhillon—what do you think of Canadian women?" Dhillon took the performance up a notch.

"White women," Dhillon said, looking at Gurmej, "are sluts." Gurmej knew Dhillon talked nonsense. But he was still taken aback. He sat stone-faced. Dhillon, pleased by the reaction of the others, bore on. "Yeah, sluts," he repeated. "Whores. All of them. Right, Gurmej?" Gurmej Khattra let it go. Dhillon was crazy. And Gurmej wasn't going to do anything that would lose him his job.

Dhillon's bluster around friends reflected his yearning for respect, his hunger for approval and his inability to sense how he was actually perceived. Dhillon lacked strength or guile. But he wielded his audacity like a weapon. And he lied, often. Others noticed something in Dhillon's eyes when he lied. Or rather, they saw the absence of something—the wavering light of conscience. But he picked his spots for boasting and buffoonery. At work, managers thought Dhillon was a quiet man—he blended in, he was unremarkable. But among the guys from India, it was different. He invited them to his home, had Parvesh cook big meals, pass around his whisky for the boys. The binges got so out of control there were times they urinated and vomited on the carpet. Whenever Dhillon was challenged to drink, he would take them up on it.

"Dhillon—think you can drink a 40-ouncer?" The story went that Dhillon did it, downing an entire bottle over one evening on a bet, then throwing up repeatedly on the floor. At J.I. Case, meanwhile, for no reason Gurmej Khattra could figure out, Dhillon became increasingly aggressive toward him, the insults turning violent. Several days after the lunchroom incident, Dhillon strapped a sharp piece of pressed metal from the factory floor, slightly longer than a knife, under his pant leg, right in front of a co-worker.

"Dhillon, what the hell are you doing?" He grinned. It was for Gurmej. After work, Dhillon followed Gurmej to the gate. He pulled out the weapon. "*Teri ma noo!*" he shouted in Punjabi, using the worst slur in the language. ("Come on, motherf—! Come here, I'll kill you!") A co-worker stepped between the two, told them to stop it, they would get fired. Gurmej got in his car.

"I don't want to fight," he said out the window. "I don't want trouble. I'm not union here, I'm not going to get fired." Dhillon marched to the car and Gurmej rolled up the window.

"I'll wait for you at your apartment!" Dhillon shouted. "I'm going to kill you. *Teri ma noo.*" Dhillon knew where Gurmej lived. How far would he take the act? Gurmej went home, but Dhillon never showed. A few days later, on a Saturday, Gurmej, his wife Cathy, and their little daughter Angel, got out of their car in the parking lot of a supermarket at Centre Mall on Barton Street.

Walking toward them, two grocery bags in his arms, was Dhillon, Parvesh alongside him holding one bag. Dhillon used the opportunity to berate Gurmej, confident that the two wives and the little girl would insulate him from a real fight. He marched purposefully toward Gurmej, put the bags down on the pavement. "*Teri ma noo*. I'll kill you. You bring your slut wife to protect you?"

It was too much. Gurmej felt fire in his chest. He met Dhillon's approach, cocked his arm, and swung. His knuckles cracked against Dhillon's eye socket. Dhillon staggered, and Gurmej chopped down on his nose like an axe. Dhillon was on a knee when Gurmej swung again, and now Parvesh said, forcefully but composed, "*Veerji*! Brother! Don't hurt him!" Gurmej paused. Parvesh was a gentle woman, honest, a hard worker. He respected her so much. "*Veerji*, let's talk about this, let's talk this over in the community," she said.

"He won't talk," Gurmej muttered. "He won't listen to anything."

Dhillon stood, blood flowing from his nose over his lip, yelling at Parvesh, his voice a guttural, raging shriek. "Call my brothers and get them down here! We'll kill him right here, right in the parking lot!"

"I'm not going anywhere," Parvesh said.

"Do whatever you want," Gurmej said.

"F—ing bitch!" Dhillon screamed. "Call my brothers, call my f—ing brothers!"

"No," Parvesh said evenly.

Monday night at 7 p.m., Gurmej answered his door. It was a police officer. Dhillon had pressed charges. Gurmej was taken to the station, sat four hours in a cell. He filed counter charges. Later, Dhillon dropped the charges and a man named Budh, a leader in the Indian community, served as mediator between the two.

"*Veerji*," Dhillon pleaded with Gurmej, "I am sorry. You were a good friend in the past. When I broke my leg, you drove me around, took me to the doctor's. It's—it's those guys, at work. The others, they forced me to say that stuff, told me what to say."

They made me do it: it was a refrain Dhillon used time and again. He was not to blame. He was a simple man. A victim.

CHAPTER 5 ~ CASE CLOSED

Dhillon stopped making an honest living on February 18, 1991. That day, he told his boss that, while working on the paint line, he had fallen off a moving trolley and hurt his back and head. He applied for and received Worker's Compensation benefits. His back was killing him, he claimed, and he couldn't bend over. That year, he received $18,838 from the Worker's Compensation Board. The next year, he received $19,000, then $22,554 in 1993. The following year, 1994, he began selling used cars but continued collecting compensation, a total of $9,353, then $8,047 in 1995, and $8,111 in 1996. Meanwhile, Dhillon's family in Ludhiana sent money each year, and so did Parvesh's. The combined value was about $10,000.

He had learned other ways to make extra cash. Soon after arriving in Canada, Dhillon heard of a scam. In the summer of 1984, he claimed he was in a fender-bender in his Oldsmobile 98 and filed a claim in the physical damage/collision category. He was paid $4,726. Five years passed before the next auto insurance claim. On October 5, 1989, Dhillon said, his 1980 Oldsmobile Delta 88 Royale was in an accident. He was listed as not at fault. He claimed disability benefits from that, was paid $2,704, plus an additional $165 in collision/physical damage, and more cash in medical expenses. Six months later, on April 4, 1990, came the next claim, this time for $358 for collision/physical damage to his 1983 Cadillac Fleetwood Brougham. On June 12, $868 on a 1982 Buick Century. This time Parvesh was listed as being at fault. Part of the payment was for collision, the rest for property damage. The next claim, five months later, was $1,869 in "other claims" and "special perils" on the Cadillac. Two months after that, on November 9, 1990, there was another small payment, for $336 in damage to the Cadillac. By December 19, the date of the next accident claim, the Cadillac jackpot: a claim that it was stolen and damaged netted Dhillon $10,034.

Great deal, insurance. Much easier than factory work. Word of Dhillon's dubious insurance claims got around in the Indian community. Even insurance agents talked about it and, ultimately,

official memos were circulated warning agents to watch out for
Sukhwinder Singh Dhillon.

There were rumors that Dhillon purchased used cars,
scratched them up with keys or a screwdriver, made damage
claims, and that he reported his car stolen in Niagara Falls,
even as it sat in a friend's driveway in Hamilton. More outra-
geous still, Dhillon arranged for others to damage his cars. A
taxi driver he knew ran into him. He invited a friend who lived
in England to visit Hamilton, rent a car, and ram his vehicle.
The friend left the country; Dhillon got the money. Dhillon was
crazy, some thought, willing to risk his personal safety to make
a bit of insurance money. Gobind, his mother, cringed at such
talk. Nasty rumors. They could not be true. Sukhwinder was a
good man. Was he not friendly with everyone? Did he not give
gifts to everyone, all the time?

Early in 1991 the claims continued: $879 for a February 25
accident in his 1982 Buick Century, and $2,632 for an April 5 claim
on a different Buick. On January 30, 1993, he filed a claim on an
Oldsmobile; the payout was $2,688. Then two more claims, for an
accident on October 20, $2,326 on the Olds again, and five months
later, on March 8, 1994, for $2,850 on the same car.

*Easy, so easy. Great deals, all of them. No one says anything
about it, apart from jealous people in the community. Some talk at
the temple. Screw them all. Let them talk.*

Less than a month later came the biggest payout yet, an accident in the 1984 Chrysler New Yorker. He cashed in a claim
that grossed more money than any of his family or friends made
in an entire year. The accident, he claimed, occurred on April 6,
1994. Dhillon was listed on the claim as 100 per cent at fault. He
received $96,706 in eight claims from the accident:

- $2,122 physical damage/collision
- $22,090 disability income benefit
- $2,037 in medical benefits, excluding rehabilitation
  and long-term care
- $22,055 in other disability income benefits
- $13,508 in rehabilitation

- $23,422 in student/preschool disability and income benefits
- $1,472 standard benefits-cost of examinations
- $10,000 bodily injury claims

Nearly a hundred thousand dollars. He never got that much again. Five months later he filed a $13,170 claim for a September 9, 1994, accident involving the Ford Aerostar van he reported stolen and which was damaged when found. The year Parvesh died, 1995, there were no claims filed. He was in India for several months. On May 10, 1996, came another claim on the van, for $5,951 for collision and property damage, and $1,274 for property damage to a third party. Three weeks later came the final claim, on May 31, 1996, a $579 claim after Dhillon reported a 1992 Ford Tempo stolen.

In an eight-year span, Dhillon was paid $145,389 in insurance money on 15 claims involving seven vehicles, an average of $18,000 a year. The jealous ones could say all they want, but Sukhwinder Dhillon was right—there was an easier way to make money. He might be an uneducated man, but even he was smart enough to see that.

* * *

"*Heblah-heblah-heblah-heblah*—Five-seven—five-seven—five-seven? Hey! Do I hear six? Six-six-six! Six? Sold! For five-seven! Hey! It's your car, Bob!" The next one was ready. The Impala. Words and numbers rolled together as they rattled off the auctioneer's tongue. "*Heblah-heblah-heblah-heblah...*"

An assistant knocked his elbow on the window. That was the signal. The Impala inched ahead on the oil-stained, concrete floor toward the yawning doorway and the pale light of the overcast morning. The auctioneer's voice pounding, the floor man's eyes met those of the East Indian man as if to say, "Well? Are you in?" Sukhwinder Dhillon nodded, and the floor man placed one foot on the back bumper, grabbed the back window frame, dragged his other foot on the floor, holding the moving car in place like Superman.

It was October 1994. Dhillon had fallen in love with the used-car business, buying autos on his own, selling to friends, buying more on credit, selling to try to catch up. In 1994 he had incorporated his own used-car dealership, naming it Aman Auto after his youngest daughter. He could fit eight cars in his driveway and up the side of the house on Berkindale Drive. That was the beauty of a corner lot, he said. He dreamed of running his own dealership on a private lot, having an office. For now, he wheeled-and-dealed right out of his home. As a registered dealer, he qualified to attend the auctions. They were like a drug for him. Used cars are worth whatever you can get for them. A game of chance. Dhillon loved it.

Early in the morning he picked up his young protégé, Ranjit Khela, for the 45-minute drive in his Ford Aerostar van with his yellow seller's licence plate to an auction in Kitchener. Whenever Dhillon arrived at an auction he greeted the young women behind the counter. They thought he was odd. Sometimes he wore those shoes, pointy white shoes, you know, like the ones you see in the Walt Disney *Aladdin* movies. Dhillon colored his hair using black shoe polish, one woman was certain. She had seen him do it out in the parking lot, actually wiping shoe polish on his graying head. And it was comical how he talked about his cars, rambling in his rapid-fire, nasal-toned English slang. "Great deal. Loaded. Loaded!" Car talk was some of the first English Dhillon learned.

The used car auction system would eventually change, become regulated by processes and procedures through The Insurance Bureau, government regulations, and agencies. Today it's a tight ship. But back in 1994 the game was different. When a car rolled through on the block, there were no computer printouts documenting the vehicle's history. Instead, the seller would merely tell the auctioneer a car's history: "Bit of frame damage years ago. All fixed. Good shape." You could get away with it.

Between 300 and 400 dealers attended each week. The big dealers were there, even agents representing sellers in the United States. There were mid-size dealers with long histories and loyal clients. And there were new upstarts nobody had heard of, small operators trying to get ahead in a game where, like in Las Vegas, you never really stayed ahead. Inside the auction garage, Dhillon could see it, feel it. The anticipation. The tension. This was what it was all about.

"Hey, everybody!" boomed the auctioneer over the loud-speaker. "It's auction time! We have an unbelievable selection of vehicles today!" The smell in the garage was a medley of exhaust, cigaret smoke, and cologne. From the huge lot in the back, auction staff drove the cars to the doors, sprayed them down with power hoses on the way. There it was in the program: Chevrolet Impala. Sedan. Blue. 234,676 km. fm/at/ht/ac. (stereo, automatic, hard top, air conditioning). Starting price, $7,555. Buy? How high should he go? There was little time to waste. Mileage, the condition of the car. The mileage was not good. Tough to sell with that kind of wear. Something would need to be done about it. No problem. A quick job. Anyone can do it. Disconnect the odometer cable from the transmission. Take a doctored odometer from the junkyard. Clip it to the cable. The guy says he can take out the old one and put in the new one in a half-hour. Easy.

"Sold! The car is yours, Sukhwinder!"

The stars of the show were the auctioneers, great mouths perched high on platforms. It was theater. A car inches into place, a floor worker behind the wheel. Black Pontiac Grand Am. Dealers mingle, the bidding begins. Two minutes to complete the deal. Haggling? Test driving? No. Two minutes. Start the bidding. "Wake up!" bellows the mouth. "I have a car to sell! *Heblah-heblah-he-blah-heblah*"—Three! Three-one, three-four, do I have three-four? FOUR!" A floor man dances across the lane, claps, eyes partners in the crowd and grabs hold of cars as they pass through. You? Are you in?

"Four-one," rolls the mouth. "Four-two, four-five! FIVE! Five-five-five-five-five! Five-seven? Do I hear SIX! Six? Six-six-six-six-six? SIX! Six-two? Six-two. Six-four-four-four-four. Three? Three-three-three-three! Sold! For six thousand, two hundred to—Gary! It's your car, Gary. And a good buy, too. And now here we go, boys: a Ford Ranger." The noise, suffocating, intoxicating, revving engines, drone of the mouths melding into one voice over the loud speakers. *"Hebuh-hebuh-hebuh-sold!-hebuh-hebu-he …*

Hey! *Hebuh-aaar-hebuh ... aaar* Hey! *Hebuh-hebuh-hebuh-sold!-hebuh-hebu-hebuh ...*" A hypnotic chant. Easy money. The cars rolled through like dice.

Late in 1994, Dhillon sensed success. He just needed more cars to get Aman Auto off the ground, to make a name. Parvesh earned steady money at the textile factory. He had money from the insurance scams. He declared making $38,500 from October 1994 to September 1995. But in September 1994, Dhillon started bouncing checks. The first one for $4,000. Then another. And another. Ten checks in all, over four months—in December, one bounced for $18,521. Later that same month he started talking to a real estate agent about buying a bigger house. And he was also planning to take a trip to India. By January 1995, Dhillon had personally run up the credit line he shared with Parvesh close to its $20,000 maximum.

On a cold Monday, January 30, Dhillon and Parvesh bought groceries at Centre Mall on Barton Street. Back at the house late that afternoon, with an unsold car sitting in the driveway, Dhillon lay on the couch watching TV while Parvesh, her head throbbing from another migraine, started to prepare dinner. Dhillon got up and brought her a capsule. Within minutes Parvesh collapsed, her body strangled by spasms and convulsions.

Life insurance money. That was the ultimate deal.

* * *

The summer of 1995 in Hamilton was hot and dry, farmers' fields hard and arid, lakes evaporating to record low levels. Dhillon was back in Canada after his trip to India, doweries in hand from two marriages, and anxiously awaiting the $200,000 payoff on Parvesh's life.

On Tuesday, June 27, a man named Cliff Elliot left his home in Burlington, a city sitting hard to the north of Hamilton along the Lake Ontario shore. He drove to work past parched brown lawns. No rain for more than a month. On this day, though, Elliot saw pellets of rain hit his windshield.

At 61 he was tall, bookish in manner. He wore glasses and had thick, dark brown hair, brushed back. People commented on

Scott Gardner

Insurance claim investigator Cliff Elliot

it, the absence of even a speck of gray. How do you do it, Cliff? He never dyed it. Cliff's mother hadn't gone gray until well into old age. It reflected Elliot's cool under pressure. He retained a British accent, having been born on a late summer's evening in Buckinghamshire, a couple of floors over top of the English pub his parents owned. His father, George, flew in the RAF against Hitler's Luftwaffe and lived to tell about it, and eventually worked on the top secret Avro Arrow fighter jet project in Canada. Dad was still around, still sipped a shot of whisky each night.

Elliot was an insurance claims investigator. This morning he was en route to east Hamilton, following up on one of the dozen or so cases on his docket. He had started in the business in 1958. Not too glamorous in the early days. There was the time he visited a woman who claimed her diamond ring was lost. He peered under her carpets on his knees, took apart pipes under the kitchen sink—*apologies, ma'am, just be a few minutes*. It was probably the neatest home he had ever seen, until he got through with it. The claim was legit. Eventually Elliot specialized in death claims. At one point in his career he directed all death claims in Canada for a company called Equifax. In 1992 he surprised his employer, Keyfacts International, by taking a retirement package. Keyfacts urged him to stay on. They needed Elliot, his thick black book packed with contacts.

Now he worked part time, easing into retirement, paid by the case. One of the new ones involved a claim on a young Punjabi-

Canadian woman. She had died four months earlier, in February.
Her name was Parvesh Dhillon. Primerica Life Insurance Company
needed more documents before paying the $200,000 benefit to her
husband, Sukhwinder Dhillon. It seemed a straightforward case.
Elliot turned off Barton Street onto Berkindale Drive, stopped
his Ford Tempo in front of Dhillon's house. There was a red fire
hydrant in the yard. Elliot pulled ahead a little farther and parked
in front of the next house, the one that had two small decorative
statues in the front yard.

Dhillon answered his door to see the lanky Elliot on the step.
The wide dark eyes affected a puzzled, even fearful, look, Dhillon's
natural shield against strangers. Dhillon nodded in greeting. Elliot
politely went into his spiel.

"Good morning, Mr. Dhillon, I am Clifton Elliot of Keyfacts
International. I'm here for you to sign some documents. It will
help expedite the processing of the claim on your deceased wife,
Parvesh."

Dhillon quickly, excitedly, invited Elliot inside, talking rough
but passable English to him. The life insurance deal. Finally. They
sat at the kitchen table. Parvesh had collapsed just over there,
on that carpet, five months earlier. "How did your wife die, Mr.
Dhillon?"

"She was at this table," Dhillon said, gesturing. "She started
to shake, then fell to the floor. She died at hospital."

Elliot studied the husband's face and waited for the words to
come from his mouth. And waited. *I am devastated … If you find
anything out about her death, please, please let me know, would
you?* Those words didn't come. No, Mr. Dhillon explained away
his wife's recent death rather blandly. Where was the pain, the
puzzlement that her death remained a mystery? Where was the
intensity that Mr. Dhillon showed at the door when the strange
man came knocking? Elliot had no idea how Parvesh died. But
her husband of—what did the form say, 12 years?—didn't know
much about it, either. And Elliot was surprised that Mr. Dhillon
didn't seem curious about it at all.

You work in this business long enough, you read people. Cliff
Elliot always insisted on seeing beneficiaries in person to read the

tea leaves, to act as a human lie detector, listening to their tone of voice, observing whether facial lines crinkled with emotion or stayed smooth in a forced cool. He would show up 30 minutes early for an appointment, or unannounced. Truth comes best off the cuff. "Terribly sorry," he would say. "Just a tad early, I'm afraid." Under different circumstances, in another life, he could have worked for Scotland Yard. The gentleman investigator, the Velvet Hammer.

Most of his cases were for accidental death. A man dies in a car accident. For the purposes of the life insurance claim, however, did he die as a result of the crash, or might he have had a heart attack in the car just before it? He needed autopsy and coroner's reports to find out. Sometimes he followed the tracks of police investigators who went before him. Sometimes he led the police. There was the Burlington man years back who made a claim after saying his wife was stabbed by thugs in a parking lot. In due course the man skipped off to Las Vegas. Elliot came calling about the claim, asked questions, gathered medical records, chatted with travel agents, police. Ultimately, the man was jailed for homicide.

There was another case—an East Indian woman filed a claim for her husband's death, saying he was kidnapped during a visit to India and killed. Elliot showed up at her house, asked to see travel documents and phone records in order to put the husband in India and confirm his disappearance. He told the wife, in his polite way: "I will contact the Canadian High Commission in New Delhi. Perhaps they have some information on the case." She got cold feet. Miraculously, the husband showed up in Canada shortly afterwards. Turns out he escaped his captors and survived. Imagine that! The insurance claim was withdrawn and Elliot phoned the police. He stood to gain little from extra work chasing people who were out to cheat the system. It was simply part of who he was.

Elliot spent about 20 minutes in Dhillon's house. Then he left with signatures on several documents. His verdict? Dhillon knew more about the death than he let on. Life insurance claims are void for a suicide if they happen within the first two years of the policy. Had Parvesh taken her own life by overdose? Died of an allergic reaction? Whatever it was, Dhillon knew something, but was not telling. Elliot got back in his Tempo and drove to Hamilton General Hospital to order records concerning the death of Parvesh Dhillon. He also requested coroner's records and those of Parvesh's family doctor.

When the hospital records came back three weeks later they offered little help. The cause of her death was listed as anoxic brain damage—lack of oxygen to the brain—but the root cause was unknown. The hospital drug screen showed Parvesh had not died from street drugs. The reporting coroner had not ordered toxicology tests in Toronto. The law did not require them. Elliot wanted to dig deeper. He called Primerica, the company that had insured Parvesh Dhillon's life. Would they like him to look into the case further, or were they content to pay Mr. Dhillon?

"The reports say we don't know how she died," he said. "She could have taken bottled Aspirin or something for all we know. It hasn't been checked, and for some reason the coroner didn't order additional toxicology." The voice on the line agreed that it sounded a little unusual, but by the end of the summer, Primerica had the documents ready to process Dhillon's claim. The company decided not to pursue any further investigation. Her husband could receive his $200,000.

Cliff Elliot had more than a dozen other cases on the go, plenty else to keep him occupied, and retirement loomed. But he was not pleased. It just didn't feel right. After getting the word from Primerica that Dhillon's check was being processed, Elliot drove to his downtown Hamilton office. He carried the brown folder over to the metal filing cabinet, the one with all the lives inside. He fingered the insurance file folders in a drawer until he hit D for Dhillon. He slid Parvesh's file into its resting place. The case was closed.

* * *

Dhillon decided to take another trip to India, a short one this time. He flew out of Toronto on July 28 and returned August 11. A visit to the market in Ludhiana for more *kuchila*? Another deal in the works? Soon after he returned, finally, the payoff arrived—the check from Primerica dated August 25, 1995, for $202,260.67. His biggest deal ever. He also would soon receive $15,000 from Parvesh's workplace life insurance policy. He had already emptied her personal account of $38,000 in savings that she had kept from him. For good measure, he forged the signature of Parvesh's father, Hardev, in order to write himself a $1,000 check from the old man's account and duly cashed it. He put $50,000 in a term deposit for both Harpreet and Aman, his young daughters. A perfect move. It looked charitable, but happened to allow him to keep his hands on the money, avoid paying tax on it, and skim interest earned on the investment to transfer into his own account. His bank adviser urged him not to do it. Revenue Canada frowned on the practice. What did Dhillon care what Revenue Canada, his adviser or anyone else thought? He was, as the car dealers put it, on a roll! On fire!

Dhillon received payments from Parvesh's life insurance policies.

In September, Dhillon went to the tax office in Hamilton and lied about his income flow, low-balled it in order to claim a Goods and Services Tax rebate. The Worker's Compensation benefits from his claim of injury in 1991 continued, and he was still selling cars. Given his mountain of debt, Dhillon was hardly set for life. But he had money to play with and two young wives in India to do with as he pleased. On November 2, 1995, Dhillon filed an immigration claim to bring his third wife, Kushpreet, to Canada. On November 7, he closed a deal for $66,100 to buy a small house on Main Street East, just east of Ottawa Street. He would rent out rooms in the house and use a large paved area behind it to park his cars. No more crowding used vehicles in his driveway on Berkindale Drive. Finally he had his dealership. He'd made it. He booked another trip to India for December. This would be a much longer visit.

CHAPTER 6 ~ BURNING CORPSE

Panj Grain, India
December 1995

Sarabjit waited for the moment, her slim young figure transformed by the offspring of Sukhwinder Dhillon growing inside her. The birth would come any day now. She had checked into Kumar Hospital, a 15-minute drive from Panj Grain. In a marriage that had been long distance at best, and nightmarish when she was with her husband, the anticipation of being a mother excited her. And Jodha, her husband? Dhillon sounded surprised when she first told him that she was expecting. But why should he be? Had they not had sex nearly every day they spent together? She wondered how he would react when he saw the baby for the first time. When she spoke to him on the phone, he told her he was due to arrive in India any day now, would likely meet her at the hospital.

In fact, Dhillon was already in Ludhiana. He had flown out of Toronto along with his mother, brother, and his daughters on Friday, December 8, arriving in New Delhi on Monday, December 11, well aware that Sarabjit would soon deliver. But he avoided her. He had other business.

On Tuesday, he arrived at his home in Ludhiana. Rai Singh Toor showed up at the door. Rai Singh was the father of Dhillon's third wife, Kushpreet. Good news, Rai said. He had medical papers for Dhillon to sign to help speed Kushpreet's entry to Canada. Dhillon had married her in April, but still had not had sex with her. Rai Singh had made it clear that would not happen until her immigration papers were finalized. The next day, Wednesday, December 13, Dhillon drove two hours to Kushpreet's village, Tibba. He arrived, exchanged pleasantries with Rai Singh, enjoyed a cold drink, and handed over the papers. Would he stay for the evening? No, he should really get home. He and Kushpreet had things to do, and he had other business to take care of.

Dhillon drove Kushpreet back to his house in Ludhiana to consummate their marriage. Rai Singh phoned the next day, determined to see the Canadian immigration expedited. Kushpreet needed to have a physical as part of the immigration process. When did Dhillon want to take her for it? Tomorrow, tomorrow, said Dhillon, stalling. The next day was Friday, December 15. At six-thirty in the morning, Sarabjit lay in her hospital bed, exhausted, a newborn baby in each arm. She had gone into labor just after six the evening before, gave birth 12 hours later. Sukhwinder Dhillon finally had a son—two sons, in fact. Twins. Sarabjit proudly told the nurses the names she picked for the twin boys: Gurmeet and Gurwinder. She just liked the sound of them. The nurses liked the names, too. The boys entered the world eight months and 10 days after Sarabjit's wedding to Dhillon.

A day after the births, Dhillon left Kushpreet long enough to phone Sarabjit in the hospital. He was in India now, finally, he told Sarabjit. She thought he sounded happy when she told him he had two sons. Or maybe just surprised. Who cared how he felt, really. Except, in Sarabjit's current state, weary from childbirth, ecstatic at the twin wonders, she let herself think that maybe Jodha would be excited. He had never had a son, and now she had given him two. It had been seven months since she last saw him. Perhaps things had changed, perhaps things would improve when they were together in Canada.

"I'll come as soon as possible," Dhillon told her. "I have some business, but will be right there."

Dhillon then phoned Sarabjit's father in Panj Grain, a man named Gurjant. Dhillon had a message for him to pass on to Sarabjit. Later, Gurjant walked into his daughter's hospital room. They chatted briefly, then he got to the point. Dhillon had called, he said.

"Why? Why did he call you?" she said.

"He has asked that you keep the babies unnamed," Gurjant said.

"What?"

"That's what he said."

Sarabjit's father didn't quite understand Dhillon's reasoning, but he also didn't want to upset him. Dhillon was his ticket to Canada, too.

"I have already named them," Sarabjit said. "Gurmeet and Gurwinder. That's it."

They argued briefly. Gurjant had never seen this side of his daughter before. Sarabjit's voice grew angry. "You married me to him, and now I have my own life. The naming will be done—it is done. I'm making my own decisions."

Gurjant left the room and Sarabjit realized she was short of breath. This was an outrage. How could Dhillon demand such a thing, and use her father as the messenger, no less? A nurse entered the room. Was she all right? "Oh yes," Sarabjit said. "When can I sign the forms registering the babies' names? I want to sign them. The names are picked."

On Wednesday, December 20, Dhillon told Kushpreet he had business in Chandigarh. He was a busy man. She should stay put. Dhillon left, bought some candy for Sarabjit, and drove two hours to the hospital. A nurse congratulated him on the news. He sat on the bed beside Sarabjit and handed her a bottle of tonic. Rub it over the babies, he said, it will make them strong. Then he held his sons. He turned to Sarabjit. Don't tell anyone about the babies, he said, don't make a big fuss over it. And do not yet name them.

"What?" she said.

"A wise man told me. The stars are not right. It will be bad luck. And another thing, do not hang the *sehara* at home." A *sehara* is a wall-hanging of flowers, often hung on a gate of a house to celebrate the birth of a son. Sarabjit was outraged. Who was this man? How could he say such things?

"It's too late," she said, defiance swelling inside her. "I've named them already."

Dhillon became angry. "How could you when I asked you not to?"

"They need names," she said. "And so I have named them."

Sarabjit was due to leave the hospital the next day, but Dhillon told her she could not yet join him in Ludhiana. He had business to tend to, and immigration matters to expedite. He told her to stay at her parents' Panj Grain home with the newborns. Dhillon left the hospital and drove back to Ludhiana to be with Kushpreet. He had something for her, something he had brought from Canada. It would help her qualify for immigration. It was a single medicine capsule.

"If you are pregnant, they won't let you come to Canada," he explained. "This pill, I brought it from Canada, it's medicine that will help. We've been having sex, this will keep you from getting pregnant."

"Yes, but not yet," she said. "I need to speak with my mother first."

Two weeks later, on December 27, Dhillon brought Kushpreet back to her home in Tibba. Dhillon saw Sukie, his wife's younger sister. "You know, we should get married, don't you think?" he said. Jodha. Always joking like that.

Dhillon left alone. He had somewhere to go, business in New Delhi, he said. He got back in his car and drove the two-hour trip (all trips on India's congested roads seemed to take at least two hours) to Panj Grain to visit Sarabjit and the twins. After Dhillon left, Kushpreet spoke to her mother, Daljit. Kushpreet was embarrassed about her relationship with Dhillon. She told her mother about the pill and what Dhillon wanted her to do.

"That's ridiculous," Daljit said. "Don't take it. You're married, after all. If you are pregnant, so be it. And I've never heard of one pill that would do that."

Later that day, Dhillon arrived in Panj Grain, driving past the village fields and the brick-walled, rectangular cemetery. Cemeteries are not common sights in Punjab. Sikhs cremate their dead, sprinkle the ashes in the river. The few cemeteries that exist are mainly for infants. Babies that die are not cremated. An infant is believed to have not yet developed a soul, and so has no relationship with God to pursue once the body is burned.

At Sarabjit's family home, Dhillon sat alone with the babies while his wife joined her mother in the kitchen to make tea. What was it that angered him so much about naming the babies? Was it that naming the kids would identify him to everyone as her husband, something he could not allow? Sarabjit and her mother came back in the room, and Dhillon said he could not stay for dinner, which is an insult in Punjabi culture. He was sorry, but he had to go, right now. He left at 8 p.m. It occurred to Sarabjit that this was the first visit since her arranged marriage with Dhillon that he had not insisted on sex. And now was he leaving, after just four hours with his new sons. Why had he even come? she wondered.

Dhillon vanished into the blackness of the country night. He drove to Tibba, picked up Kushpreet, and headed toward Ludhiana.

Sarabjit watched her babies die in agony.

Meanwhile, at 10 o'clock, back in Panj Grain, Sarabjit heard one of the babies crying. It sounded more intense than usual. As Gurmeet slept, Sarabjit picked up Gurwinder from his crib. She was frightened. She had fed him nothing but goat's milk before bed, as usual. She rocked him, tried to hum a song. She could feel his tiny body shaking. In the dim light she could see that his hands and feet had a blue tone to them. Terrified now, she felt the little body convulse, his neck, arms, and legs stiffen. He vomited a dark green fluid. Sarabjit's father took Gurwinder from her arms and rushed him to the local temple to see the priest. It was a Sikh tradition to take a sick baby to a priest for prayers. Sarabjit wanted to go, but was told to stay put. Women were told to stay indoors at night. It was cool outside, so he wrapped the baby in blankets.

At the temple the priest held the boy, blessed him, spoke soothingly. But it was no use. The baby boy died. The male members of Sarabjit's family—for tradition dictates that only males can undertake such a ritual—buried him in the cemetery. Sarabjit wanted to go to the funeral. The men told her she could not.

Her uncle Iqbal, who had first set Dhillon up with Sarabjit, phoned Dhillon to tell him the terrible news and inform him about the funeral. At the apartment in Ludhiana, Dhillon's sister-in-law answered. Dhillon told her to say he wasn't home. He did not attend the burial of his son. Later that same day, baby Gurmeet also became ill. This time the family phoned a local doctor's apprentice. He didn't know what to make of it. Take the baby to a hospital, a specialist, he said. Gurmeet's death mirrored his brother's: the convulsions, bloated stomach, blueish skin, green vomit. He died at 3:30 a.m. the next day. He was buried next to his brother. Both babies were laid to rest wearing their matching blue nylon pajamas.

Sarabjit, crushed, could only watch outside through the green steel gate guarding the pathway to the walled cemetery, tears pouring down her cheeks. Once again, her uncle Iqbal had called Dhillon's home. Again, the father of the babies did not appear to be around. He missed the second funeral as well. Later that day, Dhillon finally made the drive to Panj Grain to see his grieving wife. His face showed no emotion. He put his arm around Sarabjit. "*Udaas na ho, bachey saadey hey hee nahee see*," Dhillon said. "It's okay, don't cry. The twins never belonged to us."

Sarabjit knew, or thought she knew, what he was trying to say, clumsily as usual—that the boys belonged to God. But after his insistence that she tell no one about their newborns, and not register their names, his words carried an ominous ring to them.

Dhillon left and returned to Ludhiana. The next morning, Sunday, December 31, Dhillon was on the road again, alone. This time he headed to a village called Dhandra. He showed up at the house of a man named Narangh Singh Grewal. Dhillon walked down a dark hallway, then into a main bedroom and living area, light shining through an ornately shaped window, pistachio green walls inside, lined with prints of Sikh gurus. He was interested in marrying Narangh Singh's daughter. Dhillon had earlier directed his sister-in-law to ask around to see if there was any girl in the village who wanted to marry a Canadian man.

The young woman lined up for him was 27-year-old Sukhwinder Kaur Grewal.

Sukhwinder Kaur did not find Dhillon appealing. He had an odd aura about him. She instantly disliked him. Dhillon spoke with her briefly and mentioned his first wife, Parvesh. A sad story, yes. He had taken her to Canada. She had been fasting, was quite weak, and slipped going down the stairs of their home in Hamilton. She died from the fall. Sukhwinder Kaur was older than Sarabjit or Kushpreet. She had a feisty spirit and knew the rules. Her parents struck a deal with Dhillon that day, and she was instantly engaged. They should be married in Canada, all agreed. Dhillon vowed to return to see the family on January 12.

Courtesy of the author

Sukhwinder Kaur, Dhillon's fourth wife

Back in Ludhiana, Dhillon drove Kushpreet from his house to her uncle's place across town, her Uncle Jagdev and Aunt Iqbal Mundi. He needed to talk privately to his niece, Sarvjit, who was 20 years old. Dhillon knew that Sarvjit might one day join him in Canada to help look after Harpreet and Aman, his daughters by Parvesh. She should know the truth. She might hear vicious rumors about him. He told her that Sarabjit's babies had not been his.

"*Bholi*," Dhillon said, using Sarvjit's nickname. "You should know that Sarabjit was pregnant before I met her. It's not right, you know that. I'm divorcing her, and her parents say it's fine, to go ahead with it. They understand." Sarvjit listened. Dhillon continued, "The twins, babies, they weren't mine. But they are spreading rumors about me. Don't believe them, Bholi."

It was about 8 p.m. on Monday, January 22, when Dhillon arrived at Uncle Jagdev's house in Ludhiana to pick up Kushpreet and return her to her parents in Tibba. They had been pressing him hard about getting Kushpreet into Canada. He said he would take her the next day for the required physical examination. In the car, Dhillon talked to Kushpreet once more about the special pill he had from Canada. The pill will hide the pregnancy. It might be the only thing that gets you to Canada. We all want to make sure you get to Canada. I do, your parents do. Please, take it.

They arrived in Tibba at 10 p.m. Dhillon pulled the Maruti in front of her family's tiny home. Kushpreet got out of the car. Was Dhillon coming in? "I can't stay," Dhillon said. "Business in Chandigarh early in the morning. I'll be back tomorrow afternoon to take you for your physical."

The next day Kushpreet was preparing lunch in anticipation of Dhillon's return. She had to stop. Suddenly she was not feeling well. Her skin tingled, as though a rash had developed. She took a bath. It didn't help. The water seemed to singe her skin. She dried off. It

Scott Gardner

felt as if she couldn't breathe. She sat in the kitchen next to her younger sister, Sukie. "I don't feel well," Kushpreet said. "And look at my feet." The skin looked blue. What was going on? Kushpreet was healthy. She couldn't recall the last time she had been to a doctor. Sukie helped her out of the kitchen into the small courtyard. Kushpreet lay on a cot. Sukie noticed the spots on her sister's skin.

"Something strange is happening to me," Kushpreet said, starting to moan. "What

The courtyard where Kushpreet fell ill.

is happening? She grew tense, stiff. "Can you get me some water?" Her mother came to sit with her. Did she eat something?

"No," she replied. "But I took a pill." Then her speech slurred, her mouth clamped itself shut, her lips curled back into a grimace. She looked at her sister, Sukie, pointed her finger to her mouth. "Medicine," she moaned. "Jodha."

"We'll get you to the hospital," Sukie said. She ran out of the courtyard, up the narrow brick alleyway to summon Pargat, their tall, strong cousin. Pargat ran with Sukie to the house and found Kushpreet on the ground, her body rigid. For a brief moment, the convulsions stopped. Kushpreet could speak. "I don't know what is happening," she managed to say. "I think—I think I'm dying. I can't feel my legs. I'm gone. Quickly, take me quickly. I'm dying."

The village doctor arrived. He could do nothing. Take her to the hospital, he said. Few people in Tibba, a village of 1,200, owned a car. Pargat scooped up his suffering cousin in his arms, her back arched, face twitching. He carried her up the narrow street, then got on his tractor with her and drove to the end of the road, waiting for the car that had been summoned. Family members loaded Kushpreet into a tiny Fiat, her rigid legs sticking out the back window. Her body again shook violently. Family wept at the sight. Kushpreet urinated in the car. They drove to Bhambri Hospital. The one-storey, weathered, flesh-colored, concrete building was 20 minutes away along the rough country roads. It was named after the doctor who owned it, Dr. Mohinder Bhambri. In the car, the convulsions eased again. Kushpreet fought to speak, slurring her words.

"Mother," she said. "The medicine. I took the medicine. Jodha."

By the time they got Kushpreet to the hospital, she was unconscious. The doctor who checked her asked what she ate. Nothing, said the family.

"Take her home, unless you want to get the police involved," the doctor said.

It was not an unusual piece of advice in Punjab. When police officers are called to an emergency, victims often have to pay for their services. So Kushpreet's family took her away in the car. There was no further examination. The stiffness had gone, her body now limp. She was dead. There would be no autopsy, no investigation.

Perhaps Kushpreet's father, Rai Singh Toor, was concerned that a neighbor would frame his family for a crime they didn't commit, or bribe corrupt local police to do so. Or perhaps he was thinking of how to turn the tragedy around to get his family into Canada. He would say later that he did not suspect Dhillon of anything. Sukie was next in line. Dhillon always spoke highly of Sukie. He obviously was attracted to her, too.

The next day, Kushpreet's aunt told Dhillon the news in person. Dhillon's expression did not change. His face remained passive, bland even, as he digested the words. Had he heard what she said? He left her for a moment, made a phone call. He finally spoke.

"Why is this happening to me?" he said flatly. "Parvesh died, and now Kushpreet. All so quickly."

In Tibba, Aunt Iqbal helped the other women prepare Kushpreet for cremation. The young body was marked with bluish spots, mostly on her back but some on the inner thighs and arms. What could she have eaten that would have done this, wondered her aunt. She bathed the body, rubbed it with yogurt. She dressed Kushpreet in a new red *lehnga*. Her face would be uncovered for the first stage of prayer, then covered with the *chunni*, or scarf. Mourners began to gather in Tibba. Visitors at the funeral asked Rai Singh how his daughter died.

"It was a heart attack," he said.

Dhillon was at the funeral. Intense mourning of a death is discouraged among Sikhs, especially if the deceased is elderly. Birth and death are considered partners because they are both part of the cycle of human existence, life being merely one step toward nirvana, or complete unity with God. But Kushpreet did not live a full life, so her funeral was much darker. Her body was wrapped in sheets, a red shawl placed on top. White would have been used if she had been unmarried. Men of the family carried her body on a ceremonial wooden stretcher from the family's home down the narrow sun-baked alley.

The procession emerged onto a dirt path, fields of corn and cane as far as the eye could see on each side, along to the site of the

The funeral pyre where Kushpreet was cremated.

small white *gurdwara* and a funeral pyre block. Ancient banyan trees stood like old gray men, branches sprouting tendrils that crept down the trunk and into the ground like veins grasping for life. At the pyre was the smooth concrete floor with streaks of scorched black, surrounded by six pillars supporting a brick roof. The roof was pierced by steel grates to allow airflow to enhance burning.

The men of the family lifted the body onto the stack of dried logs on the floor, then covered her with more logs. Tradition says the husband lights the pyre. But Sukhwinder Dhillon was not there in time for the lighting. It was left to Kushpreet's father, Rai Singh, to walk around the pyre and touch a flaming stick to hay stacked at the base of the wood. Soon it burst into orange flames spewing black smoke. It burned all afternoon.

When he arrived, Dhillon hugged Kushpreet's parents in sympathy, his face now a forlorn mask.

"If I'd been with Kushpreet when she died," he said, "you'd be blaming me right now."

It was the spoiled child talking once more, taunting grieving parents, purporting to offer an alibi while at the same time blatantly, foolishly implicating himself.

As the logs crackled, a man approached Rai Singh. He said he was visiting from Canada, near Hamilton, Ontario. Dhillon's city. "My condolences," he said. Rai Singh nodded. The man continued. "Have you heard about this Dhillon guy? He was married twice before." Rai Singh did not believe him. And blaming

Dhillon would do nothing to get his family to Canada. Later that day, Dhillon mentioned Kushpreet's sister Sukie. What about her? Rai Singh said he'd support the marriage. Dhillon instantly agreed. It should be done as quickly as possible, because he had to return to Canada soon. Dhillon climbed back into his Maruti, drove down the cobblestone laneway, a smile on his face.

CHAPTER 7 ~ BIGAMY AND MURDER

Dhillon did not attend the *bhog* for Kushpreet. His absence from the family's traditional nine-day mourning period angered her grieving relatives. Nevertheless, Rai Singh pushed ahead to expedite the marriage to Sukie. He drove to Ludhiana and obtained a death certificate for Kushpreet from a city hospital. She had never been to that hospital, but this was the way bureaucracy worked in India. Any document was available for the right price, no questions asked. The bogus certificate said she died of natural causes. Rai Singh then drove to Dhillon's home to give him a copy for Sukie's immigration application and to ask for more time to raise money for the dowry and wedding.

Dhillon had other business. He returned to Sukhwinder Kaur's home in Dhandra where he spoke softly, warmly to her parents. Then Dhillon told them he had changed his mind about marrying Sukhwinder Kaur in Canada. It would take too much time, he said. They should do it here, in India, before he left. The family agreed. Ten days later Dhillon married for the fourth time. His new bride wed him at a *gurdwara* in Ludhiana, with a reception at Gurpal Palace.

Meanwhile, by the end of February, in the village of Panj Grain, Sarabjit's father grew restless with Dhillon. The tension had been building even before the babies had died. Why hadn't Dhillon taken his daughter to Canada yet? Whenever he reached Dhillon by phone in Ludhiana—a chore in itself—there was a story. Dhillon was getting papers ready. He was talking with government people. He had business deals on the go. He always had an excuse. Dhillon finally dropped in to see Sarabjit. People are spreading lies about him, he said. And he said he had heard stories about *her*—that in fact she was actually 30 years old and had been married before, already had children. Sarabjit was furious.

"You bring me the people who said that, and if I'm married, why don't you take me to the person I'm married to!"

In March, Sarabjit, her uncle Iqbal, and Dhillon visited her grandparents in a village called Mairu. They ate dinner together. In front of the grandparents, Dhillon again mentioned the "rumors" about Sarabjit. Her grandfather grew upset. "Why are you saying these things?" he demanded.

Dhillon told Sarabjit that he had to return to Ludhiana, alone, to prepare for his return trip to Canada. He would continue to make arrangements to bring her over at a later date. She didn't believe a word. He left. It was the last time Sarabjit ever saw Dhillon in India.

Once he was back in Canada, the rumors about Dhillon ran hotter than ever in Punjab. Some wrote letters that landed on the desk of Pierre Carrier at the Canadian High Commission in New Delhi. Carrier was an RCMP liaison officer. He saw accusatory, "poison-pen" letters like this all the time. There were so many of them that, without any additional query by official Indian or Canadian authorities, they went unexamined. A Sikh man who made it to Canada who is a bigamist and a murderer who should be deported? Right. In the air-conditioned cool of the High Commission office, the latest letters were filed with the rest of the stack. Case closed? There was no case.

Uncle Iqbal got wind of the stories. He was furious, embarrassed. If he had known what Dhillon was up to, he reflected, he would have phoned the police. Yes, that's what he would have done.

Scott Gardner

He was not afraid of Jodha. He visited Surinder, who was the widow of Dhillon's late brother, Darshan, and living at the family's apartment in Ludhiana. "You knew this was happening," he said to her. "Why didn't you tell me about it?"

"Jodha threatened me," she said. "He told me not to tell or he'd have me shot."

Iqbal phoned Dhillon in Hamilton. "Why have you done all this to us?" he asked. "What do I tell Sarabjit and her family?"

Iqbal Singh, Sarabjit's uncle

"Tell them to do whatever they want," Dhillon said. "Just tell them I ran away."

On April 15, 1996, Dhillon filed papers to bring Sukhwinder Kaur to Canada.

* * *

Criminal poisoning is a rare offence. A behavioral profile of the poisoner looks something like this: one with a dreamy disposition who sees the world through a child-like prism, having an illusory sense of the world and their place in it; there is a strong desire to get their own way; they may have been spoiled as a child. Poisoners try to make the world obey their will by cheating it, at first in minor ways, taking what it refuses to deliver to them. Male poisoners may be vain, pretty boys, somewhat effeminate. They tend to be non-confrontational, having little in common with the killer who attacks in an alley with a baseball bat or gun. The poisoner depersonalizes victims, an extension of their failure to accept any moral basis for life in a world they see through their own cracked lens. That profile fit Sukhwinder Dhillon in the spring of 1996. But there was no criminal profile on him. No one in law enforcement was even looking for him.

Most killers murder in a paroxysm of disorienting hate, fear, rage, or dementia, when the brain's circuits fatally cross in the blinding heat and confusion of the moment. The serial killer is different. He—and it is almost always a male—allows time to lapse between each victim in what homicide profilers call a cooling-off period. There is purpose and calculation, a rationality disturbing in its whispered suggestion that all humanity shares the capacity to kill, even if it is usually buried in a moral crevice that never sees light. The serial killer is, by definition, a successful killer. He is pushed on by his own sense of accomplishment, his ego fed but never satisfied by each murder he commits. He will not, cannot, be caught. And so he does not stop.

* * *

"*Kabaddi-kabaddi-kabaddi-kabaddi-kabaddi.*" Now it was the next boy's turn. In his pale blue uniform shirt and navy pants, little Ranjit Khela took a deep breath and ran across enemy lines on the playground, calling the word over and over again: "*Kabaddi-kabaddi-kabaddi-kabaddi-kabaddi-kabaddi.*" Ranjit touched a boy on the shoulder, sprinted to the next, just missed him, touched another, and another—"*Kabaddi-kabaddi-kabaddi!*"

The boys played the game every day. Hold your breath, run across a line in the dirt to the other side, tag as many boys as possible before escaping back. Chanting the word repeatedly ensured you could not cheat by taking a breath. Ranjit ran faster now, his lungs screaming for air, heart pounding—"*Kabaddi-kabaddi!*" Could he touch one more, push it a little further, leave himself enough oxygen to make it back across the line? "*Kabaddi-kabaddi*"—Yes! Ranjit made it back. It was a game for healthy lungs.

Every day in the Punjabi village called Mau Sahib, he was up early helping on the family farm, harvesting wheat and rice, herding buffalo. As landowning *jats* (farmers), the Khelas were not poor. After morning chores, he walked 30 minutes to school from his family's bungalow along a path made of dark brick, radiating heat, into the dusty village center where shops and produce stands lined the main dirt road. Every day, he passed the towering brick kiln and a stone-block funeral pyre. Right turn onto the main road, a canopy of banyan and eucalyptus trees, tall fields of sugar cane and rice tossing in the wind as though invisible children ran through them, and into the school courtyard. Games in the yard, then classes inside the plain gray concrete-walled rooms. It was a simple time. And the best chapter in Ranjit's life.

As a teenager he talked about the dream, making it overseas, finding his fortune. Ranjit was born on New Year's Day, 1971, the first of four children. He grew up to be a tall, handsome man, the star of the family. He was a leader, he ran the farm. A life in Canada was inevitable. Davinder and Gurmail, Ranjit's aunt and uncle, were the first to make it over, to Hamilton, Ontario. They sponsored his grandparents, Piara and Surjit, to follow. Ranjit stopped attending school after Grade 8 to work on the farm full time, drive the tractor, supervise workers the family hired for

harvest season. And, like some of his boyhood friends, he cut his
hair for the first time, divorcing himself from orthodox Sikhism.
After that he wore a turban only on formal occasions. In 1992,
when Ranjit turned 21, the road to the new world opened for him
when a woman named Lakhwinder visited him from Canada. Ranjit
embraced the opportunity to join his relatives in Hamilton.

Ranjit Khela and his sister, Karmajit

Lakhwinder Kaur Sekhon had moved to Canada in 1987 and
three years later signed on for an arranged marriage to an Indian
man. Sixteen months later they divorced. Twenty-four months
after that, she met Ranjit Khela. She had first seen him in a photo
while visiting Ranjit's relatives in Hamilton. If his family was willing
to arrange a marriage, she was interested. The couple married in
Punjab on December 13, 1992, in a village called Dakha. Ranjit's
12-year-old sister, Karmajit, cried before her big brother left. She
loved him so much, looked up to him. On October 23, 1993, Ranjit
arrived in Canada.

He soon moved into an apartment in Hamilton's east end
and met Sukhwinder Dhillon. To Ranjit, Jodha seemed success-

ful, had his own house, a beautiful wife and two kids, sold used cars. Dhillon assumed the role of Ranjit's mentor. He was 35, Ranjit—Ranna, they called him—was 23 years old. He knew little English. Dhillon spoke English, even if it was coarse. Dhillon was the wheeler-dealer, Ranjit his quiet understudy.

The two men talked about everything—cars, women, complained about their wives. Jodha's wife always had headaches. Ranjit thought his wife was overweight and confided that he was having trouble getting an erection with her. The impotence frustrated him. He was too young to go through this. Repeated visits to two local doctors, three injections of testosterone. Nothing worked.

The friends became close enough that, when Dhillon traveled back to Punjab after the death of Parvesh, Ranjit looked after his house on Berkindale Drive. While in Punjab, Dhillon drove to Mau Sahib to deliver presents from Ranjit to his family. Ranjit had sent gifts to prove he was taking advantage of his new opportunity in Canada—shoes for his brothers, a gold Nike pendant for his cousin. Dhillon was met by Ranjit's aunt. Accustomed to smaller Indian men, Dhillon appeared huge to her, like a giant. But she quickly moved from his physique to his eyes. What was it about them? What was going on in his mind? You look into a person's eyes and sometimes you just know there is something wrong. That's how it was. You could just tell. Dhillon was trouble.

* * *

In April 1996 Dhillon spoke with Ranjit about a property for sale on Barton Street East near Strathearne, a former gas station. This was where Dhillon wanted to realize his dream of building a used-car dealership. In April Dhillon signed an agreement to buy the land from Sunoco for $35,085. Now Aman Auto would have a real home. The deal was finalized on April 29. But Dhillon delayed closing the sale. May 30 was set as the new closing date. He needed more money. He delayed it again. And a third time. On May 1, Ranjit and Dhillon visited a small Allstate insurance outlet on Barton Street East. Dhillon did the talking, he knew more English, and it was his agent they met, a man named Stan

Ruhl. Dhillon said Ranjit was interested in buying car insurance. With Dhillon speaking in his rapid-fire English and Ranjit sitting quietly beside him, the talk turned to life insurance. Dhillon said they would like to name each other as beneficiary.

"What is your relationship to Ranjit?" Ruhl asked.

"I am Ranna's uncle," Dhillon lied. "He lives at my place. I take care of him. Taken care of him since he came to Canada." He wrote down their information and the pair left the office. Ruhl was a tall, engaging, 54-year-old former steelworker who brushed his silver hair straight back. He found Dhillon a curiosity, the way he spoke so quickly, out of control, careening between broken English words and phrases, all of them running together—"*Heyhow'sgoing-isthereanythingIcandoforyou?*"

"Okay, okay, slow down," Ruhl would say. "Okay? I can't understand what you're saying." Ruhl's horse sense said Dhillon was shady. Certain guys Ruhl considered to be in a gray area, character-wise. That was Dhillon. He once visited Ruhl's office after one of his many trips to India, carrying a gift for the agent. Gold slippers.

"What is this for?" Ruhl said.

"Four hundred dollars, four hundred," Dhillon said. "A gift for you."

"Where the hell do you wear them? Down to the beach?"

"The gold is real, the gold in the slippers is real," Dhillon said. "Worth a lot of money. All for you."

Ruhl said no thanks. He didn't take any gifts in his business, save for coffee and a doughnut at Tim Horton's. On May 8, seven days after the first meeting, Ruhl, Dhillon, and Ranjit met again. Ranjit and Dhillon were clear to go ahead, uncle and nephew, a policy for each. The policies were issued for $100,000 with an additional $100,000 payable in the event of accidental death. Dhillon was the beneficiary if Ranjit died.

Dhillon phoned Sunoco. He was nearly ready to close the deal on the Barton Street property. Then, on June 16, he signed an agreement to delay the sale to July. He needed more time. Just a bit more.

* * *

Ranjit awoke on Saturday morning, June 22, filled with anticipation. That day a jet carrying his parents and his sister Karmajit had taken off from India. They were coming to visit him in Canada. And he was closing a deal to sell a car. That afternoon he sold his brother-in-law, Udham "Billo" Sekhon, a Dodge Caravan for $6,500. Dhillon was there. The three of them drove the minivan to the Ministry of Transportation to register the purchase. Time to celebrate. They stopped at the liquor store in Queenston Mall, picked up a twenty-sixer of Crown Royal whisky, returned to Ranjit's place on Gainsborough Road. Ranjit rarely drank. Dhillon and Billo took turns on the bottle inside the van as it sat parked in the driveway.

Later that evening, Ranjit offered to drive Jodha home. It was only a few minutes' drive. Dhillon brought it up again, Ranna's impotence problem. He had just the remedy. Dhillon had the pill with him. He showed it to Ranjit. It was a capsule. Miracle medicine. Think about it, Ranna. In bed you will last much longer. Amazing. If anyone knows about performance with women—much younger women—it's Jodha! All those women in India, sex every day.

Ranjit said good night to Dhillon and drove back to his house, alone. That night, a late dinner. Lakhwinder served Ranjit and the family vegetables with ginger, roti bread, yogurt. Afterward Ranjit spoke upstairs with his grandmother, Surjit, then went downstairs to the area he shared with Lakhwinder. She waited for him in the bedroom, where she had tucked in their two-year-old boy, Ranjoda. After Ranjit showered he walked across the hall into the bedroom. Incense burned on top of the dresser.

The bed he shared with Lakhwinder was a mattress and some sheets on the floor. He slipped in beside her. How long had it been since he took the medicine? He felt—odd. And vigorous. The erection, yes, but more than that, his other muscles felt hard, blood pumping through them. Jodha was right. He could go all night. They had sex, then lay on the bed side by side. But Ranjit was still erect. Something did not feel right. All his muscles felt as if they were contracting against his will. The touch of the sheets felt like needles on his skin. He put on his underwear.

"Ranjit, what's wrong?" Lakhwinder asked.

"I don't know—don't touch me," Ranjit said, then yanked the sheets away from his skin as though they were on fire. Minutes later, he was convulsing, muscles clenching spastically. Somebody phoned 911 at two minutes after midnight. And then Paviter Khela, Ranjit's uncle, phoned Dhillon. Ranna is very sick. What did Jodha give him? "He had nothing at my house. I gave him nothing," Dhillon replied. "I'll come over."

Paramedics Timothy Dault and Peter Morgan were sitting in an ambulance at Barton and Kenilworth when the emergency call came in. "Emergency. Eighty-eight Gainsborough Road." The dispatcher had the wrong house number, perhaps because of a language barrier over the phone. They arrived at the correct address at 12:16 Sunday morning. They carried the stretcher inside, were shown to the basement. Incense in the air, family members, as many as 10 of them, shouting, wailing, chaos. On the bed lay Ranjit Khela, 25, in his underwear, his penis still erect. Drenched in sweat, drooling. Muffled sounds from the back of his throat. He seemed euphoric, talking to himself, his teeth clenched so tightly the gums bled, lips drawn back in a bizarre grimace.

Dhillon arrived at the house. In the kitchen upstairs, the Khelas confronted him. What did you give Ranna? "I didn't give him anything," he said. "I didn't do anything."

The paramedics fired questions at the family. Dhillon acted as translator. He was the only one who spoke any English. "He ate dinner, and felt fine," Dhillon told Dault and Morgan. "Nobody knows what happened." The paramedics strapped Ranjit onto the

Makhan Khela was on his way to visit from India when his son, Ranjit, died.

stretcher and loaded him into the ambulance and sped to Hamilton General Hospital. He lapsed in and out of consciousness.

Strychnine—*kuchila*— rapes the nervous system, sends signals from the brain that strangle muscles, but worst of all, leaves the victim aware of what is happening. At the end, Ranjit called out briefly in Punjabi. He was declared dead at 2:03 a.m. Paviter, his uncle, knelt on the floor, crying. "If I had a gun," he cried, "I'd shoot myself and then I could be with him."

Dhillon was there with the weeping family, his face creased in sorrow. He put his thick hand on Paviter's shoulder and helped him to his feet.

"God's will," Dhillon said. "We can't understand it."

* * *

The sudden, unexplained death of a young adult meant a call to the coroner. Dr. Bashir Khambalia received the call to visit the morgue at Hamilton General Hospital to examine the body and charts. The deceased was a Sikh man named Ranjit Khela. It is not known whether the coroner read the notes on Ranjit written by those who had treated him. A coroner has access to such notes, but is not required to consult them. It was another sudden death of a seemingly healthy young Indian who lived in the Riverdale neighborhood of east Hamilton. Once again, the deceased was stricken by seizures, muscle spasms, the sickly grimace, oxygen shut-off to the brain. Khambalia had also handled the mysterious death of Parvesh Dhillon 17 months earlier.

He did not order toxicology testing from the Centre of Forensic Sciences in Toronto. That was an option open to him, but was not required. Khambalia ordered an autopsy. He did not phone police. He would have done that only if he suspected something.

Chapter 8 ~ An Impossible Case

The funeral for Ranjit Khela was held July 6. His cremated ashes were taken back to India by his grandparents. Dhillon was at the funeral in Hamilton. At the visitation, he was overheard telling someone next to him to keep a distance from the body: "Be careful, stand back, there might be harmful gas coming from it." The family friend looked at Dhillon, puzzled. What does that mean? At the Khela home, friends and members of the Sikh community dropped by to express condolences. They spoke with Lakhwinder, who was still devastated and had wept through the entire service. A friend of Dhillon's named Mangat and a few others walked up to her.

"What happened that night?" Mangat asked. Lakhwinder had kept the secret to herself. Her husband's dying words were too dangerous to reveal. And Ranjit was gone, there was no changing that. But still, she spoke out. "Ranna told me just a few minutes before that he had taken a pill," Lakhwinder said.

"A pill? What kind?"

"He didn't say. He took a pill at Jodha's house."

Dhillon stood to the side, listening.

"No, Ranna ate nothing at my house," he said.

"He—he must have been joking," Lakhwinder said.

Silence filled the room.

Dhillon quickly applied for Ranjit's life insurance benefits. It was time for Ranna's "uncle" to close the deal. The first week in July, Sunoco asked Dhillon about finalizing his purchase of the vacant Barton Street property where he intended to expand his used-car dealership. He still didn't have the money. Just needed more time. He signed a second delay agreement, to July 30. And then, on July 25, Dhillon asked a local builder for an estimate on designing and building a new garage on the land. He was quoted a price of $89,000. Five days later, on July 30, Dhillon signed a new contract with Sunoco, delaying the sale to the end of August. His money was on the way. Dhillon was unstoppable.

* * *

It sits like a mirage in Agra, two hours south of New Delhi, a shimmering white beacon in the sun's harsh light at high noon; a textured, sparkling ivory colossus in the moonlight. It took 20 years to build the Taj Mahal—20,000 workers, starting in 1631, with no modern engineering technology. Yet what they built is miraculously exact, windows lined up perfectly, all of it precisely symmetrical as though designed by the hand of God. It is an architectural wonder. It is perfect. Almost. The Mughal emperor Shah Jahan ordered the Taj Mahal built as a tomb for his dead wife. It was a brash act. He succeeded. But then he ordered a second mausoleum, a black one, to be built across the Yamuna River from the original to house his own body. This act of egotism prompted his son to throw the emperor in jail for the remainder of his life to stop him bankrupting the country. And so the second tomb was never completed. When the emperor died, he was entombed beside his wife in the original Taj Mahal. But this second crypt destroyed the symmetry of his ethereal creation, which was de-signed to hold one body. The second crypt—for the emperor who went too far—is the Taj Mahal's one glaring flaw.

* * *

Central Station
Hamilton Police Service
August 13, 1996

Tuesday morning, August 13, 1996, dawned hot. The unraveling began so slowly as to be imperceptible, with a phone ringing.

"Sergeant McCulloch."

The uniformed cop's voice carried a Scottish brogue which instantly cast him as a seasoned veteran, as though his life was defined by knocking heads with toughs, maybe walking a foggy beat with a billy club years ago. In the case of David McCulloch, who was nearing retirement and worked in the Hamilton police coroner's department, that was in fact pretty much true.

He was raised in a Scottish village called Elderslie, his house a brief sprint from the monument marking the birthplace of

Braveheart, national hero William Wallace. McCulloch was born on September 3, 1939, the day Britain and France declared war on Hitler. His earliest memory was being snug in his mother's arms, peering up at a blue-black sky flecked with dots of white light, the beams searching for Luftwaffe bombers. In his adult life McCulloch had once walked the beat unarmed in London, though he used the club a few times. The Scot had met his share of nasty characters in his 30 years on the Hamilton force, too. He once rode in the courthouse prisoner's elevator beside a six-foot, 230-pound repeat child molester named James Clayton Collier, whom he had helped catch. A brilliant 34-year-old Hamilton Crown prosecutor named Brent Bentham sent Collier to federal prison for an indefinite sentence wearing the city's first danger-ous-offender tag.

"If I ever get out," Collier hissed at McCulloch, "I'm comin' back here. And you're a dead man." At the criminal trial, the jury read its verdict and Collier, enraged, jumped out of the prisoner's box, hit a court officer, and lunged at McCulloch, spitting invective. The Scot had stayed put in his chair, unblinking.

"Oh," he said, his Scottish brogue rolling over the hard con-sonants, "he did not like Sergeant McCulloch one bit."

McCulloch was now 57. The moment he picked up the phone that Tuesday morning, a faint light finally shone on the trail of the serial killer. This fella, McCulloch reflected, was an original. "Just about slipped through the cracks, too."

The caller was not a cop or a medical official or a relative of one of the victims. But McCulloch used his horse sense, believed what he heard. And he acted. Dave McCulloch was the first police officer to get involved. He phoned the forensic pathology depart-ment at Hamilton General Hospital. Later, he walked into the office of Hamilton police inspector Bruce Elwood. "Bruce, I think we might have ourselves a double homicide here."

It seemed like an end, of sorts. In fact it was just the begin-ning, because Sergeant McCulloch would be well into retirement, his old billy club a decoration in his basement den, before much of anything was resolved.

* * *

Cliff Elliot never worked Fridays, not anymore. That was for junior claims investigators. But, for some reason, he had worked on Friday, August 2, 1996. Shirley, his assistant, put the fax on his desk early that morning before he arrived at the office on Main Street West. It was from Metropolitan Life Insurance, asking for documents regarding a claim for the death of a man named Ranjit Khela. Elliot read the details in the fax. Deceased's date of birth: January 1, 1971. Village of Mau Sahib, District of Jalandhar, Punjab. That made him about 25.

Young, thought Elliot. Had to be a sudden death, some kind of accident. Auto, probably. The reporting coroner was Dr. Bashir Khambalia, a family physician. As a matter of protocol, Elliot needed to call the coroner for more information. Khambalia was not available. Elliot, as usual, was not going to wait around. He left his office. The fax said Ranjit's insurance policy had come into effect on June 18, 1996. The date of his death was June 23, 1996. He dies five days after the policy was taken out? Elliott drove to the downtown public library, flipped through back issues of *The Hamilton Spectator*, *The Toronto Star*, and *The Toronto Sun* to see if there had been any recent coverage of a young East Indian man's sudden death in east Hamilton. Nothing. It was now 3 p.m., a long weekend looming, but Elliot returned to the office. He phoned the beneficiary listed on the fax. Fellow named Sukhwinder Singh Dhillon. Relation to deceased: uncle. A woman answered the phone and said Dhillon wasn't due home until later.

"I'll call back," Elliot said. He phoned the next week, on Wednesday, August 7. He got Dhillon on the phone, introduced himself. "Mr. Dhillon, what was your relationship to the deceased?" Elliot asked.

"I am his uncle," Dhillon said.

"I will need some signed authorizations to get medical records and so on that will be needed in order to process the claim," Elliot said.

"Okay."

Dhillon agreed to meet on Monday, August 12 at 10 a.m. It was hot and muggy that morning. The air trapped over the lower city felt like a warm wet rag over the mouth. Cliff Elliot didn't know it, but he was about to meet Sukhwinder Dhillon for the second time. He drove to the house on Berkindale Drive.

Scott Gardner

Dhillon's house on Berkindale Drive in east Hamilton

Next door was Olga Vidal's place, Parvesh Dhillon's old friend. The Vidals were originally from Portugal. A few years back, they had placed two small statues out front, one of a lion, the other of an eagle. And they hung a tiled plaque on the front brick wall, a depiction of Christ. An inscription on it, in Portuguese, translated as "God of miracles." On a nondescript suburban street like Berkindale, the place stood out. To someone like Cliff Elliot, it was unforgettable. He pulled his Tempo in front of Dhillon's house, but there was the fire hydrant. Elliot, the straight arrow, pulled ahead in front of the house. It all seemed so familiar.

I've been here before, he thought. But with so many cases and contacts filling his head, it was hard to say when. Dhillon greeted Elliot at the door. They spoke in the basement, filled out forms, Elliot asking questions.

"How did your nephew die?" Elliot asked.

"Ranna was watching TV, said he had a pain in his chest, then fell to the ground and died in the hospital. That was it."

Elliot stared at Dhillon. The nonplussed attitude—he'd seen that before, too.

"Yes. Well, did the police or coroner get involved?"

"I don't know," Dhillon said.

"I need to contact the closest next of kin for Mr. Khela."

"That's me. I am his uncle."

"Where are Mr. Khela's parents?" Elliot asked.

The Khelas had arrived in Hamilton shortly after Ranjit's death, and since then Dhillon had seen them frequently. They were staying on Gainsborough Road, minutes from Dhillon's home.

"They live in India."

Elliot continued. "Some medical institutions won't accept just your signature on the forms. I need an address for Mr. Khela's parents."

"I think they're traveling in the United States somewhere, or B.C.," he said. "I could have them come to Hamilton."

"What about Mr. Khela's wife?"

"Nobody knows where she is."

Elliot tried to determine how well he understood English vernacular. "Can I see some ID?" he asked, using the acronym on purpose. Dhillon quickly produced his driver's license number, then his social insurance card. Elliot copied the numbers in his book. Elliot asked to see some of Ranjit's documents that Dhillon had in hand, including Ranjit's driver's license.

"Mr. Dhillon, the insurance claim says Ranjit lived at your address, 362 Berkindale. But Ranjit's driver's license says his address is 188 Gainsborough."

"My brother lives at 188," Dhillon said. "Ranna spent time at each house, he just used 188 for his records."

"I will try to get the information that Met Life needs from the doctors and hospitals," Elliot concluded, "but I have to tell you there is usually a hiccup. I still need to get signatures from his parents, whenever they arrive."

Elliot left the house, looked once more at Dhillon's house, and the Vidals' next door. Back at the office, he asked around. Khela? Ranjit Khela? Anyone hear that name before? No. Elliot shuffled to the filing cabinet. Under K, nothing. No Khela. Well. What about the beneficiary, Mr. Dhillon? There were several Dhillon files. But just one with the address where Elliot had just been: 362 Berkindale: Dhillon, Parvesh Kaur. Born in Punjab, July 15, 1958. Died on February 3, 1995, in Hamilton. Life insurance policy beneficiary: Sukhwinder Dhillon. Husband. It was the file Elliot himself had put away the year before. Holy mackerel, thought the Velvet Hammer. He sat at his desk and read the file more closely, then looked over at his secretary.

"Shirley, there's something not right here. Two young people with the same beneficiary—one was his wife and one was his nephew, apparently. Both died suddenly, no cause for either."

Elliot wound back the tape in his mind. Parvesh. Mr. Dhillon's nonchalant reaction when they discussed her death. Now he remembered.

"Honey," he said to his wife, Amelia, as he came through the door at home that night, "I had the biggest case of déja vu today."

Cliff Elliot thought of nothing else that evening. First thing the next morning, Tuesday, August 13, he was on the phone with Dave McCulloch. "Sergeant, I've got some information I think you should know about."

That afternoon, McCulloch visited forensic pathology in the basement of Hamilton General Hospital. He met with forensic pathologist Dr. Chitra Rao. She listened to McCulloch relay details and speculation passed to him by Cliff Elliot. Two sudden deaths. Two healthy, relatively young adults. Both from India. Unknown cause of death. One insurance beneficiary. Rao retrieved the files on Parvesh and Ranjit. She noted that the postmortem report for Ranjit was not yet finished by Dr. Chris Clague, a medical pathologist who had conducted Ranjit's autopsy because he was on call helping out the forensic pathologists, Rao and Dr. David King. Clague was a Brit who had lived for several years in Canada but would soon be returning to the United Kingdom to work at the Isle of Man hospital. So far Clague had hypothesized noncriminal drug poisoning or perhaps infection. As a matter of course, Ranjit's tissue and blood samples were kept for further study. The coroner who handled Ranjit's death, Dr. Bashir Khambalia, did not order advanced toxicology. He was not required to do so.

Chitra Rao was from a town in India called Kerala. Her father had died before her second birthday, and she was sent to live with a guardian in Sri Lanka. She was thoroughly acquainted with the dark side of human nature. Young Chitra had hungrily observed her guardian's career as a criminal lawyer. At 10 years old she sat at the kitchen table with him as he talked about cases, let her read his papers. He hoped she'd be a lawyer. Instead Chitra went to medical school in Bihar, in northern India, with an eye toward forensic pathology. As an intern, she became well versed in criminal poisoning, saw cases frequently in the hospital, victims of poisoning from chloroform, arsenic—all substances that were readily available. Later, she became a devotee of forensic mystery writer Patricia Cornwell, even striking up a friendship with her. Back in 1983 Rao solved the murder of McMaster University professor Edith Wightman. The professor was found dead in her office, a white towel stuffed in her mouth. No sign of a struggle, Rao noticed. Curious, she thought.

She had turned to a Hamilton cop and said, "What about chloroform?"

Dr. Chitra Rao, forensic pathologist

The cop smiled. Chloroform? Who uses chloroform these days? Rao sent the towel to the Centre of Forensic Sciences in Toronto for testing. Chloroform. That's how Wightman had been subdued before she was robbed, then suffocated on the towel. The killer was eventually caught. Case closed.

She listened to McCulloch's story. Two sudden deaths in the Indian community. Coincidence? Natural causes, though unexplainable? Instinctively, darkly, Rao thought poison. She phoned CFS. She was sending samples from Ranjit Khela's tissue and blood for a tox screen. In 1996, the CFS general drug screen could detect only a handful of poisons. But Rao wasn't fishing. She knew she was looking for murder and was already speculating on the weapon. She told a CFS toxicologist to narrow the scope of the screen.

"Check for chloroform," she said on the phone. "And strychnine."

* * *

Dhillon's next deal was coming together. On Friday, September 6, 1996, he wrote a letter:

Piari Sukhwinder Kaur,
Sat siri Akal, Tera Kee haal hey?
Dear Sukhwinder Kaur,
Hi, how are you? We are fine here. I think your interview will be held on October 3. I am sending you the papers you wanted. Don't be nervous. Don't worry about anything. Everything is in God's hands.
Yours,
Sukhwinder Dhillon

Five days later, on Wednesday, September 11, the propane-flame blue eyes peered through the car windshield. Hamilton homicide detective Warren Korol drove downtown to Central Station through a veil of fog. By noon it lifted and all was clear. Korol had been posted to the homicide branch less than a year and was still getting his feet wet. His supervisor, veteran investigator Steve Hrab, poked his head out the office door and saw the detective at his desk.

"Hey, Warren. You're not doing anything. I've got a good one here for you."

The smirk Korol often wore deepened, the eyes smiled. "*A good one.*" Translation: an impossible case, or nearly so. Two deaths in the city that were "historical," as the cops put it: closed-book cases where detectives had not been called to the scene in the precious moments after the death. The bodies of the victims—if they had been murdered—were gone. Both had been cremated.

Korol looked over the files. Ranjit Khela and Parvesh Dhillon. Two young adults. Their deaths, 17 months apart, were considered to have been from natural but unknown causes at the time, but foul play was now suspected yet unproven in both cases. No smoking gun, no murder weapon. Ambulances had attended to the victims, but the tapes of the 911 calls had already been deleted. The deaths were witnessed by family members, but language would be a barrier in both cases.

Warren Korol was still fresh enough in homicide to relish the challenge. The idealist in a detective makes him believe he speaks for the victims. It is a noble calling. Experience would make Korol a realist. You do what it takes to investigate a case, but within the often frustrating confines of the legal system. If you don't, you won't win. And that was what the game was about. Veterans of homicide work know the job is tougher than it used to be. Yes, more forensic bells and whistles to assist, but then there are also more legal hoops to jump through than 20 or 30 years ago. It wasn't enough to catch the bad guy and roll up evidence against him—evidence that, in the court of common sense, was plenty for a conviction. No, in a court of law you battled to get slivers of truth before a judge or jury. Korol had seen judges throw out evidence on minor procedural issues, leaving lawyers to present juries with a filtered version of the facts. It burned him. Most of the time, Korol had an inviting casualness about him and those who barely knew him gravitated to his easygoing manner. The new assignment? It didn't faze him. Not yet. But ultimately the case would test him like nothing ever had, eat him up, rub his patience so raw it could have bled.

* * *

At the Centre of Forensic Sciences in Toronto, in a cramped lab with shiny black counters, a sample of Ranjit Khela's blood rotated in a tube, combined with a chemical solvent. Turning, turning, methodically mixing in the spinning machine. Toxicology technicians liken the process to mixing oil and vinegar. Separate then break down the blood, isolate the foreign substance a killer might have put there. Remove the natural material such as protein and fat. The techs call these "the dirt." Examine what's left: routine compounds, cholesterol, caffeine, nicotine, medication—and, perhaps, poison. Mix blood with a special solvent and its chemical balance is altered. The drugs no longer pack an electrical charge and they attach to the solvent. There were 130 to 140 drugs that could be detected in the blood screen.

Ranjit's blood was subjected to this process and placed in a thumbnail-size glass vial. Then it went into a gas chromatography machine, the size of a large microwave oven. The sample began its journey through a copper tube, pushed along by gas pressure. The tube, if stretched out, is about 15 to 30 meters in length, maximizing travel distance. It is coated inside with a material similar to car wax. As the sample blows through, individual drugs stick to the wax at different intervals based on their chemical affinities. The time spent moving and sticking—the retention time—differs from drug to drug.

The lab had developed a catalogue of retention times that ranged from under a minute to 50 minutes for more than 100 drugs, poisons, and other compounds. As the components of Ranjit's treated blood shot through the machine, each in turn hit the end of the copper tube and was burned off, creating a signal that registered on a computer screen. A technician monitored the signals, noting spikes in the line—sharp, high peaks, then flatter ones, then sharp again—a blueprint of components in his blood. The tech recognized the patterns of most of the peaks. Routine stuff. Caffeine. Cholesterol. The computer churned out a printed list naming each detected common chemical and compound.

Suddenly an unfamiliar peak appeared. Whatever it was, it represented a minute quantity in the blood. The computer assigned the unknown peak a number, representing its retention time. The technician had never seen that number before. No one in the lab ever had. She left the room, walked down the hall, pulled out a thick binder, and flipped to a chart. The peak was for an exotic poison. Strychnine. Just as Dr. Chitra Rao had predicted.

Strychnine is a crystalline powder, colorless, odorless but extremely bitter. CFS almost never came across it. They tested blood samples for 2,500 deaths each year, and in the 12 years they had kept records, CFS had found strychnine in a blood sample just three times before. Strychnine was once sold off the shelf in Canada as rat poison, under brand names such as Kwik Kill. But that was back in the 60s. Nobody could buy it off the shelf anymore, at least not in Canada. Ranjit Khela's blood sample showed a trace amount of strychnine, a concentration of 0.07 milligrams per 100 milliliters of blood. Enough to kill.

CHAPTER 9 ~ BLACK EYES

The man behind the counter handed Warren Korol the paper cup filled with tea.

"Thanks," he said, digging coins from his pocket then reaching for the door. "You take care." Korol's polished black shoes clicked down the steps at Val's, the coffee shop across from the station that was frequented by police officers. Korol looked imposing in a charcoal suit wide enough to hang comfortably from his broad frame and conceal the .40-caliber Glock in the holster underneath.

Every so often Korol was reminded that you never stop being a regular cop. The other day, he'd seen a kid trying to break into a car, right there, a couple of blocks from Val's and the station. Not only that, the car was a cop's private vehicle. So Korol, in his suit, chased down the teenager, his dress shoes slapping the pavement, grabbed him by the collar, and, gasping for breath, radioed for assistance. "For chrissakes," he thought. "I'm not supposed to be doing this kind of thing anymore."

He claimed to have no nicknames. Korol's surname, of Ukrainian origin, sounded clean and angular. His first name was formal, with no phonetic option to add a "y" to the end—no Jimmy or Johnny or Danny. It was just: Warren. Married, three young kids. Square-shouldered handsome, with light brown hair that grayed nearly imperceptibly, cropped tight on the sides. When it grew longer he moussed it on top, creating a look that suggested he had just come out of a swimming pool. His approach to the job was measured, businesslike. Korol sat at his desk in Central Station, took a sip of the tea, a stray curl of hair falling onto his forehead. His eyes scanned documents on his desk provided by forensic pathologist Dr. Chitra Rao.

"Strychnine is an alkaloid found in the seeds of the *Strychnos nux-vomica*, the botanical name given to a tree indigenous to the Indian subcontinent." Strychnine. That was a new one in an era of sniper and drive-by shootings, machete attacks, mail-bomb murders. In his career Korol would see lacerated bodies, bullet holes in skulls. But poisoning from a tropical plant? He needed to learn more.

"It is a potent central nervous system stimulant and convul-
sant, acting by the selective blockade of postsynaptic neuronal
inhibition. Death may occur ... due to paralysis of muscles of
respiration." Strychnine was closely restricted in Canada. Two
companies were licensed to sell it for agricultural use. What about
in India, Korol wondered? How easy would it be for someone
to smuggle it out of India? At some point he should give it the
test. He continued studying the background papers. There is
no acceptable therapeutic use for strychnine, at any dosage, in
conventional medicine. It is technically a stimulant but if used
in the wrong amount, muscles spasm so violently and repeatedly they rip apart, sucking oxygen from the brain, plunging the
victim toward certain death.

In Canada a highly diluted byproduct of strychnine, called
nux vomica, is available as a homeopathic remedy. Drinking even
a full bottle would do little harm. But in India and Southeast Asia,
strychnine tonics are available in much higher, riskier concentrations. As little as five milligrams of pure strychnine kills. A
milligram is a thousandth of a gram. An ordinary headache pill
contains 325 milligrams of active ingredient. Divide that into 65
pieces, and if one of them is pure strychnine, swallowing it could
be fatal. Strychnine comes in clear crystals or white powder form
and is absorbed rapidly in the bloodstream. Reactions to ingestion
vary, but seizures commonly occur in five minutes, heart attacks in
20 minutes, and brain damage can cause more drawn-out death.
Most deaths occur in three to six hours, from asphyxia.

It is one of the most bitter substances in the world. Dissolve
one cup of salt in 50 cups of water, and a hint of salt would be
tasted. Dissolve one cup of salt in 1,000 cups of water, and the salt
would be undetectable. But if one cup of strychnine was dissolved
in 100,000 cups of water, you would still taste it. A poisoner would
need extremely sour or bitter food to mask the taste of strychnine.
Much better to pack it into something the victim swallows whole.
Like a capsule.

* * *

The death of Ranjit Khela was recent; the tox screen would give Korol a good starting point. But what about Parvesh Dhillon more than a year earlier? She had collapsed and died in early 1995. There had been no detailed toxicology performed. The oldest motives for murder are love and money. Korol knew there was one man who benefited from both deaths—Sukhwinder Singh Dhillon, husband of the former and friend and mentor of the latter. He was also the sole beneficiary of both their life insurance policies, worth a total of $400,000.

But Korol worked methodically. He did not jump to conclusions, or if he did, he didn't announce his thoughts. He was trained to keep an open mind. Hunches and common sense don't land first-degree murder convictions. Hard evidence wins in the courtroom. Gather evidence, forensics, and interview, interview, interview. Still, from the start his gut instinct said this was a double homicide. Korol logged on to criminal records and punched in the name. Dhillon, Sukhwinder Singh. Information raced across the screen:

REM: Korol
ROYAL CANADIAN MOUNTED POLICE IDENTIFICATION SERVICES
RESTRICTED—INFORMATION SUPPORTED BY FINGER-PRINTS SUBMITTED BY LAW ENFORCEMENT AGENCIES—DISTRIBUTION TO AUTHORIZED AGENCIES ONLY.
FPS: 15923OD
Dhillon. Sukhwinder Singh
CRIMINAL CONVICTIONS CONDITIONAL AND ABSOLUTE DISCHARGES AND RELATED INFORMATION. 1992-11-13 Assault Sec 266 CC $300 Hamilton Wentworth REG PF. 92-2518
END OF CONVICTIONS AND DISCHARGES

Korol logged off the system and turned to a folder containing a Hamilton police report on the same charge. Dhillon's first name was misspelled. It read:

92-08-14 8:30 DHILLON SUKHBINDER
Assault Level One

The report covered an incident of wife abuse. For four years it had sat in darkness in a police filing cabinet. Now it was a brief, ugly glimpse into Parvesh Dhillon's life, two sheets of paper with a few words and dates. Korol kept his mind focused. It is quite a step—a huge step, from a man striking his wife to murdering her. An ugly fact of life, but some men hit their wives. They aren't all killers. But then, while men who beat their wives don't necessarily kill, men who kill their wives frequently have a history of domestic abuse. The assault was a clue, although Korol knew that it would probably never be aired in court. A judge would almost certainly refuse to let the jury in a murder trial hear about a domestic assault. It would be prejudicial to the accused. That was the language the lawyers used. Korol stuck to the rules, respected them. That didn't mean he had to like them.

But court is one thing, a police investigation another. Homicide detectives seek the whole story, not one scrubbed of prejudicial notions. Sukhwinder Dhillon was a murder suspect. And you could add wife-beater to his resumé. Parvesh's husband was a cruel man. A cowardly one. In time, after investigating, interviewing, researching, Warren Korol learned Parvesh's story. It was not a pretty one.

* * *

As a little girl, Parvesh Kaur Grewal would walk from her house, past the large banyan tree in the street, up the dusty laneway, through the black gate to the public school. She loved school and her teachers. It would be wonderful if she could be a teacher herself. She lived in a crowded urban neighborhood in a village called Sahkewal, within Ludhiana's city boundary. Her family owned a dairy and crop farm—larger than the Dhillons'—and their home adjoined several other bungalow-style units that over time they purchased. It was, for Ludhiana, a quiet residential area, none of the buzzing markets seen in other parts of the city. There were pockets of poverty, but also well-kept homes. Near the Grewal house, kids played in the narrow streets. At night it was quiet. The neighborhood contrasted with Birk Barsal, Dhillon's neighborhood nearby, bursting with bustle and commerce.

Deep inside, beyond the expectations of her parents and culture, Parvesh had, like other educated Punjabi women, an inner sense of the possible, of other life destinations. But she kept those thoughts at bay. There was no other choice. The plan was laid out. As a young woman in a traditional Punjabi family, the paramount concern was ensuring you did not dishonor your parents in the eyes of the community. Her destiny changed forever in 1981, the year she was introduced and engaged by her parents to Sukhwinder Dhillon. When she arrived in Canada in 1983, Parvesh was 25, one year older than her husband.

They were entirely different people. Sukhwinder had a thick, lumbering physique, dark skin. Parvesh was tall and slim, with uncommonly fair skin—almost like a white woman, Indians said. Fair skin on a female is revered in Indian society. Parvesh had teardrop-shaped green eyes, as though suggesting an unspoken inner pain that only she knew. Her husband's eyes were like a slap in the face, with an intensity that seemed born of anger or wild-eyed confusion, as if he were trying desperately to absorb information about surroundings and people he did not understand. Parvesh was educated, he was not. She knew English and something of the world. He was a dreamer, brash and boastful. Parvesh lived to adulthood with both her mother and father alive; Dhillon's father died when he was a boy, thrusting his mother into the center of his world. At their wedding, upon seeing the jewelry collected by Parvesh's family for the dowry, Dhillon demanded more on the spot.

In Hamilton, while Dhillon avoided hard work, Parvesh labored at a mushroom farm. In the summer of 1984, each morning, she boarded a bus before dawn for the farm in Campbellville, north of Hamilton. She was a harvester, and harvest was every day. That meant slicing individual mushrooms from their trays, one by one, all day long. It was similar to working in a greenhouse, with one notable exception: no light. No light except for the one strapped to her head as if she were a miner, a tiny beacon guiding her way. "Women's work" was how her husband described it, but he constantly pestered Parvesh to hand over her hard-earned money.

Parvesh Dhillon

On July 26, 1985, she gave birth to their first child, Harpreet, by caesarean section. Six months later she returned to work, a new job at a textile factory. The following year, Parvesh miscarried her second pregnancy. Then she started work at a shoe factory. In 1988, the Dhillons' second daughter, Aman, was born. Sukhwinder Dhillon was anxious to have a son. In May 1991, Parvesh was pregnant again. She traveled to India to have the fetus tested to determine its gender. She discovered it was a girl and had an abortion performed. Dhillon was so determined to have a son that he hired an immigration consultant to bring Parvesh's eight-year-old nephew from India to live with them. His plan was to adopt the boy. He and Parvesh visited the consultant, a man named Parmagit Singh Mangat, in Etobicoke on September 18, 1992. Parvesh wore Western-style clothes, blue jeans. Mangat was struck by the contrast between the boorish Dhillon and Parvesh, who was gentle, sophisticated, beautiful. Nevertheless, her husband did most of the talking and made the decisions, even as they argued frequently.

Mangat did not know that Dhillon was out of work, on compensation. As the official sponsor for the boy, Dhillon signed a form claiming he worked at a place called Continental Auto Body in Hamilton and made $32,240 a year. Parvesh's family in India fought Dhillon's attempt at adoption. Parvesh and Sukhwinder returned to Mangat's office a second time, and bickered even more. On the final visit, Dhillon came alone to see Mangat and cancelled the sponsorship attempt.

"We don't want to do it any more," Dhillon said. "I don't want someone from my wife's side of the family as a son anyway."

Parvesh, daughters Harpreet and Aman, and Sukhwinder

* * *

Home movie: Aman's birthday party. Harpreet is there, friends, in the basement of the house on Berkindale Drive. Children gather on the dark red carpet to watch the presents opened, excited young voices alternating between Punjabi and English. Parvesh, in a yellow dress, laughing with the girls, radiant smile, serving ice cream. The video camera is placed on a tripod. A man enters the frame. Her husband. Parvesh is on the couch and he sits beside her. Her smile vanishes, she glares at him. He playfully grabs at her dress, she swats his hand away. Parvesh rises from the couch, walks toward the camera, looks directly into the lens. A brief, silent stare, as though sending a message, no wink, no playful exasperation. For one moment the eyes are not aqua, they look black, as though offering an open window into her future with Sukhwinder Dhillon.

In August 1992, Parvesh worked at a factory on South Service Road called Narroflex, which made elasticized bands for clothing. It was the coolest, dampest, grayest summer anyone could remember in southern Ontario, oppressive in its bleakness. Her night shift over one day, Parvesh eased the car out of the parking lot, the factory noises still echoing in her head, another migraine beginning to build. She had worked at one of the machines for 12 hours straight. Great mounds of elastic cloth bands fed together through her machine, then into smaller piles in boxes, appearing like mounds of snakes. She manned the machine—chick-chick-chick/whap-whap-whap/chick-chick-chick/whap-whap-whap. Her job was making sure boxes were properly packed then taped shut and sent along a steel conveyor belt for delivery. 11:03 p.m. Chick-chick-chick/whap-whap-whap/chick-chick-chick/whap-whap-whap. 11:05 p.m. Fifty-five minutes until her first hour finished, and the first $7.50 of the day. More bands, another box packed and taped and onto the belt. And on and on. The night grew old. Morning arrived. Chick-chick-chick/whap-whap-whap/chick-chick-chick/whap-whap-whap. Last box sealed. Parvesh was free to go home.

She had just turned 34. She was weary, feeling what many Punjabi women experience after the initial excitement of Canada wears off. In Canada, everything is so busy, everyone works all the time. There is no escape from it. It was late morning. Parvesh drove along the quiet two-lane service road while, on the other side of the fence, beyond the road, cars on the QEW highway ripped by. Farther still, on the other side of the highway, was Van Wagner's Beach. On a clear day, if she slowed her car, she could see Burlington across the water, and farther along the shore, like a miniature, the skyline of Toronto, the place she had landed nearly 10 years earlier. Her eyes heavy, Parvesh drove the 10 minutes to her house, excited at seeing her two daughters. Aman was four, Harpreet, seven. The girls were her life's joy, they were all she talked about. Her husband wasn't home. When was he going to return to work? How long had he been on compensation now? Parvesh had opened four bank accounts at three banks, trying to keep her money from his greedy hands.

Parvesh lay on her bed, closed her eyes. The headaches came so frequently, it seemed like every day. She saw a doctor regularly. Her overall health was fine, but the fist of pain in her back that spread to her head never stopped. She had a CT scan and an electroencephalogram. Both came up normal. The doctors described her pain as "ordinary muscle tension headaches." Relax more, they told her. Remove the source of the stress. But she couldn't just remove her husband. The nights when Jodha had friends over were awful. Drinking downstairs, shot after shot of whisky, then the expectation, followed by the loud demand, that she make them all dinner. She would have to face the mess the next morning—leftover food, even on occasion vomit on the floor—and clean it up. This while she worked obsessively to keep a spotless house. But even the drinking parties weren't as bad as the abuse, the moments when Jodha wrapped his thick hand around her slender neck and screamed threats in her ear, even that he would kill her.

He once took Parvesh to one of the used-car auctions he attended as a dealer. He introduced her to the man who ran the place. The manager saw Parvesh, her head covered with a scarf, eyes glazed and distant. "So how d'ya put up with this guy?" he said, using a folksy expression. Dhillon smiled. Parvesh said nothing, her face frozen.

Her mother and father lived with them for stretches of time. Dhillon treated them with violent contempt. Friends heard that Dhillon swatted his in-laws with newspapers, hit them with kitchen utensils, used gutter language in their presence, or swore directly at them. The rumor was that Dhillon even stood naked in front of the parents, a sickening insult in the Punjabi culture. On Friday, August 14, Parvesh's father, Hardev, was living there, working days on a chicken farm gathering eggs. At 6:30 a.m. the phone rang in the Dhillons' home. The call was for Hardev. It woke Dhillon up. Six-thirty? The wife's old man does nothing around here, and the phone rings for him at 6:30 in the morning? Parvesh, still asleep, felt a heavy hand grab her shoulder. She awoke to hear Jodha yelling at her, his voice stinging inside her head. She talked back. Parvesh was so much smarter. He never forgave her for that.

The hard back of his thick hand smashed across the right side of her small, soft face. The force of the blow snapped her head around. Parvesh tasted her own blood on the inside of her lip, her cheek bone ached, a red welt forming, shooting pain up through her sinuses and head. Jodha continued yelling, but her hand was on the phone now. There had been other opportunities in the past

Parvesh and her girls

to report her husband. Two years earlier, on a February day in 1990, Parvesh went to the ER at St. Joseph's Hospital. Jodha had hit her in the face and delivered a blow to her chest. Her face was sore and her head ached, along with her shoulder, and her chest felt crushed from within. The nurse X-rayed her and found part of a lung had collapsed. He had broken the seal covering the lung. The doctor asked how it happened, and Parvesh said Dhillon had kicked and punched her. But she would not call police, would not press charges. The assault wasn't the first. There were two black eyes on separate occasions. She had gone to the family doctor for one of them and told him it was caused by a doorknob. It wasn't time to tell the police. Still, as if sensing that proof might be needed some day, Parvesh had a friend take photos of her black eyes.

This time, the morning of August 14, would be different. The radio in the Hamilton police cruiser crackled. Doug Rees and Rick Abelson had just come on duty. "Domestic," the voice said. "Three-six-two Berkindale Drive." Rees wheeled the car around. They pulled up in front of the house. A knock on the door. Parvesh answered, Dhillon was in the basement. She told her story in English, opened her mouth to show the cut. Rees and Abelson went downstairs.

"So what happened here this morning?" Rees said to Dhillon. Dhillon's face showed no emotion. No yelling, no exaggerated movements. He was calm. His English, while broken, was easily understood.

"Hardev does nothing around here."

Rees, a 10-year veteran, put his hand around Dhillon's arm. "You are under arrest, sir. Will you please follow me to the car?"

Rees waited for a reaction. He always gave them a choice. You can come outside and struggle, be cuffed, humiliated for neighbors to see, or you can leave like a gentleman. Dhillon, despite his size and his attempts to portray himself as an unhinged tough guy to friends, never physically challenged Hamilton police officers. He walked to the car quietly, with Rees guiding him by the arm. He rode in the back seat of the cruiser, saying nothing.

Rees stopped at the Stoney Creek station to write the report while Abelson took Dhillon to the downtown police station. The charge was Level One assault. He spent the day in a cell, then was shackled and driven to the court on Main Street. He was released on bail. Parvesh testified against him. He was convicted and fined.

"What happened, Jodha?" one of his friends asked him later.

"Three hundred dollars," Dhillon said, his face placid, as though discussing the weather. "Family problem."

Chapter 10 ~ God's Will

Warren Korol checked out an unmarked white Crown Victoria from the carpool at Central Station and drove to Hamilton General Hospital. He had an appointment with forensic pathologist Dr. David King, the one who had performed the postmortem on Parvesh Dhillon. They now had proof that Ranjit had been killed by strychnine. But proving Parvesh had met the same fate was a much greater challenge.

King, when consulted on reopening the investigation into her death, had an idea. Parvesh had been dead 19 months now, but he had filed away a box of Parvesh's tissue samples sealed in wax in the storage room. Minute quantities of poison in her system could have already disappeared with time, or been eliminated when the samples were sliced and packed in wax at the autopsy. But it was worth a shot. He walked to the storage room, just around the corner from his office in the forensic pathology department, the smell of formaldehyde present as always. He had a staffer take photos of him at every step. The box was still there. Inside were 32 square blue-gray plastic cartridges, each about the size of a watch face, each containing a tiny piece of Parvesh's organ tissue sealed in wax. King wrapped tape around the box.

Scott Gardner

Parvesh's tissue samples were stored in cartridges like these.

Korol greeted King, who handed over the box. Then Korol was back in the car, the box on the seat beside him, on the QEW bound for Toronto, driving in silence, thinking about the case. The Crown Vic descended from the Gardiner Expressway. Korol drove up Bay Street and parked next to the undistinguished building of dirty gray concrete and brown brick, two flags snapping high atop poles outside. He entered the George Drew Building, which housed the Centre of Forensic Sciences. He signed in on the second floor, then delivered the box to the lab.

Korol next headed to east Hamilton with his partner, an officer named Billy Paynter, and parked at Ranjit Khela's house on Gainsborough Road. His family still lived there, including those who had clustered around him crying the night he died. Korol knocked on the door. Paviter Khela, Ranjit's uncle, answered. He said nothing and let the detectives in. Sitting inside was Lakhwinder Sekhon, Ranjit's widow.

"I am Detective Sergeant Warren Korol and I am investigating the death of Ranjit Khela."

The family stared blankly at him. Paviter said something in Punjabi. Now Korol returned the stare with one of his own. What the hell were they saying? Korol had hoped they would know a bit of English. The visit was over. The cold case was difficult enough, but Korol couldn't even communicate with witnesses. It wasn't just the language barrier. There was a cultural divide, too. Even some members of Hamilton's growing Indian community who spoke English were reluctant to talk to two white cops. It was their protective mechanism, a shield when feeling threatened by a cop, a journalist, a stranger. *No speak English*. Korol needed help or the case of his career was finished.

* * *

The rookie's dark eyes narrowed and focused, trying to interpret the movement of the silhouettes in the back windshield of the idling car. He walked slowly toward the vehicle.

It was May 1, 1989. Kevin Dhinsa had joined the Hamilton police force less than a year earlier. Now he had pulled over a car that had run a stoplight on Bay Street. Dhinsa checked the plate, ran the number on the computer of his cruiser. Stolen car. He made quick mental notes as he drew closer. Two occupants in vehicle. Appear to be male. Movement? No—yes. Yes, one of them reaching behind the seat.

The pale brown skin tightened on Dhinsa's face, his heart beat faster. Right hand on the grooved plastic grip of the Glock, out of the holster, pointing the muzzle at the ground. He was almost even with the car. The rest happened so fast. Suddenly the vehicle was moving, right back on top of him, on an angle. He reacted. Dodge, turn, raise the Glock, fire, an explosion, rear tire blown. But one shattered tire wasn't enough. The driver hit the gas and took off. Dhinsa had slowed him down, however, and other cops made the collar a few blocks away. Commendation? No. Instead the rookie had to defend himself against a charge under the Police Act because he had pulled his gun in public. A few days earlier, a Toronto cop had shot a young man by mistake. Police brass across Ontario were on edge. If he was found guilty, Dhinsa was off the force. That possibility made him think of his parents, Sawaran and Ajit. They would be so upset.

His family had moved from India to Hamilton in 1976. Dhinsa's grandfather had been the deputy fire chief in Bombay. Growing up, his family moved frequently because his father was a civil engineer who worked for a university that regularly relocated him. Kevin came to Canada at 15. Back then he still used his Sikh first name, Kamaljit. When he was in his early twenties in Hamilton, before his life as a cop, an Irish boss he worked for anglicized his name and Dhinsa eagerly adopted it. He worked at his English, so much so that he lost nearly any trace of an Indian accent, speaking in a perfect, measured baritone. In Hamilton, his parents were so proud he was a police officer. Kevin Dhinsa, in the eyes of his family and the local Indian community, had made it.

In the end he was found innocent of any wrongdoing in the tire shooting incident. A rough ride for the rookie, but it did not inhibit his brashness on the job. There was also the case where he was alone on foot patrol, took on four young men he suspected of drug dealing on the street, grappled with one of them, and they both plunged through a plate-glass window. Dhinsa got to his feet and saw the other man down, lying on shattered glass—and a perfectly clean gash in the man's neck, blood pumping out rhythmically. Dhinsa's chest went hollow, his breath gone. Had he just killed an unarmed man? While executing a simple drug arrest? Police investigated the incident internally, Dhinsa's career on the line again. Again he was found innocent. And the injured man lived.

One day in 1988, Dhinsa, a rookie in uniform, rode an elevator up a city building with his training officer. A woman in the elevator whispered to her child, "Behave yourself or the policeman will take you away." It was a joke. Dhinsa said nothing. The training officer, whose face usually bore a mirthful look, wheeled around, serious.

"Listen, I don't appreciate that," he said. "That's not a nice thing to say to a child. We are police officers, we're his friends. Don't scare him like that."

The officer was Warren Korol. Korol and Dhinsa went their separate ways. They were reunited in the fall of 1996. At that time Dhinsa worked in vice and drugs. He was seconded out of the branch to assist lead investigator Korol in the possible double-homicide case. Dhinsa, a Sikh, fluent in Punjabi, was the logical choice. Korol and Dhinsa now embarked on the case of their lives, one of the most expensive and complicated homicide investigations in Canadian history, one that one day would even make headlines back in Kevin Dhinsa's home country.

* * *

Scott Gardner

Kevin Dhinsa

"Ranjit lait gia tey kehan lagaa, mein theek naheeen. Usdi ghar wali, Lakhwinder ney ambulance nu phone keeta. Mein usdey maalish karnee chahee tey usdey theek hon dee ardas keetee. Oh meinu ehi kahee gia, meinu hath naa laao."

It was Tuesday afternoon, September 17. In the east end station, Kevin Dhinsa listened to Surjit Khela, Ranjit Khela's grandmother, recount what happened the night he died. He translated her words to English as Warren Korol typed on his laptop: "Ranjit lay down, said he wasn't feeling well. Lakhwinder, his wife, called an ambulance. I wanted to rub his body and pray to help him get better, he kept telling me not to touch his body or feet.... The ambulance came, put an oxygen mask on his face and took him away on a stretcher. Paviter also phoned Ranjit's friend, I think his name is Sukhwinder. They came to the house just before the ambulance arrived."

"Do you think this happened," Dhinsa interjected in Punjabi, "because Ranjit ate something?"

"*Naheen, eh taan rab dee marjee hey.*" ("No. It is God's will.")

This was the routine for all the interviews. Dhinsa asked questions that were typed on Korol's laptop, the answer came back in Punjabi, Dhinsa translated. Then Dhinsa read the answer back to the witness in Punjabi for confirmation. That was how it went from interview number one with Surjit Khela, through interviews 10, 20, 60, 80, and more. A few of the people being questioned spoke English. Most did not.

Korol and Dhinsa were different, and the same. They were both 36, but Korol had nearly 10 years more experience as a police officer. The roots of both their family trees were outside Canada, Dhinsa's in India, Korol's in Ukraine. Both men stood more than six feet, pushing over 200 pounds apiece, Korol with a thicker physique, Dhinsa slighter. Korol had the light brown-graying hair, Dhinsa's black hair was cropped short. With his tanned, often serious face and dark eyes, Dhinsa radiated intensity. Korol came off easy-going. He was the lead investigator, but the pair were more like equals in the heat of the investigation. "Meet the brains of the operation," was the way Korol eventually came to introduce his partner. "Indispensable."

Scott Gardner

Detectives Warren Korol and Kevin Dhinsa

They finished interviewing Surjit, and then Ranjit's grandfather, Piara. Why, the detectives asked Surjit, did Ranjit name Sukhwinder Dhillon the sole beneficiary of his life insurance policy?

"I don't know," Surjit said in Punjabi. "But we trust Jodha, he was like our own family. When Jodha went to India, my family would look after his house. Since Ranjit's death, he drops in all the time. He takes us places."

After Korol and Dhinsa finished they walked the elderly couple to the police station lobby. Waiting for them was Ranjit's uncle, Paviter, and a man with a dark beard, short black hair, wide eyes, and a burly physique. Dhillon. Korol had seen his photo in the report of his assault on Parvesh. Grandfather Piara spoke Punjabi to both the uncle and Dhillon.

"*Police kehndee hey ki, Ranjit dee mot zehar naal hoee hey.*"

Dhillon's eyes widened, as though he was surprised by what he was hearing.

"*Eh kiven hoea?*" Dhillon replied.

The group of them left the station. Dhinsa turned to Korol.

"Warren. I overheard them."

"And?"

"Piara told them that the police say poison killed Ranjit. Then the uncle repeated it to Dhillon. And Dhillon said, 'Well, how did that happen?'"

Later that day, the detectives interviewed Lakhwinder, Ranjit's widow. She talked about the dinner she served him, nothing out of the ordinary. She said little else, said nothing about Dhillon, or anyone else, giving Ranjit anything. There was no shortage of suspects as far as Korol was concerned. Ranjit's family said Ranjit and Lakhwinder were going through a divorce. The pair may have had a difficult relationship. Lakhwinder was a suspect. So too were Ranjit's grand-

Piara, Ranjit Khela's grandfather

parents, who practiced homeopathic medicine. Did they give him strychnine, by accident or otherwise? Dhillon was, of course, the main suspect. Only he stood to gain financially from his friend's death.

The next day, Wednesday, Korol sat in front of a computer at the station. He planned to interview Lakhwinder's brother, Udham Singh Sekhon, and Harmail Singh, Ranjit's brother-in-law. Korol logged on to CPIC, the Canadian Police Information Computer. He usually did a check for any criminal record before each interview. He typed in the name Sekhon, Udham Singh, and his address in Hamilton. The computer spat out the information:

1. 92/01/08 DWI $400
2. 92/09/23 Driving with more than 80 mg of alcohol in the blood. Two charges, 21 days on each.
3. 94/07/25 Oakville: a) care or control while impaired, 3 months. b) driving while license disqualified, 1 month consec. c) driving while impaired, 3 months consecutive proh dri 3 years. d) driving while disqualified, 1 month consec and proh dri one year
4. 96/01/02, assault, susp sent and two years probation

Korol typed in Harmail Singh's name. The first six counts were from Vancouver, the last two in Hamilton.

1. 1980: 80 mgs alcohol, 30 days
2. 1982: Impaired, 14 days
3. 1985: refuse breathalyzer, 3 months
4. Theft under $100
5. 1988: Impaired, fail to attend
6. 1988: Impaired, fail to attend
7. 1989: Assault, utter death threats
8. 1994: DWI, refuse sample

Neither man was an exemplary citizen, it appeared. But Korol didn't discriminate when it came to getting information.

* * *

"Vistinduk, jahar, kuchila, vishtinduk, nux vomica."

The naturopath listed Punjabi words for strychnine. "*Kuchila* comes from the kapilo tree, the leaves and berries are poisonous," he continued. It was Thursday and Korol and Dhinsa were interviewing an east Indian naturopath in east Hamilton.

"Could you mask it?" Korol asked.

"To an extent. *Kuchila* has no odor if mixed with alcohol or spices like ginger. But it is very bitter tasting." He added that when *kuchila* is diluted, it does have healing powers. People use it as a pain killer, or for stiffness, mental sharpness. Impotency, too. But in its pure form, it kills. "Once in the bloodstream, to the central nervous system, the body spasms. Convulsions, muscles contract, blood pressure increases and the heart rate quickens until the heart fails."

The naturopath knew nothing of the homicide investigation, but he had just described perfectly the symptoms exhibited by Ranjit and Parvesh shortly before they died.

"Thank you," Korol said. "I'll be in touch if we need anything more."

Next the detectives interviewed Billo, Lakhwinder's brother. He reconstructed his view of the last evening he'd seen Ranjit, on June 23. Billo had purchased a used Dodge Caravan van from Ranjit on June 23 for $6,500. That same day he, Ranjit, and Jodha drove it to a government office to get it certified. At 4:30 in the afternoon they returned to the Khela home on Gainsborough Road.

"Billo, you just bought a new van," Ranjit said. "You should party. We should get some drinks."

"What for? You don't even drink, Ranna."

"So what? Paviter is home, he'll help you drink."

At 6 p.m., the three men drove to buy whisky at a liquor store in the mall. Billo and Dhillon downed shots in the parking lot. Then Ranjit drove them back to his house on Gainsborough. Paviter came out to join them. Ranjit didn't drink, but the other three men sat in the van in the driveway, swigging from the bottle. Ranjit went into the house and came back out with some food on a plate. Then he left the others to go visit his grandmother in hospital. Ranjit returned to the house at 9:30 p.m. to find Dhillon, Billo, and Paviter still sitting in the van, drinking and talking.

"Ranna, how about some more food?" Billo said. Ranjit shook his head.

"Come on, join us! Join us for some drinks!"

Soon afterwards, Ranjit drove Dhillon home. He offered to drive Billo home, too. "I'm just around the corner, I'm fine to drive," Billo replied, whisky on his breath. Billo drove off in his new van, but Ranjit followed him to make sure he got home safe. Ranjit phoned Billo's wife later, about 10 p.m., to make sure he was okay.

Korol's laptop clicked as Dhinsa translated the story. By Billo's account, Dhillon definitely had time alone with Ranjit. Was Billo telling it straight? He did admit to driving home while probably impaired. Given his record, he was probably telling the truth about that. He had offered a glimpse into the complicated issues within the Khela family. The divorce Ranjit and Lakhwinder were supposedly going through was "only on paper," a sham, he said, so each could marry another Indian and bring them to Canada. There was a custody dispute over their boy, who was named Ranjod.

"Lakhwinder, my sister, is a timid woman, she does what elders tell her," Billo said. "Some people wonder if the poison was meant for my sister and Ranjit took it by accident. Ranjit's father wants custody of Lakhwinder's son."

Dhinsa asked if there was anything else Billo could tell them about Ranjit's death.

"*Eh taan rab dee marjee hey.*"

"It is God's will," Dhinsa repeated for Korol. God's will —that was the second time the detectives heard the phrase in relation to Ranjit's death. It would not be the last. Outside the Khela home that same day, Thursday, Piara, Ranjit's grandfather, told the detectives he didn't believe Ranjit was murdered. Korol was amazed. He was learning about Sikh belief in fate, but he also wanted to give the old man a wake-up call.

"Kevin," Korol said to Dhinsa, "tell the grandfather the toxicologists found poison in Ranjit's blood, and that someone put it there. Tell him about the autopsy, the whole process. Give it to him straight."

Dhinsa spoke, and Piara's face tightened. Then the old man broke down and cried.

* * *

On October 8, the detectives pulled up in front of an apartment building on Grandville Avenue, in the neighborhood where Dhillon lived. There they spoke with a man named Yog Raj Rathour, an insurance agent and respected member of the Indian community whom Ranjit had dealt with when he first came to Canada. Ranjit had once purchased a life insurance policy through Yog, but had canceled it without explanation a few weeks before he died.

Yog told the police about bizarre rumors floating within the community. Ranjit had a friend named Jodha. Yog himself had never met him. Jodha's wife died suddenly last year. She had a stiff back, a painful grimace on her face. Very strange. Then Jodha went to India. They say he married several women, received dowry money. And one of the women died a death similar to Jodha's first wife. It was all just rumors, some of it came all the way from India, and who knows how it got twisted or who was trying to get at Jodha. Korol looked at Dhinsa. They knew that Jodha was Sukhwinder Dhillon's nickname. Korol's thoughts raced. The trail might lead to India. He and Dhinsa could be taking a trip.

It was time to interview Dhillon himself. Korol wanted to keep the questions confined to Ranjit's death. Don't let Dhillon know they have him in their sights for Parvesh's murder, or that they have heard rumors about a possible India connection. Korol punched in the number on his cellphone.

"Mr. Dhillon. This is Detective Sergeant Warren Korol of Hamilton police. Detective Kevin Dhinsa and I plan to drop by your house for an interview."

"Yes, yes, yes—don't speak much English," Dhillon replied.

"That's fine," Korol said. "Detective Dhinsa speaks Punjabi."

The detectives drove along Barton Street, past Aman Auto, Dhillon's car dealership, then onto Berkindale Drive and pulled up in front of number 362. Dhillon answered the door.

"I'm Detective Warren Korol. This is Detective Kevin Dhinsa."

Dhillon smiled and shook their hands vigorously.

"Yes, hello, come in, come in," he said.

They sat in the kitchen and Korol hooked up his laptop. Dhillon spoke excitedly.

"Anything I can do, anything, fine, fine."

His English was fast and rough, and he lapsed back and forth between bursts of English and Punjabi. Dhillon pulled a long tube from a shelf, removed a roll of paper from inside and unfurled it on the table. It was a blueprint for a new garage he was going to build on the house. After showing it off, Dhillon sat down.

"You can ask me anything," Dhillon said, smiling. Dhinsa began, in Punjabi.

"Have you ever heard of strychnine, also known as *vistinduk*, *kuchila*, *jahar*, *kuchola*, *vishtinduk*, or *nux vomica*?"

"I've never heard of them," Dhillon said. "I'm not an educated man. I have only heard of these names from you. I went to school three or four years. I'm just a dairy farmer."

"Can you tell us how this poison might have got into Ranjit's body?"

"I don't know. I don't know if he had any problems in the house, don't know if there was any fighting. I never saw anything."

"On your dairy farm, do you or your servants give anything to the animals to help them reproduce or enhance fertility?"

"No. We didn't give them anything. Just grain."

Dhillon talked of the last day he spent with Ranjit. He said Billo, Ranna, and he all went to register the car at 2 p.m., then to the liquor store. They returned to Ranjit's house, then he, Dhillon, went home alone. His story did not mesh with Billo's, who said Ranjit drove Dhillon home. Korol jumped in.

"What time did you leave Ranjit's home after returning from the liquor store?"

"Around two or three," Dhillon said in English. "I usually have one or two shots then slip out. Billo starts talking nonsense when he has a few drinks."

"How could you have left Ranjit's home at two or three o'clock to go home when you already said it was two when Ranjit and Billo picked you up to go to the ministry?"

"They weren't very long in the ministry. It couldn't have been more than two-thirty, three."

"After you returned from Ranjit's house, did you see him again that day?"

"No, I didn't. I was working in my garden, planting."

"How was the death of Ranjit explained to you?"

"I don't know, I don't speak much English," Dhillon said.

Dhinsa finished with the final statement they gave all the witnesses: "We are sorry about the death of Ranjit Khela. It is important that we investigate this case thoroughly to find out how the poison got into his body. Is there anything we can do for you at this time?"

"I don't know anything about it," Dhillon replied. "I am just a simple *jat* man."

Chapter11 ~ Lie Detector

On Wednesday, October 23, Korol started chasing the India connection. He visited the Canadian immigration office on King Street and asked an official named Paul Bassi to dig for information on Sukhwinder Singh Dhillon. Bassi produced a document.

"Mr. Dhillon filled out two applications to sponsor two different females to enter Canada as his wife," Bassi said.

The blue eyes narrowed.

"The first was for a Kushpreet Kaur Dhillon, made on November 2, 1995. The second was for a Sukhwinder Kaur Dhillon, made on April 15, 1996. Neither woman has ever landed in Canada."

Korol hurried back to Central Station and began drafting a letter to Interpol in India, requesting information on the possible deaths of the two women and, if they were dead, the cause of death. He sent it the next morning. Then Korol phoned a contact with the RCMP, who put him in touch with Pierre Carrier, a liaison officer with the Canadian High Commission in New Delhi.

"Things happen pretty slow around here with the Indian authorities," Carrier told Korol. "And rumors fly all the time. But we'll do what we can."

A week later, on Thursday, October 31, Korol and Dhinsa visited Ranjit's family on Gainsborough Road again.

"Stop bothering us," Ranjit's grandfather, Piara, told Dhinsa in Punjabi. Dhinsa said nothing. "I want you to guarantee," Piara continued, "that if any of us should die because of our cooperation with police, you will bear full responsibility."

Later that afternoon a fax arrived from New Delhi. Pierre Carrier confirmed some interesting information about Dhillon. Sukhwinder Dhillon married a Sarabjit Kaur Brar on April 5, 1995, in India. They had two children. There is now a petition for divorce. Dhillon married a Kushpreet Kaur Toor on April 30, 1995, in India. She died in her village on January 23, 1996, of a heart attack. Dhillon married Sukhwinder Kaur Dhillon on February 16, 1996, and is sponsoring her to come to Canada but she has been refused entry by Canadian immigration authorities due to the number and timing of the marriages.

Korol had barely finished the fax when he grabbed the phone and called New Delhi, where the time was 10 hours ahead.

"Pierre?"

Carrier answered the phone at home, in bed, then took the call in his kitchen.

"What can I do for you, Warren?"

"Sorry about the hour, Pierre," Korol said. "But I had to confirm—is the information on this report legit?" Carrier replied that the facts were correct. Korol asked for copies of any documents about Dhillon.

"And Pierre, don't start asking questions about Kushpreet in India. I want to get Dhillon in for a polygraph first, and I don't want word getting back to him that we know what he's been up to over there."

* * *

The air was thick with moisture and the smell of cedar. Beads of water formed on Sukhwinder Dhillon's shoulders.

"*Bhara, mein kujh naheen keeta. Mein kujh vee galat naheen keeta.*" (Brother, I didn't do it. I didn't do anything wrong.) Dhillon sat on the bench in the sauna with his friend, Kalwinder Singh, at Family Fitness Center on Barton Street. Kalwinder looked over at Dhillon, who sat with his elbows on his knees, his paunch straining forward. The friends rarely talked about family. It was always business. But not this time. Kalwinder had already heard the rumors at the temple. The police were after Dhillon, accusing him of killing his wife and his business friend. He married a bunch of women in India, probably killed there, too. Kalwinder didn't know what to believe. Dhillon seemed so sincere in his manner. And he was a good guy. Kalwinder said nothing to get him going on the rumors. Dhillon had just started talking.

"They say I got the woman pregnant," Dhillon said. "It's not true. I'm all clear on that. It was someone else. And the dead babies, they were dead at birth." Kalwinder said nothing. Dhillon continued. "I don't know why everyone is saying this about me. I am innocent. They think I killed Ranna, too. I didn't do anything,

I'm telling you." They left the gym. A few weeks later, Dhillon pulled up in front of the truck repair shop his friend owned.

"Brother!" Dhillon said.

Kalwinder grinned.

"Jodha."

Kalwinder figured the police were getting closer to Dhillon. He even believed that a cop had been in the sauna with the two of them on at least one occasion, a white guy, listening to their conversation. But Dhillon hardly seemed concerned by the attention.

"How are things?" Kalwinder said.

"There's a cop over there," Dhillon replied, gesturing to a vehicle parked down the street. "He's following me." Dhillon kept a straight face, then broke into a grin and laughed. One of Kalwinder's workers walked over. He liked Dhillon. Thought he was a good guy.

"Hey Jodha, if you were in India, whether you did it or not, if they thought you did it you'd be in jail already."

Dhillon nodded in agreement. His brother, Sukhbir, had been a cop in India. And his father, too. Jodha, he knew all about cops. Was friendly with the Hamilton cops here, too, especially the Indian guy, Dhinsa.

"In India you'd be in jail," the worker repeated, "and if you weren't in jail, they'd beat you. They'd say, 'Did you do it?' And if you said no, they'd beat you. They'd say, 'Did you do it?' And if you said no, they'd beat you until you said yes."

Dhillon nodded and laughed. The worker shook his head, grinning. "Here, they can't touch you! They're not allowed to."

"You're right," Dhillon said. "You're right."

Police surveillance on Dhillon continued through the fall. One afternoon, Dhillon left his house carrying a brown paper bag. He drove to Eastgate Square mall and entered carrying the bag, its bottom straining from the weight of what was inside. How many cars had he sold with a bogus mileage reading? He approached a garbage can in the food court and stuffed the bag in, then turned and left. A couple of minutes later, a hand reached into the garbage can, retrieved the paper bag, and pulled it out. The undercover Hamilton police officer opened the bag and peered inside. There were several of them, metal cylinders. The cop walked out of the mall, got into his unmarked car, and drove back to the station. You'll never guess what Dhillon dropped in a garbage pail at the mall, he reported. Odometers. A whole bag of them.

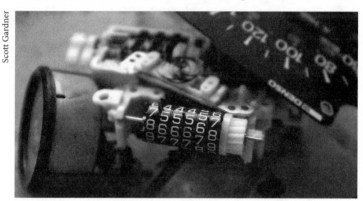

Scott Gardner

Police found a bag of odometers that Dhillon had tossed in the garbage.

* * *

On Wednesday, November 13, Korol and Dhinsa again paid a visit to Dhillon's home. Korol wanted to get him to agree to take a lie detector test. The three men sat at his kitchen table. Dhillon stood up, opened the fridge, and turned to Dhinsa. Speaking Punjabi, he asked Dhinsa a question. Dhinsa shook his head no. Korol smirked. "Dhillon, we know you can speak English," he said. "We found out that you helped the Khela family as a translator in the past. You should also know that the polygraph test will go much quicker if you speak English."

"I can speak some English," Dhillon replied. "But some of it I don't understand."

"That's what Kevin will be there for, to help."

"Yes."

Dhillon agreed to take the test on Sunday. Korol and Dhinsa returned to their car and drove away.

"Warren," Dhinsa said, "remember when we first got in the house and Dhillon asked me something in Punjabi? He offered us a drink." Korol grinned.

"You're kidding."

"I politely declined," Dhinsa said.

"Good call, partner."

On Sunday, the detectives arrived at Dhillon's home. He wasn't there. They waited. When he showed up, they drove him to a police station in nearby Oakville, where the polygraph would be done. A video camera tapes the questioning in one room, detectives watch it live on a monitor in an adjoining room. Dhillon was introduced to Sergeant Steve Tanner, the polygraph operator. Korol and Dhinsa entered the adjacent room to watch the test on the monitor. Tanner spoke with Dhillon in English. The test will take two or three hours, he said. You have the right to call a lawyer. And then Tanner said he would be asking Dhillon if he gave poison to Ranjit.

"The test doesn't lie," Tanner said. "It will tell us if you are lying and if you killed Ranjit Khela." Dhillon suddenly looked confused.

"I don't understand," Dhillon said, a blank look on his face. Dhinsa left Korol's side and entered the polygraph room. He repeated Tanner's statement in Punjabi. Dhillon's English had suddenly taken a turn for the worse, and remained that way. Korol burned. He had hoped to get Dhillon speaking freely today, but now he saw problems down the road in court if they didn't do it by the book. Dhinsa could translate, but he was hardly a neutral observer. Korol decided they needed to get an official interpreter for the polygraph.

"What about later today, Dhillon?" he asked.

"I have a wedding to attend," Dhillon replied.

The detectives drove Dhillon home at 11 a.m. When would he be free to take the test? He couldn't do it until next week. On December 2, the detectives went to the house to nail down a date. Dhillon wasn't there but his mother, Gobind, was. Dhillon's niece, Sarvjit, was also at the house. She had been brought from India to help look after the children and Gobind. They interviewed both women. After Gobind gave her statement, she signed the bottom marking a large X as her signature. Then she looked at Dhinsa.

"*Tusee chaah lavongey*?" Gobind said.

Dhinsa turned to Korol.

"She would like us to have some tea," he said.

Korol smirked.

"Tea? I'm not having any tea in this place," he said.

"Warren, it's a slap in the face to refuse tea in an Indian home."

"Well then, you better get in the kitchen and watch her make it."

In the car afterward, the partners laughed about it.

"You know," Korol said, "we could always have played the old switcheroo." Gobind brings in the mugs, places them on the table, turns away for a moment, the cops switch the mugs—ah, but maybe that's what she wanted them to do! Switch back, the shell game continuing. Dhinsa roared with laughter.

Gobind had told them her son was at the Pizza Pizza at Queenston and Parkdale. The detectives found him there sitting with Ranjit's father, Makhan Singh Khela.

"You have nothing to fear from the polygraph," Dhinsa told Dhillon in Punjabi, "unless you are guilty of something. If you pass the test, our suspicions will be removed."

"Kevin," Korol said, "tell Dhillon that the insurance company knows we are investigating, and nobody gets paid until we finish."

Dhillon agreed to take the polygraph test on December 8 at 10 a.m. But the day before the appointment, Dhillon phoned Dhinsa, said his mouth was hurt and he couldn't talk. He had been involved in a car accident in a McDonald's parking lot, although he hadn't reported it. On December 10, on surveillance, detective Mike Martin watched a healthy-looking Dhillon enter his house and emerge a short time later wearing a bandage wrapped around his chin and neck, to take his daughter to school. Later in the day Dhillon was seen in his car again, but the bandage had vanished.

Korol and Dhinsa went to see Dhillon the following day. He spoke to Dhinsa awkwardly, his jaw seemingly frozen. Korol smirked. Dhillon pulled down his bottom lip to show him.

"I don't see anything, Dhillon," Korol said.

"Warren," Dhinsa said, "he says he wants to call us later in the week to set up the polygraph."

"Dhillon," Korol said, "I think you're making excuses to avoid taking the lie detector."

Dhillon turned to Dhinsa, a confused, hurt look on his face, his English again failing him.

"Look at me, Dhillon," Korol snapped. "Look at me—you know what I'm saying, so don't turn to Kevin. Why don't you just reply to me in English and stop making excuses?"

"I know—a little English," Dhillon said. "But I am sick, I am in pain. I'm going to the dentist for it."

"Are you scared to take the lie detector because you gave Ranjit strychnine?"

Dhillon turned to Dhinsa. "*Mein kujh naheen keta. Mein kisey nu zehar naheen ditta.*"

"I didn't do it," Dhinsa translated for Korol. "I didn't give anyone any poison."

The detectives got back in their car and drove through the neighborhood to the Khela family home. Dhillon got into his own car and followed them. Korol parked on the street, Dhillon in the driveway. Dhillon started honking his horn and got out of the car as Ranjit's grandparents, Piara and Surjit, emerged from the house. Dhinsa spoke to all three of them.

"If Ranjit has been murdered," Piara said in Punjabi, "his soul will not be at rest. That's what I believe."

"Piara," Dhinsa said, "Dhillon is delaying our investigation into Ranjit's death by not taking the polygraph test."

"Jodha did nothing, the test will be a waste of time," Piara said.

"It is not a waste of time," Dhinsa said. "Look, there is also the insurance claim. The sooner Jodha takes the polygraph, the sooner the claim can be settled."

Dhillon, listening, volunteered again to take the polygraph.

"I know you're not feeling well," Dhinsa said, turning to Dhillon. "But if you're worried about your jaw, you'll be talking less during the polygraph than you have already been talking today."

Later that day, Korol opened a large envelope that arrived at his office. It was from Pierre Carrier in New Delhi. The documents included:

- Two letters from Sarabjit Kaur Dhillon, wife No. 2, addressed to the Canadian High Commission, dated April 4, 1996, and September 13, 1996. They cited Dhillon's bigamy, warned that Dhillon's third wife, Kushpreet, had died mysteriously, and urged Canadian officials to reject the bid of Sukhwinder Kaur, Dhillon's fourth wife, to come to Canada.
- A divorce document, with Dhillon the applicant and Sarabjit the respondent.
- An application for permanent residence in Canada for Kushpreet Kaur Dhillon, dated August 2, 1995.
- An application for permanent residence in Canada for Sukhwinder Kaur Dhillon, dated May 18, 1996.

On the morning of December 15, the detectives picked up Dhillon to take him for the polygraph. They stopped for coffee on the way to Oakville. Korol drove, Dhinsa beside him and Dhillon in the back. Dhillon sat in the middle of the seat, leaning forward and talking casually.

"How's the new business coming?" Dhinsa said. "Are you going to have a gas bar on the property, too?"

"No gas bar, just a garage," Dhillon said. "The whole thing, the lot, everything, is going to cost between $200,000 to $250,000. My house is paid off, but now there's a mortgage on the house against the business."

Dhinsa brought up Parvesh's name.

"My first wife died February 3," Dhillon said.

"How?"

"Brain damage," Dhillon said, his expression unchanged. "She was in hospital five days before dying. They never operated on her."

"Any word about the insurance settlement for Ranjit's death?"

"Makhan Singh Khela wants to return to India after he gets the insurance money," Dhillon said. "I'm giving him the money as soon as I get it."

Dhinsa said nothing.

"If Ranjit was killed," Dhillon added, "then it makes the insurance money blood money. God willing, not even an enemy should ever receive blood money."

They arrived at the police station at 9:19 a.m. They met their supervisor, Detective Sergeant Steve Hrab, plus Steve Tanner and the official Punjabi interpreter. The test would be conducted by Tanner, then Korol, Dhinsa, and Hrab would each question Dhillon. The three detectives watched Tanner's interrogation on a monitor in a separate room. A polygraph machine measures changes in blood pressure, respiration, and "galvanic skin resistance"—sweat—during questioning. Tanner prepared Dhillon for the test. That process took more than two hours. Using an interpreter, he explained to Dhillon, at length, how the test works.

"We are interested in monitoring the heart," Tanner said, "because when a person tells a lie and knows they are telling a lie, their heart will always fight against that lie. Everyone knows the difference between what is right and wrong. It's taught by elders and church people."

"I'm not telling lies, sir," Dhillon said.

Tanner fastened two straps to Dhillon, one across his chest, the other across his stomach. Sensors were attached to his left hand and a blood pressure strap on the right biceps.

"I need you to sit perfectly still, Dhillon. Keep your feet flat on the floor in front of you, do not move when we go through the test. When I start the test, keep your head up, look straight ahead."

Before the real test, Tanner said, they'd do a dry run. "Dhillon, have you ever fixed odometers to produce false readouts?"

"No."

The needle quivered. Dhillon asked for a Tylenol. He had a headache. Tanner asked another question, one of the standards of the polygraph, a litmus test of sorts.

"Have you ever told a lie in your life?" It's a trick question. Everyone has told a lie.

"No," he said.

Finally, Tanner got to the real test.

"In June of this year, did you give poison to Ranjit?"

"No."

"In June of this year, were you the person who gave poison to Ranjit?"

"No."

"In June of this year, was it you who gave the poison to Ranjit?"

"No."

"Did you have any involvement in the poisoning of Ranjit?"

"No."

Scott Gardner

Later, Tanner unhooked the machine from Dhillon and left the room. Dhillon remained in his chair, alone, staring at a wall, rubbing his beard, picking lint off his shirt, an unconcerned look on his face. Tanner returned at 8:06 p.m.

Police video of Dhillon taking lie detector test

"Dhillon, I have very carefully looked at the results. It is obvious to me that you are lying about Ranjit. Now there are other things we need to talk about."

Tanner explained his rights. Dhillon was not charged with anything, he could call a lawyer. But his evening was just beginning. Dhinsa entered the room. Dhillon had already been read his rights, so Dhinsa did not repeat them. It was a seemingly minor oversight, but one that would come back to bite him. Dhinsa asked questions, then it was Korol's turn. Both detectives used the methodical, measured, business-like approach with which Dhillon was familiar. But things were about to change. It was 10:30 p.m. Now it was Steve Hrab's turn.

CHAPTER 12 ~ NO PLACE TO HIDE

Detective Sergeant Steve Hrab stood five-foot-nine, wore glasses, and had a brown mustache and goatee flecked with gray. He looked unimposing physically next to Korol and Dhinsa. But Hrab, 45, chased bad guys with a zeal that, on occasion, got him in hot water. Outwardly, detectives like Korol and Dhinsa wore an orderly detachment. But with Hrab things seemed to get personal. Some of the guys Hrab came across, well, he came to hate them—especially the ones who abused women and children. He'd see the criminal in court, or in a cell, and unsuccessfully fight to keep the words from escaping. "You ... piece ... of ... shit."

Scott Gardner

Detective Sergeant Steve Hrab interrogated Dhillon.

He could keep a lid on his anger. Most of the time. Once, a convicted murderer sat in a holding cell at the station. Hrab felt his loathing build, wanted to plant a little fear in the killer's head. Hrab walked down to the cell by himself, then right up to the bars.

"You know what?" he sneered. "I'm glad you're going to prison. So glad. 'Cause you know, in federal prison there will be a lot of guys like you, a lot of predators. But this time they will prey on you—terrorize you the way you terrorized others. A bit of advice: you might want to think about growing eyes in the back of your head."

The criminal, shocked and enraged, complained to his lawyer. Hrab was forced to write an official letter of apology to the man at Kingston pen. Obviously Hrab had got to the guy. He felt it was worth it.

While not certified in the field, Steve Hrab counted homicide profiling among his professional interests. It was still a relatively new discipline for investigators, made famous in psychological thriller movies like *Manhunter* and its sequel, *Silence of the Lambs*. Hrab took the courses, traveled to FBI headquarters in Quantico, Virginia, studied under the first FBI profilers, men like John Douglas. In his book *Journey Into Darkness*, Douglas explains interrogation techniques used on killers. You meet the subject on his own psychological level: "Deal with them on their own level or else they can bullshit you for their own self-serving purposes. Remember, most serial offenders are expert manipulators of other people. If you're not willing to come to their level and see things through their eyes, they won't open up and confide."

Hrab knew how to use provocative tactics. Fourteen hours into his questioning by police, Dhillon was about to experience it for himself. He was tired, said his head hurt. It was 10:40 p.m. The Punjabi interpreter who had been Dhillon's comfort blanket left. Hrab entered the room. Time to play bad cop.

"Okay, Dhillon," Hrab began, "I'm part of the team investigating the death of Ranjit Khela. I want to tell you before I continue that anything you say can be used in evidence.... It can be used at your trial. You understand that?" Dhillon nodded. "Do you remember a few years ago when you beat up your wife Parvesh, you had to go to court?"

"No."

"You went to court. You beat up your wife."

"Oh yeah, yeah, three, four years ago," Dhillon said, as though he was discussing nothing more than a parking ticket. "Three hundred fine."

"You got a three-hundred-dollar fine?" Hrab asked.

"Yeah."

"Right," Hrab said. "Okay. Today we're here because Ranjit was murdered. He was killed. Ranjit was murdered and today this machine told us it was you. So what's gonna happen to you is that you're gonna have to go to court for killing Ranjit."

"I no kill him."

"You killed him."

"I no kill him."

"Yeah, you did, and I'm gonna tell you why. Are you a religious man?" Hrab asked.

Dhillon nodded, clasped his hands on his lap. "Do you believe in—"

"Go to the *gurdwara*."

"Do you believe in God?"

"Yeah, I believe in God."

"That's a lie!" Hrab snapped back.

"Me no lie."

"You're lying."

"No lie, sir."

"Yes, a lie. A lie. You are a very cold man. And there's only one thing in your life you worship, and that's money. That's your God."

"No, no money. God."

"Money. Money."

"No, sir."

"That is your God. Right there, you do everything for money."

Hrab placed a $5 bill on the arm of Dhillon's chair. Dhillon put it back on the desk.

"No."

"This is what you live for, money. Don't say no when I know it's a lie. Don't say no. Because I believe in God," Hrab said.

"I believe in God too," Dhillon said, placing his hand on his heart.

"No, no, you don't. You believe in this—this is your God. Money…. Why did you beat up Parvesh?" Hrab asked. "Why did you hit Parvesh?"

"Family problem."

"What was the problem?"

"Sometime I go mad and drink a little bit."

"Why were you mad? What made Dhillon mad?"

"No mad."

"You were mad and you hit her. Why did you hit her?"

"I drink, I told you."

"That's a lie."

"I no lie, sir."

Hrab paced the room, toward Dhillon, back again.

"You were lying to me. I have the record from court," Hrab continued. "You hit Parvesh because you were mad because her family wasn't paying any money to live with you. Your God, money."

"No," Dhillon said.

"Yes. It's in the records. So don't tell me I'm a *liar*!" Hrab's voice suddenly boomed. "There's only one liar here! You! Don't lie any more!"

"I don't understand," Dhillon said, looking unperturbed.

"Oh," Hrab sneered, "you understand *everything*. You hit Parvesh for money."

Hrab placed the $5 bill on the arm of Dhillon's chair again. Dhillon picked it up and put it back on the desk. "You know when someone dies, they do an autopsy?" Hrab asked. "A doctor looks at her when she's dead and he cuts little pieces out of her. He takes little pieces. What he does is cut little pieces out of her, from the body, cuts them out and keeps them." He motioned with his hand toward Dhillon, as though digging pieces of flesh. "They don't know why she died, she's a young woman. People 36 years old don't die in Canada for no reason."

"Maybe I go tomorrow die?"

"I don't care about you dying."

"Okay."

"I wouldn't care less. But Parvesh died, and nobody knows why. She didn't have a heart attack."

"Talk to the doctors," Dhillon said.

"I talked to the doctors!" Hrab shouted. "They have the little pieces of your wife. You cremated her but we still have these little pieces." Hrab gestured as if he was ripping the heart out of Dhillon's chest. "They took little pieces from Ranjit that they cut out of his body and they send it to the laboratory in Toronto. The doctor asks why is Ranjit dead and the laboratory says we find strychnine, a poison."

"I no give poison to him."

"Strychnine. Strychnine. Which is *kuchila*."

"I no remember, no."

Hrab turned to a white board hanging on the wall. He drew arrows to show the trail of death—Parvesh, Ranjit, the Indian marriages. "Parvesh dies, two months later you're in India, you marry one young woman, you don't like her, you throw her out, you go marry another one."

At 10:59 p.m. Hrab pulled a pill out of his pocket, held it in front of Dhillon's face.

"Did you give Ranjit a pill the day he died? Right? 'Hey, Ranjit—*kuchila*. Makes you very strong with a woman so you can perform.'"

"I don't tell that to you, sir, no."

"No, not to me, but you tell Ranjit. Ranjit is saying he needs something to be strong with his wife. 'Tonight when I go to bed I want to be strong.'"

"No, I no give to him."

"Six days before, you signed a $200,000 life insurance policy on Ranjit."

Dhillon said he planned to give the money to Ranjit's father.

"No, *you* get the money," Hrab said.

"No, sir."

"Liar."

Hrab pointed at the polygraph machine. "This is the truth, not you. The machine is the truth, not you. The machine says you're a liar."

Later, Hrab told Dhillon the police in India were waiting for him.

"'They're gonna arrest you. 'Cause you killed a girl in India."

"I no kill."

"Yeah, just like you killed Ranjit here. Didn't ya."

"No."

Later, Hrab called Kevin Dhinsa into the room to translate. "If he starts with the bullshit here, Kevin, you tell me right away. I don't want any bullshit."

"I swear to God," Dhillon said after several questions, "I didn't give any medication to anybody, even if you cut me into pieces, every piece will say the same thing. From now on, even if somebody asks me for a headache pill at my home, I am not going to do that."

"Even if I believe you, for now my suspicion is that three young people died and you are right in the middle of it," Dhinsa said.

"Yeah, everybody is blaming me."

Hrab spoke. "I hate to interrupt this, but is he telling us the truth now, Kevin?"

"No," Dhinsa said.

"Why are you wasting our time, why are you talking bullshit?" Hrab said.

Dhillon said nothing.

"I'm the boss here!" Hrab shouted. "I'm the boss! No more lies and bullshit. Don't look at Kevin. Look at me! *Me!* Why are you telling Kevin anything? You killed because of money, so tell us the truth. Don't look at him. Tell me the truth." Dhillon said nothing.

"Tell me the truth. Tell me the truth."

Dhillon looked at Dhinsa.

"No, tell *me* the truth. No more lies."

"If you're going to kill me, kill me," Dhillon said.

"I'm not gonna kill you," Hrab said. "In India they might kill you. Kevin, tell him—ask him what they do to murderers."

"Death sentence," Dhinsa said.

"Yeah, hanging," Dhillon added.

"Hanging? You're going to go there and hang?" asked Hrab.

"I—"

"For killing that girl?"

"I don't kill her."

"Well, they say you did."

"You hang me, shoot me."

"I'm not going to kill you, *you're* the killer. You kill people. You killed those people, people in India. Yeah! Tell him Kevin, he's caught. You've been caught."

"You kill me," Dhillon said.

"We don't do that in Canada. I'm not a killer, I'm not like you. I have a job to do. My job is to put people like you in jail."

"Are you going to take me home?"

"I'm not taking you home right now, I want to hear the truth. Do you work hard?"

"Yes, I work hard."

"You like money."

"You want my money, house."

"I don't want those. You love money so much you killed for it. Six days after you took out life insurance on Ranjit, he died. A couple of months after Parvesh took out life insurance, she died. It had to be you. Your kids didn't give it to her. It's you."

Dhillon said nothing.

"Who killed them?"

"I don't know."

"It was you! You killed them!" Hrab was thundering again. "Tell me the truth! Tell me who killed them! Right now. You haven't told the truth once here tonight. You are the killer, and we will tell everyone you are the killer, and we will find out about more people you killed. We will find them all. Because they will find out in India."

"I'll go to India, no problem."

"The Indian police will take care of you and we'll never hear of you again. You'll go to India and will never come back."

Dhillon said nothing. Hrab approached the end of his inquisition.

"You use the word f—k a number of times," he said. "You understand the English language really, really well eh? You know what? Don't f—k me over. Okay? Don't f—k me over because you are f—ing me over and you are f—ing Kevin over by lying. You know, you're a used-car salesman. That's what you do for a living and you lie every f—ing day of your life. You lie about everything you do in your life. You lie for money."

"Yeah."

"You lie every f—ing day. Lie, lie and it's always money, money, money, money, money and you lie. You kill for money, you lie for money."

Remarkably, Dhillon sat through Hrab's verbal attack, outwardly showing no emotion, offering denials but not taking the bait, not arguing back, showing little exasperation. He did not crack.

"Tomorrow morning I'm gonna talk to the newspaper, the television, I'm gonna tell them that Ranjit Khela was murdered. I'm gonna call your lawyer tomorrow and I'm gonna tell him the truth."

"Can I go now? Would you send me now?"

Dhinsa answered him in Punjabi. "If you want to go, go. You should go and talk to your lawyer, all right."

"Yes, yes."

"And also tell him that you murdered Ranjit."

"I haven't murdered him, why should I tell him? Send me home."

"We will be back in a minute," Hrab said. "You have no place to hide now, Mr. Dhillon. No place to hide."

Hrab and Dhinsa left the room. Dhillon fiddled with the lie detector attachments still on the desk, took a sip of coffee, made a circular pattern with the chains from the polygraph, set the mug down, took another sip. He rubbed his head, picked fluff off his pants. Then, tired, he put his right hand under his jaw, holding up his head, rubbed his mustache. He looked bored. The time was 11:41 p.m. Three minutes later, the door opened and he was led from the room. The interrogation was over.

It was 10 minutes past midnight. Korol and Dhinsa drove Dhillon home. Dhillon spoke to Dhinsa.

"*Mein kujh naheen keeta. Mein kisey nu zehar naheen ditta.*" (I didn't do anything. I didn't give anyone any poison.)

"You failed the polygraph test," Dhinsa said in Punjabi. "We believe the results. We think you poisoned Ranjit."

"I did not, I did not," Dhillon said, his English returning.

Korol shook his head, turned it to one side and spoke out of the corner of his mouth.

"Dhillon," he said, "you are a pathological liar."

Warren Korol's day did not get any better. That afternoon, he filed a request with a justice of the peace for a search warrant for 362 Berkindale Drive. The form came back to him. "Process not

issued," it said. Korol steamed over the rejection. There had to be
enough information to warrant a search. He needed to look for
traces of strychnine in Dhillon's house. The JP said any search
was too far removed from the time of the deaths to find anything.
How would he know? You never know what a search will unearth.
Things got no better two days later, when Korol read a faxed letter
sent from a local lawyer named Richard Startek:

December 18, 1996
"Without Prejudice"
Attention: Detective Warren Korol
Re. Ranjit Singh Khela

Dear Sir,
I act on behalf of Sukhwinder Singh Dhillon, Makhan Singh Khela,
Lakhwinder Khela, Surjit Khela, Piara Khela, Mohinder Khela,
Paviter Khela, Jaswinder Khela, Davinder Dhillon, Harmail Dhillon,
Mandeep Dhillon, and Gurpreet Kaur. My clients were concerned
with respect to the manner in which they were being questioned with
respect to Ranjit's death and a number of them had been accused of
having played a part in this death.

In fact, polygraph tests were conducted on a number of in-
dividuals some of whom were not aware of their rights and can
barely speak English. In fact, Mr. Dhillon apparently had a poly-
graph test conducted this past weekend and when he questioned
Detective Dhinsa with respect to being able to contact me, he ap-
parently was advised by Detective Dhinsa that Detective Dhinsa
had already spoken to me. This of course is not so. My concern
is that my clients' rights have been violated. I am requesting that
there be no further questioning of any of my clients without my
consent and my presence.

Yours very truly,
Richard P. Startek

Korol spoke with Dhinsa. Dhinsa said he never told Dhillon
that Startek gave approval for the polygraph. Then Korol visited

assistant Crown attorney Brent Bentham, who had been assigned the case, and gave him a copy of Startek's letter. Korol smirked. Startek. He had nothing against the man personally. But the homicide detective had rarely encountered him in court. Startek was predominantly a family lawyer.

On Tuesday, barely 30 hours after the polygraph test ended, Steve Hrab's promise to Dhillon about media exposure came true. The headline on the front page of *The Hamilton Spectator* said: "Pair were poisoned, police now believe."

* * *

On the other side of the country, 4,500 kilometers away, a man named Gurbachan Singh visited his son's paper mill near Surrey, British Columbia. Gurbachan was from the Punjabi village of Panj Grain. He still kept a house there, just down the street from the Brar family—including Sarabjit, the young woman who married Dhillon. At the mill Gurbachan, who understood English, saw a local newspaper spread out on a table. He picked it up and read a familiar name in a brief article. Newspapers in B.C., which has a large population of East Indian descent, had picked up the story that Hamilton police suspected that someone had murdered a man named Ranjit Khela using poison. The article said another person, Parvesh Dhillon, may have been poisoned earlier and it quoted Steve Hrab: "The circumstances surrounding her death are very similar in medical terms. The symptoms and signs of her sudden illness were similar. It's a very, very acute reaction." Hrab added that police knew who the killer was. "The individual who is doing this is targeting people for a reason. But I don't want anyone to fear there's a lunatic running around out there."

The story said Parvesh, who lived with her husband, Sukhwinder, became violently ill and was rushed to hospital last year. Gurbachan paused on the name. Sukhwinder Dhillon? The same man who had married Sarabjit from his village? And fathered her children? Perhaps the police in Hamilton would be interested to hear what he, Gurbachan, knew.

The phone rang in Hrab's office. Tips come in all the time. But this one was more than a bit interesting. Hrab spoke with Warren Korol, who had unearthed the Indian connection in the case—the multiple marriages, the death of the third wife, Kushpreet. But now there appeared to be more.

Korol phoned Gurbachan. The Indian man told Korol about Sarabjit's newborn boys—Dhillon's sons—dying in the middle of the night soon after Dhillon's only visit with them. Rumor had it that Dhillon had earlier warned Sarabjit not to name the babies, not to register their births with authorities. He gave Korol Sarabjit's phone number in Panj Grain. Korol let the information sink in. Parvesh. Ranjit. Kushpreet. And newborn boys? Could Dhillon have murdered his own children? Later, he phoned Pierre Carrier in New Delhi. Korol gave Carrier Sarabjit's phone number.

"You should know, Warren," Carrier said, "I'm a liaison officer, not an investigator."

"I understand."

"We'll need to involve the Indian authorities in this, to contact Sarabjit and so on. Warren, if you come to India I could arrange for you to see the people you need to interview. Otherwise an investigation here will probably take two or three years. Things move very slowly. You should seriously think about coming over yourself."

CHAPTER 13 ~ THE INDIAN CONNECTION

On December 18, Korol met with Ontario's deputy chief coroner, Dr. Bonnie Porter. She called Dr. Michael McGuigan at Toronto's Hospital for Sick Children. McGuigan was also medical director of the Ontario Regional Poison Information Center. McGuigan agreed to review the symptoms exhibited by Parvesh Dhillon at the time of her death. But even if McGuigan confirmed the symptoms were the same as those caused by strychnine poisoning, Korol still had no forensic proof. He spoke to Joel Mayer, head of the biology section at the Centre of Forensic Sciences. CFS still had Parvesh's tissue samples, which Korol had delivered two months ago. No progress to report yet, but Mayer was still optimistic they could detect strychnine with further testing. Korol knew that without toxicology, it would be next to impossible to prove in court that Parvesh had been poisoned.

The next night, back in Hamilton, Korol and Dhinsa interviewed a man named Inderjit Singh Mangat. Mangat told them about a gathering four days after Ranjit's death. He said Lakhwinder told several people that Ranjit's dying declaration to her was that Jodha had given him a pill. At that moment, Dhillon had heard Lakhwinder, Mangat said, and walked over to her. "Dhillon said 'No, Ranjit didn't eat anything at my house,'" Mangat recalled. "And then Lakhwinder said Ranjit must have been joking. The other people there offered no reaction."

Korol and Dhinsa had suspected it before but now they were convinced—the Khela family's cone of silence wasn't rooted entirely in a belief that death is God's will. It was a coverup. Korol recorded his suspicions in his notes. *I believe it is possible that the Khela family know more than they are telling us. They may be trying to cover up the death so they can collect insurance money that Sukhwinder Singh Dhillon will give them."*

* * *

On January 2, 1997, Korol got the call from Joel Mayer at CFS. He had news Korol did not want to hear. They had been unable to detect strychnine in Parvesh's tissue samples. Strychnine might well have been present, but over time it had leached out of the tissue, perhaps during the testing process itself. They just didn't have the technology to detect whatever minuscule traces might remain.

Korol's heart sank. It was a huge blow to the case. But perhaps there was other evidence that could tip the scales against Dhillon in court. They had Ranjit's cause of death confirmed. Perhaps they could prove that Dhillon had easy access to strychnine, possibly find some in his house. And there was the Indian connection. They could prove their case indirectly, circumstantially. Look at all these people close to Dhillon who had dropped dead from the same symptoms. Korol boned up on the *Mutual Legal Assistance Treaty*. It is an agreement, signed between Canada and India in 1996, allowing smoother cooperation between the two countries on matters of criminal justice. He sent a request through the Department of Justice in Ottawa for advice on applying under the treaty to gather evidence in India.

* * *

On March 15, Korol applied again to a justice of the peace for a search warrant for 362 Berkindale Drive. In his written application, Korol said he believed that Dhillon had emptied a Fiorinal headache capsule and packed it with strychnine. There might be traces of the powder in the house. This time, a different JP approved the request. Police put the house under surveillance. On March 17, Dhillon left the house along with his two young daughters. A few minutes later, the police swept in and executed the search warrant. Dhillon's niece, Sarvjit, and his mother, Gobind, were there, and were told to leave. A police search van backed into the driveway. Dhillon came home and stood outside, watching. Kevin Dhinsa walked up to him.

"Dhillon, you could save us all a lot of trouble if you just told me where I can find the *kuchila*."

"I never had it," Dhillon said. "I could never kill my wife. Or Ranna."

The house appeared as though it had been recently cleaned. And the medicine cabinets had been emptied. Among items seized in the house were a mortar and pestle; contents of a vacuum cleaner bag; Ranjit Khela's checkbook and his proof of death certificate; Canada Trust bank books for Parvesh and her father; a proof of death statement for Parvesh signed by a doctor; statement of death for Kushpreet Kaur Toor; handwritten addresses for Kushpreet and Sarabjit; marriage certificate from Dhillon's wedding to Sukhwinder Kaur; divorce judgment with Sarabjit; checks to a local lawyer handling the purchase of properties for Dhillon's used-car dealership on Barton Street East and Main Street East; six photographs from a family album showing bruising to Parvesh's eyes.

They also seized an insurance policy on Dhillon's niece, Sarvjit, that named her uncle Sukhwinder Dhillon as beneficiary. And in the bedroom dresser, they found a blister package of Fiorinal capsules, with one missing. Korol smirked. Dhillon was trying to be clever. Leave the open package in the bedroom dresser, as if that would prove Parvesh had taken the Fiorinal as he claimed to paramedics. Dhillon was unaware that the drug screen in fact proved that Parvesh had no Fiorinal in her system.

They vacuumed the place top to bottom, but the search failed to unearth any evidence of strychnine in the house. The only way to prove Dhillon had access to strychnine was to prove it in India. The search uncovered Dhillon's passport, and one of the stamps showed that he had traveled to India prior to Parvesh's death, and again prior to Ranjit's death. On March 21, Korol received word that Police Chief Robert Middaugh had given him the green light to go to India. On April 1, Korol visited the Crown attorney's office downtown to see Brent Bentham. The prosecutor had been considered a young prodigy by lawyers senior to him when he started in the office 12 years earlier. Now just 39, Bentham already had a long resumé of tough prosecutions in Hamilton. The bespectacled Bentham was a slim, quiet family man with straight brown hair, blue-gray eyes. A detail guy, taciturn, relentless, and without pretension, he spoke in a deep baritone with a measured, bookish manner. Korol gave him the final draft of his request for treaty assistance to go to India.

Korol received a fax from Pierre Carrier in New Delhi on April 15. It was a report on the preliminary investigation into the rumors about Dhillon in and around Ludhiana, conducted by an Indian Central Bureau of Investigation inspector named Subhash Kundu. The report confirmed the stories Korol had heard about Dhillon's multiple wives and the sudden deaths of Kushpreet and the newborn twins. Korol phoned Carrier, told him the request for treaty assistance was on the way from Ottawa. Carrier said he would speak with his contact at the CBI. The next day, Korol faxed Carrier their itinerary.

On March 24 the search of Dhillon's house ended and police packed up their hulking command vehicle and left. Now the media were deep into the story. A *Hamilton Spectator* reporter named Jim Holt spoke to Dhillon at his house. "It's terrible," Dhillon said. "My English is bad. Speak to my lawyer." Dhillon stepped into the house, then re-emerged with his brother, Sukhbir.

"Of course we are angry, what do you think?" Sukhbir said. "Who wouldn't be angry if police force them from their home? It's all just gossip, 100 percent gossip."

Ben Chin, a TV reporter from Toronto, rolled into town. He spoke to Korol. "Do you know where I could find Mr. Dhillon's lawyer, Richard Startek?" he asked.

"Mr. Startek does a lot of family court matters," Korol replied. "You might find him in Unified Family Court." Chin said he knew there were other deaths in India being investigated. Korol asked Chin if he knew anything about strychnine.

"No."

"You might want to familiarize yourself with it. And by the way, have you asked Dhillon where he was when the people in India died?"

"No."

"You might find the answers interesting."

Korol planted a couple more questions in Chin's head. The reporter might also ask Dhillon if his first wife had used homeo-pathic medicine. Warren Korol worked with the media—and *worked* the media. Through the reporter he saw an opportunity for Dhillon to lie and hang himself on the record. He was sure Dhillon wouldn't disappoint.

Chin, his straight black hair flowing to the shoulders of his white trench coat, showed up near Dhillon's home two days later and gave him a taste of hard-core TV news on the fly. He cornered Dhillon in his car, parked on a neighborhood street. He didn't let his subject go, led him with his questions, offered empathy.

"Did the police tell you they were going to come?" Chin asked.

"No, I don't understand English so well. Please leave me alone," Dhillon said, speaking quickly.

"I just want to tell your side of the story," Chin replied earnestly. "Do you think the police are picking on you?"

Dhillon nodded.

"You are an innocent man," Chin said. "You open your door to police. They can check your house all they want, they won't find anything, right?"

Scott Gardner

Video from a TV reporter's interview with Dhillon

"No, no, nothing."

"They are saying it's poison that killed your wife."

"No, no poison. I am 100 per cent clear, no problem. Police investigate, no problem."

"What about the people who are dead in India?"

"She's not my wife."

"How many wives have you had?"

"Please, no more, I'm upset. I was divorced, that's it."

"To set the record straight," Chin continued, "you are a victim here. You've done nothing wrong."

"I'm 100 per cent clear."

"If anything, you've had very bad luck, people dying."

"Right. He was a son to me. Please, talk to my lawyer."

"Thank you very much."

"I'm 100 per cent clear. Clear, clear, clear, clear."

"Somebody in your community is trying to make you look bad."

"Yes. Some people very nice, some people bad. Making stuff up. I'm 100 per cent clear in my heart."

"And what about the twins? Are they dead?"

"No—I never saw them. Never touched them."

Korol and Dhinsa met with Brent Bentham on April 24 to discuss the points to be covered in India. They needed to find out every detail about the deaths there from witnesses, obtain documents from government offices to confirm births, marriages, and deaths, determine whether doctors were called for all of the deaths and why autopsies were not performed. They also had to ask witnesses to the three deaths exactly what symptoms the victims had exhibited. And they needed to go shopping for strychnine. On April 28, a jet took off from Toronto's Pearson Airport with the two detectives on board.

* * *

Chandigarh, India
May 1, 1997

Each morning, CBI Inspector Subhash Kundu woke by 6:30 a.m. His wife, Jogi, whom he had married as arranged by his Hindu parents, made him breakfast, usually toast or an omelet, perhaps *bratha*—a type of bread—with yogurt. Then he reported to his office at the Central Bureau of Investigation building in Chandigarh, the Punjabi capital. But there were other times when the CBI inspector rose much earlier, answering a phone call in the middle of the night. A suspect in a corruption case to be questioned.

Kundu should pay him a visit. He'd dress, load his firearm, and drive his cream-colored Pajha motorcycle through the dark streets and hot air, past rows of towering eucalyptus trees shedding their fine bark, the trunks like polished bone in the moonlight. At the apartment, a rap on the door and the suspect was invited to join Kundu back at the CBI station. Then the interrogation in a gray windowless concrete room with a rattling fan.

Inspector Subhash Kundu in his office in Chandigarh

On the morning of May 1, 28-year-old Subhash Kundu woke early for a different reason. It was one of those mornings when he needed no alarm. The Canadian detectives were arriving today at the train station. CBI officials occasionally cooperated with a Canadian RCMP liaison in New Delhi on immigration matters. But it was unheard of for a CBI man to work hand in hand with Canadian police officers on a murder investigation.

India's CBI has a role comparable to that of the RCMP or FBI. Its officers enjoy a measure of respect as a result. That's quite different from India's regular uniformed police, who are infamous for petty corruption. There is a saying that, in India, a police officer can turn a suicide into a murder, or a murder into a suicide, for the right price. Even after a car accident, witnesses and victims are reluctant to phone police for fear they'll end up having to pay for their services on the spot. As with all things that shock foreigners about India, the root cause is complicated. Uniformed local police in India are paid poorly for difficult and often grisly work.

By the time Korol and Dhinsa arrived in India, Kundu had already completed much of the leg work. All that remained was for the Canadians to confirm what he had discovered. Kundu had been on the road gathering information for several weeks after being assigned to the Dhillon case, interviewing family members of victims.

Kundu knew well the fleeting nature of life in India. He had a dark sense of humor about it. Off duty, over a couple of beers and cigarets, Kundu observed that in the event of a nuclear war between India and Pakistan, Pakistan could strike first and kill more than a million Indians, but India would win the war. And the million dead? "India is overpopulated anyway," he said, "so that wouldn't be such a bad thing." Then Subhash Kundu waited, his face deadpan, for the reaction of his audience before he grinned and the dark eyes danced.

Still, even Kundu was shocked by the trail Dhillon left. He thought the man was a bastard. No matter what happened, he believed Dhillon would be judged and found guilty in a higher court some day. You can escape human justice. But not God's.

Kundu drove to the CBI office, the flesh-toned building in Sector 30-A, on Thursday morning. Two guards with rifles stood out front in their tan uniforms. Kundu, wearing his usual dress shirt and pants, strode past the CBI logo in the lobby, up the four flights of steps, the air still and stale, then down a darkened, pistachio-green hallway. He unlocked the padlock on his office door. Two desks faced each other. A tattered ceiling fan shook as it rotated thanks to the crack in its base. The walls in the dreary, windowless room were ivory-colored concrete marked with splotches of greenish blue that looked like chunks of torn rain clouds. It was a pitiless room, no character or warmth, not one photo, no medals or diplomas, no certificate attesting to the fact that Subhash Kundu was one of India's elite, a man who scored high enough on the Indian Police Service test to merit immediate appointment as Inspector.

Kundu was born in the pitched heat of summer in 1968, in a village called Kinals in the province of Haryana, south of Punjab. His father, Birmati, served in the Indian army, so the family moved frequently. In 1990 he took the police exam to obtain a position in the CBI. He was appointed a sub-inspector the following year. He was just 23. He was posted in New Delhi for a year, then transferred for the next four years to remote areas in Kashmir—the flashpoint between nuclear rivals Pakistan and India. In 1996 he was transferred to Chandigarh. He lived a good life with his wife and two children, Shilpa and Abhishek. They had their own apartment in the most orderly and clean major city in northern India, which sits two hours from the Himalayan foothills. They took day trips to mountainous Simla, rode the cable car at Parwanoo, lunched overlooking the ridges and green valleys.

He left his office, walked down the hall to the weapons room, wrapped his hand around the black plastic grip of a revolver, and returned to the office. The gun was a vestige of India's colonial days. The British had granted India independence in 1947 but their influence lingered in many ways, from bits of English that became part of the Hindi and Punjabi languages to steering wheels on the right side of cars, to the Webley & Scott handguns still used by police. The Mark IV .38-caliber revolver was a break-top—it snapped open for loading. It was now considered an antique of sorts, but was still reliable and a man-stopper when required. Kundu loaded the gun with six round-nosed bullets, then wedged it into the belt holster in the back of his pants. He usually kept his gun at work and wore it only when necessary. It was uncomfortable, for one thing, but today it felt right.

The Dhillon assignment was potentially dangerous. Dhillon and his friends would know the police were on the case. They would not be pleased. It wouldn't take much for a friend or ally of Dhillon to catch the detectives in a remote village or even in a crowded market. The Canadians would not be permitted to carry firearms in India. So he, Subhash Kundu, would protect them. He couldn't rely on local police in the villages, among whom Dhillon had friends. Korol and Dhinsa wouldn't know Kundu was armed. That wasn't necessary.

* * *

Seven hours after taking off from Toronto, Korol and Dhinsa's flight touched down at London's Heathrow Airport, at 9:45 a.m. local time on April 29. A two-hour layover, then they boarded the plane for the eight-hour flight to New Delhi. It was 1 a.m. local time on April 30 when they touched down. The trip to India is exhausting. The body's internal clock has to adjust to the 10-hour time difference from Eastern Standard Time. The detectives disembarked at Indira Gandhi International Airport and headed to the baggage claim under colored sashes and streamers, decorative dolls hanging from a ceiling that was as low as a parking garage's. They spotted a driver from the Canadian High Commission holding a sign with their names on it.

Exiting the car at the hotel, the heat, even at 1:30 a.m., hit them like hot water exploding from a burst pipe. Pierre Carrier had put them up at the Hyatt, a six-star palatial oasis with walls made of Indian sandstone, a sprawling pool in back. It was the finest hotel the detectives had ever stayed in. They shared a room and were asleep by 2:30 a.m. Five hours later they were up, showered and dressed, and headed down to meet Carrier in the hotel lobby. Carrier's driver took them through New Delhi to the Canadian embassy—still called a High Commission, in keeping with the tradition for British Commonwealth countries (even though India does not recognize the Queen as its head of state). Korol learned that anyone who can afford to do so hires a professional driver in India to navigate the chaos on the roads. Hindu drivers place little god figurines on their dashboards to look over them on the roads. "Three things you need driving in India," the driver said. "One, good brakes. Two, good horn. Three, good luck."

Chapter 14 ~ To Live and Die

Warren Korol had done the Caribbean vacation thing, but had never ventured further afield, so he was instantly overwhelmed by New Delhi. With its 12 million people, the city is home to India's central government. It was planned and built by the British in 1932 when they decided to move the capital from Calcutta. The city embodies India's contradictions. There's the stench of poverty in Old Delhi, the seventeenth-century Muslim walled city within the capital where merchants still slit the throats of lambs in open-air markets, the blood trickling across the pavement. In the modern part of the city are the attractive white bungalows ("bungalow" is an Indian word) that once housed British generals and are now occupied by Indian government officials whose children, dressed in their powder-blue uniforms, walk home from government schools.

Scott Gardner

The aerial view from a tower in Old Delhi

New Delhi tries to do what no other Indian city can: regulate order in the midst of chaos. Signs at intersections warn that horn honking is outlawed to cut back on noise pollution, even as traffic chokes the roads every hour of the day. Air-pollution laws ban diesel fuel for auto rickshaws, which line up for five hours at a time for government-approved clean gas pumps. There is a seat-belt law, but most of the cars are designed without belts in the back. There is a helmet law for motorcyclists, but only for the driver, not the women in flowing dresses who ride on the back side-saddle (a more modest position than straddling) or the bare-headed sleeping babies perched precariously on their laps. The well-kept paved streets are often shaded by a canopy of trees; men stand in rows and casually urinate in public against elegantly designed bridge walls.

Korol, Dhinsa, and Carrier were chauffeured up the long boulevard called Shanti Path, or "peace way," home to several embassies. The German mission was across the street from Canada's. The American embassy was a walled fortress with a massive stars and stripes in front, and a huge fountain ("There's Big Brother," the driver quipped). They passed the embassy of India's neighbor and rival, Pakistan ("There is India's true friend, *Pakeestahn*," the driver said, sarcastically). Barbed wire lined the top of the wall that surrounded the Canadian High Commission, where a sentry holding a rifle stood on guard. Not far from the embassy gate, a group of Sikhs sat in the shade of trees lining the boulevard, waiting to apply for visas for Canada. Inside the building, Carrier introduced the detectives to the High Commission's staff physician, Dr. Govind Prasad.

Scott Gardner

The Canadian High Commission in New Delhi

"Where can we buy strychnine?" Korol asked, anxious to get started, adrenalin masking his jetlag. Prasad suggested Bhogal market. New Delhi has hundreds of markets, but tour guides suggest avoiding taking first-time visitors to Bhogal, one of the largest and most congested.

The driver parked at the market and the three Canadians stepped from the air-conditioned car. It was now high noon and the heat hit like a brick. Korol had heard about Indian heat. It was another thing to feel it. Even the breeze against his damp forehead was hot. The heat beats up newcomers, the body instantly bathed in sweat as the heart pumps harder to adjust. The head feels compressed, feet roast inside shoes, a pouch strapped around the waist burns like a hot coal. Most Indians carry cloths to wipe their faces, although few seem to wear hats or sunglasses. No Indian man wears shorts;

better to wear pants to shield the skin. There is a walk, notable among Indian men, a loping stride, feet barely leaving the ground, arms heavy and swinging with their own momentum, the body shutting down every unnecessary muscle, storing energy.

Scott Gardner

The heat and bustle of the markets overwhelmed the detectives.

The bustle of the market assaults the senses. Cars, bikes, and rickshaws squeeze among the many stores and kiosks and merchants—the cobbler, tailor, outdoor barber, dye man twirling cloth in a vat of hot blue liquid, auto repair, appliance repair, fruit and vegetable stands, the thin man with ribs and vertebrae pressing through his leathery dark skin as he squats barefoot beside a large pot of oil, cooking samosas. Young boys stroll the streets in pairs, holding hands or arm in arm. It is a common yet paradoxical sight in India, with its macho male culture, this unabashed affection that young men show each other. Men rarely show any public affection toward women, no hand-holding and absolutely no kissing.

Their size alone made Korol and Dhinsa stand out in the crowd. Children called out, "Hey Jim!" as Korol walked down the street. Men stared; women were more subtle in casting glances. Dhinsa approached a shopkeeper who sold pesticides and asked in Punjabi for *kuchila*. Dhinsa bought a brown envelope labeled "rat poison" for five rupees, mere pennies in Canadian money. It was not quite what they were looking for. They wanted to buy raw *kuchila*.

Later, they headed to the CBI. On the main floor, the trio met
Superintendent H.C. Singh, in charge of Interpol affairs. Singh's
assistant presented a tray of tea and ice water. It would be the
same everywhere the detectives went, drinks always offered in
the Indian tradition. Singh gave Korol a copy of sections 161 and
162 of the Indian Criminal Code, stipulating that if Indian police
take a witness statement, the witness must not sign it, a legacy of
India's tradition of coerced statements.

The next day Korol and Dhinsa rode from their hotel to the
New Delhi train station. Taking the train north to Chandigarh was
Dhinsa's idea. They could have been chauffeured in a car, a four-
hour drive, or could have flown. But the train was a throwback
to Dhinsa's childhood, the days when he reveled in riding the
rails to his grandfather's farm in Haryana province, watching the
scenery whip past. It would be a good chance for Warren to see
the countryside up close. And they could afford to ride first class.
But the trip turned out to be a rude homecoming for Dhinsa. They
boarded the Shatabdi Express. It was early morning, the platform
at Delhi's train station slowly stirring to life. People slept on the
concrete floor. A little boy walked up and down the platform with
his shoe polishing kit, calling, "Shine? Shine?" There was litter on
the platform, human excrement between the tracks. Dhinsa was
appalled. It wasn't how he remembered it.

The Shatabdi's "deluxe air-conditioned seat car" is the pride
of the railway. But this, too, was hardly the experience Dhinsa
remembered. It was indeed air conditioned and it had seats—in
Indian terms that made it deluxe. Most Indians ride rail cars with
wooden benches and hang out the windows to beat the heat inside.
A one-way ticket in the cheap seats costs 100 rupees, about three
Canadian dollars. As the train inched away from the platform,
stray cows and wild dogs crossed the tracks ahead. The train picked
up speed, providing a collage of images. There were the shanties,
looking as though they had been thrown up by the earth, barely
standing, smashed brick and wooden shacks with crumpled tin
roofs. Land along train tracks is considered public in India, and
officials allow squatters to live there. The heat of the morning rose,
the sun burning off the haze like a hot ember through tissue paper.

And then the view suddenly shifted, a contrast to the bleakness, the picture out the window shifting to color, the fields green with cane and corn and elephant grass, a pump house pouring water onto a rice paddy. Women far off in the fields hunched over in their purple and orange dresses, backs bent to the sun now high in the sky. The flooded rice paddies glowed like green neon under the hazy pewter sky.

Scott Gardner

The detectives rode the train to Chandigarh.

More settlements passed, the train shaking and clacking through them, signs declaring places such as Narela, Bhani Khurd, Kurukshetra, Ambala. Women and children huddled in an abandoned rail car and in the shade of an underpass.

The train glided past the station platform of a town called Panipat. The developed part of Panipat is situated along the road from Delhi to Chandigarh and is a typical beehive of markets and commerce. Panipat is best known for its pickles. But along the tracks was the other Panipat, the underbelly. Cloistered inside the train, Korol and Dhinsa looked out on the most brutal existence they had ever seen, a life of black and gray interrupted by an occasional flicker of orange from piles of burning garbage. In this wasteland, women picked through trash, cows and naked children waded in stagnant water as black as tar, trying to escape the heat. A thin old man sat in dirt with his head clasped in his hands.

Perhaps things had been just as bad in Kevin Dhinsa's youth but his vision had been more selective, his senses lulled and numbed by the beat and rocking motion of the train. Or maybe life along the rail line had simply grown worse. Dhinsa made a vow to Korol right there: they would not take the train on the return trip. And he would never ride the train in India again.

* * *

Korol and Dhinsa saw the foothills of the Himalayas come into view as the train neared Chandigarh station and its sign of greeting: "Northern Railway and Chandigarh Railway Station Welcomes You." As the train slowed to a halt, the conductor opened a door and heat gushed in. The platform was smooth hard stone, cleaner than in Delhi. A little girl labored to tug a huge burlap sack across the floor. There were two other signs inside the station. One was a warning: "Do not pay bribes. If anybody of this office asks for a bribe or if you have any information on corruption in this office, you can complain to the head of this department." The other was a quote: "Let all of us Hindus, Mussalmans, Parsis, Sikhs, Christians, live amicably, as Indians, pledged to live and die for our motherland—Mahatma Gandhi."

Inspector Subhash Kundu tossed his cigaret to the ground and strode toward the designated train car with his unaffected swagger, his arms slightly out from his sides, head tilted, palms open as if challenging anyone to approach.

Indian men are, on average, shorter than Europeans or Canadians. But Subhash Kundu, while slim, stood over six feet tall. He had a neatly trimmed mustache, his skin deep brown, thick black hair brushed to one side. He immediately identified Warren Korol, the only white passenger in the car. And the tall Indian beside him must be Kevin Dhinsa. In India, men commonly say hello by placing the palms of their hands together as if in prayer, bowing. Touching strangers in greeting, in Indian culture, is rare. It is too hot and dirty to engage in that. But Subhash Kundu did not put his palms together and bow. He reached out his long hand and shook Korol's, and then Dhinsa's, and smiled, bobbing his head slightly in Indian greeting.

"We go?"

As cab drivers descended on the men, Kundu waved them away like flies, escorting them to the private car. "What is the plan, the agenda?" Kundu asked, alternating between broken English and talking to Dhinsa in Punjabi. The rules were that the Hamilton detectives could record witness statements during interviews, but

Kundu would have to be present. Dhinsa would read a statement back to a subject so that person could make any alterations or deletions. The witness must not sign the statement.

"We need to find a place where we can buy *kuchila*," Dhinsa said. Kundu said nothing, but his head cocked to the side and bobbed in agreement.

"I know a place."

The car drove through the bustle of horse-drawn carts and rickshaws and cars and scooters and bikes. A cow stood at the side of the road rubbing its head against a signpost. The cow is revered in India. When a dairy cow has produced all the milk it is capable of, the farmer frees it to wander wherever it pleases for the rest of its life. Kundu directed the driver up a back alley, emerging in the parking lot of the coral-pink Piccadilly, Chandigarh's only five-star hotel. The lobby was cool and clean, with a shining black marble floor, but the rooms were spartan by Western standards, the beds hard and short, the carpet worn. This would be a low-level hotel in Canada, but to Warren Korol it was perfect. The Hyatt in New Delhi was palatial but the "Pic" was more like home, the staff warm and friendly. He felt comfortable.

The detectives again shared a room, just as they would for the entire trip. Korol was in a strange country, pursuing a serial killer. The detectives' presence might not be welcomed by certain people. The two cops, by now becoming close friends, had to watch each other's backs. Kundu had lined up witnesses who could talk about Dhillon's activities in India. He would bring some to the hotel, they would visit others in the field.

At 3:45 p.m. that Thursday afternoon, the detectives stared into serene green eyes that resembled those of Parvesh Dhillon. It was her brother, Seva Singh Grewal. Seva told of Parvesh's dark life with Dhillon, the late-night whisky-drinking binges with the boys that she dreaded. Dhillon always harassed her for money, and hit her.

"My belief is that he killed her by hitting her on the head with something," Seva said.

They interviewed Parvesh's mother, Hardial Kaur Grewal. She, too, believed Dhillon had killed Parvesh. More than that, she gave

Korol and Dhinsa a glimpse into the private hell that her daughter had lived, described Dhillon's routine boorishness and abuse. As the statements unfolded, Korol and Dhinsa were struck by Dhillon's foolishness. It was as though he had choreographed evidence of his guilt at every opportunity. He had a reputation for ruthlessness among people who knew him, and that was clearly merited. Some even felt he was a criminal mastermind. But Dhillon left deep footprints that anyone could see if they knew where to look.

At 6:30 p.m., the detectives and Kundu piled into the car. There were no interviews scheduled, but Korol was anxious to see the place where Dhillon's third wife had died. They drove two hours toward Ludhiana and then the village of Tibba. It was Korol's first exposure to unruly Punjabi roads. The highway was studded with bumps. Vehicles engaged in a constant struggle to pass one another, any opening good enough to try, horns blowing incessantly, bumper stickers on thundering trucks urging car drivers—as though they needed urging—to "blow horn" in warning. The volume of traffic was incredible. A cyclist was forced off the road into a ditch. There were man-drawn rickshaws, horse-drawn carts, goat herders, pedestrians, women carrying crops on their heads.

The police officers stopped for a break on the way to the village. The Canadians had been warned not to drink water unless it was out of a sealed bottle. Sealed was the key word. At the side of the road, at a kiosk, a man filled empty labeled water bottles from a hose, then screwed the lid back on. Instant purification. They crossed the Sutlej River, slowed to pass through dusty villages like Rupnagar, Morinda, Kajauli, Samrala, with their bustling markets. An odd mix of Punjabi and English signs advertised stores such as Lovely Auto or Lovely Appliance. At the farming village of Tibba, they walked through the black gate guarding the courtyard to Rai Singh Toor's home—the courtyard where his daughter Kushpreet had suddenly died.

Korol and Dhinsa both had young children. They greeted Rai Singh with the deference and compassion they would show any person whose daughter had died. The detectives had no way of knowing that one day they would curse Rai Singh's name.

He showed them the spot on the ground where Kushpreet had collapsed. It was getting late. Dhinsa arranged for the family to visit

Scott Gardner

The village of Tibba

their hotel for interviews. The next morning the detectives and Kundu questioned Rai Singh and five others, reconstructing the day Kushpreet died. Daljit Kaur, the mother, said Dhillon gave her daughter poison— Kushpreet told her she had swallowed a pill as he had asked. Dhillon insisted on giving her the medicine so she would not be pregnant when she took the medical exam for her entry to Canada. Korol asked the next question, which Dhinsa translated into Punjabi.

"Did he ever discuss Parvesh Dhillon?" he asked.

"All he would do is show me her photo and say, 'See how pretty she was.'"

Rai Singh told the story of Kushpreet's wedding, her death, and his subsequent attempt to marry another daughter to Dhillon.

"Dhillon asked me if he could marry our younger daughter, Sukie," Rai Singh said. "I agreed to it because I didn't suspect anything."

This, thought Korol, is a man desperate to get to Canada. That afternoon Korol, Dhinsa, and Kundu went shopping for *kuchila*. Unlike the chaos in Delhi and Ludhiana, the markets in orderly Chandigarh were like outdoor strip malls. They passed an area selling leather goods. Suddenly two men sprinted past them. Korol's police instincts kicked in. Thieves. He turned to chase them, but Kundu grabbed his arm and smiled. Korol then saw the police officers in pursuit. The fleeing men were vendors.

"They haven't paid police for the right to sell here," Kundu explained.

"Paid—the police?" Korol asked.

Kundu nodded.

"What will they do when they catch them?" Korol said.

"Take their money, their goods, for payment."

Later, they found a spice shop. *Kuchila?* Korol had already discovered that a six-foot-plus white man arouses curiosity in Punjab. He stayed in the car while Dhinsa and Kundu entered the place.

"*Kuchila?*" Dhinsa asked.

The shop owner was

Detective Kevin Dhinsa in a Punjabi market.

suspicious. No. They had none to sell. Kundu was convinced they had asked the wrong way. He sauntered into another spice store, told the merchant he needed *kuchila* to kill a rabid dog, and paid 10 rupees for it. In the car he handed Korol the paper bag with the simple yet deadly flat brown seeds inside. Easy.

They woke at 4:30 a.m. the next day, their routine settling in. They picked up a boxed lunch of cucumber sandwiches from the hotel kitchen in order to avoid buying food from roadside vendors, and were on the road by 5 a.m. to miss the traffic. On the map, Punjabi cities and villages appear close together, but the rough, congested roads make every drive a long one. Each trip consumed an entire day. On May 5, Korol and Dhinsa drove nearly five hours to the village of Moga, where Dhinsa photocopied the marriage certificate of Dhillon and his fourth wife, Sukhwinder Kaur. Later in the day, they drove to the police station in the town of Faridkot, where Kundu asked for an update on the investigation of a complaint against Dhillon made by Sarabjit. Then it was off to Sadar police station in Kot Kapura, where they saw copies of the birth and death certificates for the twin boys. They also obtained copies of documents from Dhillon's marriage to Kushpreet in the town of Payal.

Panj Grain, Sarabjit's village, was next.

Chapter 15 ~ Invisible Graves

Korol and Dhinsa called at the home of Gurbachan Singh, the man who had phoned them from B.C. back in Canada. He led them farther down the street, turned into the courtyard where Sarabjit lived. The house was a gray concrete box with wooden doors painted bright green. Behind one of the green doors was Sarabjit's room, where she and Dhillon had slept on occasion, with the rock-hard woven rope mattress on the bed. Korol took photos of the house and the room. Sarabjit handed Dhinsa the original death certificates for the twins.

Korol and Dhinsa interviewed Gurjant, Sarabjit's father, then Sarabjit, and Baldev Singh Brar, a village elder. The room was dark and the air was oppressively hot. Light slipped past the door and shone on the concrete floor. Sweat soaked the detectives' shirts, flies nipped at their feet. Gurjant Singh talked of the night the first boy died. In his mind's eye, Korol pictured the baby wrapped in blankets against the night air, his tiny legs and arms stiffening. He said the family took the baby to the local priest for prayers, for divine intervention. "He did not profit from the prayer," Gurjant said quietly.

Scott Gardner

The symptoms sounded like strychnine poisoning. Korol and Dhinsa assumed the babies were cremated, which meant there was no forensic evidence to be found. Sarabjit told the detectives how Dhillon had insisted she not name the newborns. He had said it would bring bad luck. Sarabjit said Dhillon had visited his sons just once, here at her home, and had been alone with them for several minutes. She talked hesitantly about her life with Dhillon.

Sarabjit's brother, in the family home in Panj Grain

"My parents kept telling him that he should take me to Canada," she said quietly. "He just kept saying, 'I'm getting the papers ready.'"

She stared at the floor as she spoke, averting her eyes from the men.

"Jodha told people that I had been married before, and that I was really 40 years old, and that I had children before. My grandfather yelled at him, swore at him. 'Take me to the one who said this,' he said."

They were nearly finished the interview. Then Gurjant said to Dhinsa, "Would you like to see where they were buried?"

Buried? They were buried in the village cemetery. Dhinsa, a Sikh who had attended a Catholic school in India, didn't know that infants were not cremated. Gurjant led the detectives from the courtyard, turned left up the dirt road, then right. They passed through a large green metal gate and along a narrow 100-meter path through a corn field toward a five-foot-high brick wall enclosing a rectangular area. Korol, Dhinsa, Kundu, and Sarabjit's family marched up the path, the same one they had walked to bury the boys. Inside the brick wall lay a funeral pyre block. The rest of the cemetery was dirt baked hard as concrete, weeds and sharp-edged shrubs and plants growing wild.

"This is the cemetery?" Korol said to Kundu. "There are no grave markers."

"No."

Korol's mind leaped ahead. Forensic evidence. We have to find these bodies and dig them up. "Kevin, ask Gurjant to locate the graves. Don't let Sarabjit's brother see what he does." Gurjant walked to the far end of the cemetery and pointed to the ground. He said the names Sarabjit had given the

Inspector Subhash Kundu at the gates of the cemetery

boys in defiance of Dhillon. That's Gurmeet. That's Gurwinder. Then it was the brother's turn to independently locate the graves. He got the names reversed but pointed to the exact same two spots in the hard earth. Korol was now thinking way beyond the legal jurisdiction of this trip.

"Kevin, we have to exhume these kids."

Dhinsa looked at the unmarked graves, saying nothing. He agreed with his partner. But his mind instantly started calculating possibilities. Budgets for the police, the Crown's office. The decision wasn't up to Korol and Dhinsa. They would have to go through channels, take nothing for granted.

"I'm telling you right now, buddy," Korol continued, "you'll be making the return trip to dig them up."

The detectives were so focused they didn't notice the crowd gathering. At least 50 children had followed them to the cemetery. Some were standing on the brick wall. The Canadians were on display, especially the big white one. Foreigners like Korol visited places like New Delhi, or Chandigarh or the Taj Mahal in Agra. But they did not visit rural villages like Panj Grain. Many of the children had never seen a white person before. Children surrounded him. He had never experienced anything like it. He looked down into the faces of the kids with chocolate skin and bright eyes. They looked up at him with a mixture of curiosity, bewilderment, and challenge.

Fair skin is revered in India. Television ads push "fairness" cream for the less than 10 per cent of the population who can afford a TV set and who brood over such things as the hue of their skin. To see this six-foot-plus white-skinned giant stride among them was the biggest thing to happen in the village in a long time. They all watched as the investigators got back into their air-conditioned car. In a cloud of dust, the strangers were gone.

The next day, Korol and Dhinsa visited the M/S Duggal homeopathic store. Korol browsed the book collection. Prices were dirt cheap, like everything in India. With their budget, he joked, they could buy a fleet of Indian cars. He bought two books: *Modi's Medical Jurisprudence and Toxicology*, a faded blue 900-page doorstopper with a taped spine, and a bible-sized 1,040-page book called *Ruddock's Homeopathic Vade Mecum*. He flipped to the index in *Ruddock's* and looked under strychnine. On page 260 there was an illustration of the *kuchila* seeds that were the same kind that Subhash Kundu had purchased in the market days before.

"Homicidal poisoning by strychnine is rare in India," it said. "A case occurred in Seoni, in which a man suffered from the effects of poisoning as a result of taking betels (leaves and nuts chewed by many Indians) offered to him at a singing party by two persons with whom he was not on good terms."

Poor terms indeed.

"There was a case in which a person in Moradabad District was given some wine mixed with strychnine, but he threw it out of his mouth suspecting it to be soap water. Some of the wine remained in the cup, and was drunk by his son, who died within half an hour."

That night the detectives had dinner with Kundu in the Empress Room, the hotel's in-house restaurant, then turned in for the night, the raw strychnine seeds in a bag in one suitcase.

In his hotel bed that night, Korol again cracked open *Modi's*. He thought back to the cemetery in Panj Grain. Chapter V: Exhumation. "It becomes necessary to exhume bodies from graves when a suspicion of poisoning or some foul play such as criminal abortion, homicide or disputed cause of death arises. In India, such a procedure is not so common owing to the custom of cremating dead bodies." The key point: exhumations do take place here. "In India and in England, no time limit is fixed for the disinterment of a body. In France, this period is limited to ten years and is 30 years in Germany."

There was, of course, nothing said about foreigners coming to India to exhume a body—much less foreigners coming to India to exhume two newborns. *Modi's* would need some updating by the time Korol and Dhinsa were through with the Dhillon case. Korol inserted a beige hotel pamphlet between the pages as a bookmark and turned out the light.

The next morning, they drove to Tibba and Bhambri Hospital, the place where Kushpreet's family had taken her the day she collapsed. It was a run-down building painted peach in the village of Sahnewal. Dr. Mohinder Bhambri, the hospital's doctor and owner, shook the detectives' hands and offered them water and Pepsi. He spoke English, wore a golf shirt, and had a black mustache. He smiled often as he spoke with the detectives. The drinking glasses sweating from the heat in the room, the doctor told Korol he had no record or memory of Kushpreet.

Scott Gardner

Dr. Mohinder Bhambri

"She arrived dead at the hospital," Korol said.

"If that was the case, then there would not be any need for me to keep a record of her attendance," he said.

"Are you aware of other cases of strychnine poisoning?" Korol asked.

"I've heard of them, yes," Bhambri said. "Opium addicts. It usually happens to addicts when they mix strychnine with opium. Enhances the stimulative effect. Truck drivers use it to stay awake at night on the road."

"Where do the addicts get the strychnine?"

"I don't know, although there is probably a black market in Punjab where you could buy it."

Korol read Bhambri the witness statements from Kushpreet's family. They had brought her to the hospital, her body stiff. The doctor had told them she was dead, that they might as well go home.

"I'm sorry," Bhambri said when Korol was finished. "I don't recall that situation."

Korol and Dhinsa went to the local police station in Sahnewal, ordered criminal record checks on members of Kushpreet's family. None had ever been involved with police. They drove to Ludhiana, Dhillon's home town. The blanket of smog over the city actually helped moderate the blazing heat of the sun, even while

choking the lungs. Visitors were greeted by the bronze statue of
three revered figures in modern Indian history, their fists raised
defiantly: father of modern India Mahatma Gandhi, independent India's first prime minister, Jawaharlal Nehru, and Sikh hero
Bhagat Singh. "Not much to see in Ludhiana." That was the city's
description in a popular Indian travel guide. Foreign faces were
an uncommon sight.

Ludhiana overloaded the senses. It was raw, supercharged
modern India without the British refinements of Chandigarh.
Chandigarh's orderly streets bustled; Ludhiana's screamed. There
was little to distinguish where one market ended and another
began. The city was one endless line of fruit and vegetable stands,
silk and sari shops with their chartreuse and fuchsia and emerald
fabrics flapping in the hot breeze, appliance repairs, homeopathic
and medicine shops, tailors, street vendors roasting ears of corn
over open fires on the sidewalk. Down one street there was a
shingle announcing the services of B.P. Singh, Advocate. Next to
his, Narrinder Singh, Advocate. And another advocate. Then five,
10, 15, 20 more lawyers' kiosks in a row.

Dhillon's neighborhood in Ludhiana

They headed to an administration office, obtained marriage
documents for Dhillon and Sarabjit. Then it was to the civil surgeon's
office for Kushpreet's death certificate. They tried to find Birk Barsal,
Dhillon's old neighborhood. It is so buried in Ludhiana's urban maw

that even people who lived within the city weren't sure of how to get there. Kundu was able to locate it, however. At Dhillon's family apartment, they interviewed Surinder Kaur Dhillon, his sister-in-law, the widow of Dhillon's eldest brother, Darshan.

Yes, she knew Dhillon was married to three women. She knew he had hit his eldest daughter when she objected to his marrying Sarabjit. Surinder had heard about the twins' fate, and Kushpreet's. She herself had gone to the funeral. Surinder told the detectives that Dhillon had cried after Kushpreet's death.

"If he cried so much, why did he marry again in 10 days?" Kundu asked in Punjabi.

"He said that he can't keep coming back here all the time," she replied. "His house is in Canada and he wants to get this over with."

Dhinsa asked if Dhillon had ever threatened to hurt Surinder if she told others about his multiple marriages.

"He said there would be a fight in the house," she answered. "He has a short temper and I am afraid of him."

Before they left, Dulla arrived—Manjit Singh Sidhu, Dhillon's old friend and an officer with the Punjabi state police. He seemed to hover over them, saying little. Korol thought he looked like Ali Baba. It was not the last time Dulla appeared out of nowhere when the detectives were poking around Ludhiana. They returned to Tibba, retrieved photo negatives of Kushpreet's wedding to Dhillon. As evening fell, they visited Parvesh's brother, Seva. He was a generous, friendly man, a practicing Sikh who wore the turban, a symbol of his devotion. Once, a visitor asked him what it felt like to wear a turban, and Seva promptly removed the sacred head-wrapping and placed it on the guest's head. He had his own business in Ludhiana, and there was still the family farm, a 25-acre property a few kilometers from their home. He missed his sister terribly.

"I am a God-fearing man," he said. "I believe in my religion. But many times I've asked God, 'Why did this happen?' It is still in my head. Why?"

Seva insisted that Korol, Dhinsa, and Kundu join him in a toast to his late sister. He beckoned his son to open a new bottle of Aristocrat whisky, then splashed the golden liquid over the ice in the glasses. They made a toast. And then another. Seva reveled in entertaining. It was past midnight now. Korol turned to Dhinsa.

"Kevin, let's just grab a hotel room in town," he said.

Dhinsa would have none of it.

"Warren, we just can't. It's deplorable here."

Their driver took them all the way back to Chandigarh.

On May 8, they returned to Birk Barsal once more, this time to visit Dhillon's farm, a small patch of green in the middle of the urban craziness. There was a barn, cattle, and workers.

Scott Gardner

The Dhillon family farm

"Do you know Dhillon?" Dhinsa asked one of the workers.

"Only to see him."

"Are you familiar with *kuchila*?"

"No."

They knocked again at Dhillon's walk-up apartment. Dhillon's nephew, Manminder, was home.

"What was Sukhwinder Dhillon's reaction to the news of Kushpreet's death?" Dhinsa asked.

"He cried when he heard," Manminder said.

"Did you see tears, or did he just cry out loud?"

"There were tears."

"How could a man be sad about a death and then marry another woman very shortly after?" Dhinsa continued.

"That I don't know. Only he would know that."

The detectives had not been at the apartment for long when big Dulla arrived. This time he spoke with the detectives in broken English. They learned that Dulla had earned his reputation some 13 years earlier when the Indian government sent the army to quell a bloody uprising by Sikh nationalists in Amritsar. Dulla had fought for the army and was repaid for his service with a rapid rise through police ranks.

"So how many people did you kill up there?" Korol asked.

"Twenty-five."

Dhinsa nudged Korol. He noticed the bump under Dulla's shirt, the revolver.

"Mind if I take a look?" Korol said. He reached over, lifted the tail of Dulla's shirt, and slid out the small revolver. He examined it and emptied out the ammunition. Then he handed it back. Dulla said nothing. Maybe his appearance and reputation were exaggerated. Or perhaps he feared a reprisal from the CBI man, Subhash Kundu.

"Did you attend the wedding of Sukhwinder Dhillon and Sukhwinder Kaur?" Dhinsa asked.

"No. I didn't have time," replied Dulla.

"We have a signed document that says you were at the wedding."

Dulla looked at the officers.

"I signed it," he admitted.

"You just told us you didn't go to the wedding."

"I went to the wedding."

Kundu interjected. "What is your duty as a police officer?" he asked.

"Wherever the criminal is, catch him."

"As a police officer, didn't you think something was suspicious with all these marriages involving Dhillon?"

"He used to say, 'My wife is dead, I need a mother for my children.'"

Dulla stood to leave. Korol lifted his camera. Dulla held up his hand. There would be no photos.

* * *

Back on the road, they drove two hours out of Ludhiana, past straw huts that were used to store cow dung for fuel, through dusty markets and along creeks where cows gathered to cool off. They arrived in Dhandra, home to Dhillon's fourth wife, Sukhwinder Kaur. The village name wasn't even on a map. It was just there, had always been there. Along the tight cobblestone streets, cars turned in their side mirrors to avoid scraping the walls of buildings on either side.

"How the hell do you find these places?" Korol said. Kundu grinned.

In a narrow alleyway, they stopped, got out of the car, the heat striking like a chorus of sun lamps, no breeze, taking their breath away. Their driver parked in a sliver of shade, shut off the engine, locked the doors, pulled out a cloth to wipe his face and waited. A woman appeared in a doorway and beckoned them inside through a dark hallway, then into a dimly lit main bedroom and living area. A fan labored, light streamed through an arched window revealing pale green walls festooned with prints of Sikh gurus. Like other homes they visited, this one was colorful and inviting inside, a stark contrast to the nondescript exterior.

Sukhwinder Kaur was plump and had an oval, expressive face. She seemed outgoing, made eye contact with the men and always seemed ready to break into a smile. Kundu sat beside her on the large bed while Korol and Dhinsa went to the couch. Korol opened his laptop and began typing.

"What did Dhillon tell you about his first wife, Parvesh?" Dhinsa asked.

"Dhillon told me that Parvesh had been fasting before she died," she said. "He said she slipped down the stairs and fell, then died several days later."

"Are you aware," Dhinsa asked, "of the investigation in Canada into the deaths of Parvesh Dhillon and Ranjit Khela, and that Sukhwinder Dhillon is the prime suspect?"

"He told me that no one could kill their own wife and their best friend."

At 28 she was both older and better educated than either Sarabjit or Kushpreet—she had gone to a women's college in

Ludhiana for three years—and carried herself in a more assertive manner. She's a feisty woman, thought Korol. Kundu did not
consider Sukhwinder Kaur a victim. He believed she was well
aware that, when she married Dhillon, he had committed bigamy.
Perhaps she thought the last two marriages had been annulled in
some way. But she knew about them. She simply yearned to get
to Canada. She handed Korol a copy of a Canadian immigration
application that showed Dhillon was sponsoring her. She believed
she still deserved the opportunity to get to Canada. Was there still
hope? The Canadian police were here, perhaps there would be a
trial, perhaps they would take witnesses like Sukhwinder Kaur to
Canada to tell their story.

CHAPTER 16 ~ "DHINSA IS DEAD"

The Hamilton detectives and the Indian CBI inspector became close friends. Near the end of their stay, Kundu showed the Canadians a place in Chandigarh to buy tailored suits, and the detectives left their measurements with the tailor for future orders. On their last night together, they ate dinner in the Piccadilly Hotel's Empress Room. For Kundu, reputation was everything. He led a comfortable life in Chandigarh. But his apartment and his motorcycle were merely material possessions. His goal, ultimately, by the grace of God, was passage into heaven. He would actually pose the question directly.

"What do you think of me? What do you think of Inspector Kundu? What do you feel, in your heart?"

At dinner, Korol suggested they invite the man who had been their driver, a young man they called Bubaloo, to join them. Kundu closed his eyes, pursed his lips, and shook his head, not bobbing it in the Indian way of saying yes, but in the negative. It wasn't done. Drivers in India drive. They are proud of their job, it is what they do. They associate with other drivers.

"The driver? He can't come in here."

It hit Korol—here they were, two police officers, but culturally worlds apart. Status is part of India's fabric. That could be said for any society, but in India, with its caste system, status is defined at birth and there is no escaping it. Europeans joke that, in the United States, the customer calls the waiter "sir." Not in India. Kundu, a man with a generous spirit, would hold up his hand to a waiter, wave him over, barely looking at him. The waiter was not offended in the least. It was his role.

Korol could never get his head around the caste system. Sikhs had rejected it, too, centuries ago. But here was the caste system alive and well in Punjab, he thought. In the West, status matters, but Korol himself was proof that life can be what you make it. Raised by working-class parents, a family with no university graduates, he climbed the career ladder and educated himself at a top university. In their trips to the villages, after parking, Bubaloo would scramble out of the car and hold the door open for Korol.

"Get outta here—don't be opening doors for me," Korol play-fully growled.

At the end of the trip Bubaloo asked Korol for his autograph. Korol chuckled. "No, Bubaloo, I won't do that," he said, as though the rejection would awaken Bubaloo to the notion that he, a driver, was every bit as important as a big police officer from Canada. But when Bubaloo became upset at the slight, Korol relented, signed a scrap of paper, and gave it to him.

In the Empress Room with Dhinsa and Kundu, Korol wasn't about to take on the caste system on his own and insist Bubaloo eat with them. But he wasn't giving up, either.

"Subhash, tell the waiter to get some food to the kid." The waiter, a puzzled look on his face, carried a plate of food out the door into the parking lot to Bubaloo, courtesy of Detective Warren Korol.

* * *

The next day Korol and Dhinsa said goodbye to their friend Kundu and returned to New Delhi by airbus from Chandigarh airport. No more train rides. On May 13 they met again with RCMP liaison officer Pierre Carrier at the Canadian High Commission on Shanti Path in New Delhi.

"After I return to Hamilton I'm going to send a letter, through you, to the Indian authorities to see where they stand on exhuming the twins," Korol said.

Carrier, from Chicoutimi, Quebec, was impressed. During his three years in New Delhi, he had frequently served as a go-between with Canadian police and Indian authorities, but had never heard such a request. Later, he would inch his way through the Indian penal code, a document that dates back to 1858. There was not one reference to exhumations.

Korol pulled out a photocopy of the Canadian immigration application that showed Dhillon falsely claiming Sukhwinder Kaur as his lawful wife.

"I'll pass this on to the immigration office," Carrier said. The woman had still held out hope of making it to Canada. Korol

Pierre Carrier

had just ensured that it was highly unlikely to happen.

"One more thing Pierre," Korol said. "I have to say I have...concerns...about how vigorous the local Indian police investigation will be of the deaths here with this Dulla guy around. I think he has a lot of influence with the witnesses and the police."

Their business concluded, Carrier offered Korol and Dhinsa a chance to unwind.

India is beautiful, dirty, fantastic, frustrating. To a first-time visitor the impact on the body and mind is considerable. There is the heat, the Indian version of Montezuma's revenge, and fear of contracting malaria. It starts weeks before arrival, the shots for hepatitis, boosters for polio and diphtheria, reimmunization against diseases long ago defeated in the West. Malaria pills, such as mefloquin, must be taken before and after the trip. The side-effects can be what are called "vivid dreams." Perhaps it is not the pills at all, though, but India infiltrating the psyche that rouses the visitor from sleep in full sweat, a crack of moonlight between hotel curtains in the dark room, hallucinating and—whatever you do—do not allow that lone stray mosquito to bite, stay covered under the blankets no matter how hot it gets, wait for daylight.

"Perhaps you would like to cool off in the pool?"

By Indian standards the Canadian High Commission property was like a resort. There were volleyball courts, even a couple of nets for a version of road hockey. The grass was kept neatly trimmed with a power mower—a rarity in India. Lounging by a pool was something of a mixed blessing. It is, in fact, too hot to enjoy lying on the skillet that the patio becomes in the sun. Still, after long days in the stink and heat of Ludhiana and the villages, Korol could not believe how good the tepid water felt when he lowered himself in. It was the Indian effect. For Westerners making their first trip, a whole new appreciation is felt for the simplest conveniences. The detectives savored their modest oasis, a hot wind whipping through the compound, while large black crows swooped in to sip at the water's edge.

* * *

Korol and Dhinsa landed in Toronto on May 14, 1997, with briefcases full of witness statements from India—and several bags of strychnine, in liquid and raw seed form. At customs neither detective declared he was a police officer. Korol wanted to see how easy it was to smuggle poison like strychnine.

"Anything else to declare?" the customs official asked the two men returning from a two-week stay in India.

"No," said Korol.

"No," said Dhinsa.

A week later, on Wednesday, May 21, Korol gingerly placed the strychnine samples into official plastic drug bags and filled out a request for the Centre of Forensic Sciences to test the material. The next day, Dhinsa and Korol drove to Toronto to deliver the samples. They met with Jim Cairns, Ontario's new deputy chief coroner. Korol briefed Cairns on the investigation. The detectives needed more evidence, more scientific proof in the case.

"I'd like to get your opinion on exhuming the twin boys in India," Korol said.

Cairns immediately thought of Dr. Charles Smith at the Hospital for Sick Children. Smith, Ontario's best-known pediatric pathologist, was at that time considered Canada's foremost hands-on expert in exhumations. Korol spoke with Joel Mayer, head of toxicology at CFS, and asked him to test the potency of the strychnine samples. Then he broached the question of the exhumation.

"Dr. Mayer, we're pursuing a plan to exhume the twin boys in India and bring the tissue back here to CFS," Korol said.

"If there is strychnine in the body," Mayer said, "the liver, kidney, body contents, and the cloth that surrounds the bodies would show its presence."

The next week, Korol decided it was time to let the media in on some of what was going on. Korol and police communications officer Ken Bond met to prepare a news release announcing that

Parvesh Dhillon's death was now being treated as a homicide and that detectives Dhinsa and Korol had been to India to investigate other fatalities as well. What the release did not say was that they still had no forensic evidence that Parvesh had been murdered.

Dr. Charles Smith

Hamilton Spectator archives

* * *

Warren Korol had been after Dhillon for nine months. Time to turn up the heat. Korol and Dhinsa knocked on the door at Dhillon's home. Nobody home. They drove away, then saw Sarvjit Dhillon, his niece, on the sidewalk.

"Where is your uncle?" Dhinsa asked.

"Milton. His car broke down," she said. "I can't speak with you any more."

She handed them a business card. Richard Startek. Attorney-at-Law. Korol smirked. That was the next stop. Korol and Dhinsa walked into the office on Queenston Road. Dhillon was there. He was not in Milton, and he did not have car trouble. Startek, a slight man with thick silver hair, was in an adjoining office. Startek was not on Korol's list of favorite people. He had sent the letter in December suggesting that Dhillon's rights to counsel had been violated by the detectives during the polygraph test.

"Mr. Startek," Korol now said to the lawyer. "Let's talk. All of us."

The four men sat in Startek's office. Korol nodded to Dhinsa. "Tell Dhillon that we think he murdered his business partner—and his wife."

Dhinsa began speaking to Dhillon in Punjabi. Dhillon tried to interrupt. Startek motioned at Dhillon to listen.

"Your deceased wife," Dhinsa continued, "Parvesh Kaur Dhillon, was poisoned and we have publicly committed her death as a homicide and you are the prime suspect. Do you understand?"

"*Mein kuch naheen keeta*," Dhillon said. I didn't do anything.

Startek held up his hand to Dhillon and said, in English, "You don't have to say anything."

"I know, I know," Dhillon replied in English.

Korol shook his head. This is a joke, he thought to himself. Gee, Dhillon, aren't we supposed to need a translator here?

"Dhillon," Korol said, "could you leave the room now? We'd like to talk to your lawyer."

Dhillon complied, then Korol turned to Startek, his eyes narrowing. "We are conducting an investigation here," he said. "And I have to tell you I don't appreciate you telling witnesses not to speak to us."

"I told Sarvjit Dhillon," Startek said, "that if she wished to talk to the police, she can do it in my presence. Sarvjit just left my office before Dhillon showed up. Dhillon's family and the Khelas have an underlying fear of the police."

Korol kept his tone even.

"Richard, we seek the truth. That's it. We don't tell people what to say. We only want the truth. And if we find out that people lied to us, we'll tell them. And one more thing. It appears you have a conflict of issue here that you engaged in while instructing the victim's family, the Khelas, and Sukhwinder Dhillon, who is our suspect, in relating police matters."

Korol later recorded the exchange with Startek in his notes.

Two days later, a fax machine beeped in the office of an Ottawa law firm called Gowling, Strathy and Henderson. It was a statement of claim in a lawsuit. Gowling, Strathy and Henderson represented Metropolitan Life insurance. Dhillon knew how the system worked. He had rights. He remained the sole beneficiary of Ranjit's life insurance, a tidy $200,000. So what if the police believed he had killed Ranjit? They had proved nothing. He was clear. No arrest. He was not about to let the money slip through his fingers. Dhillon was suing for it—and then some. The date on the fax was May 30, 1997. The statement read:

Sukhwinder Singh Dhillon vs. Metropolitan Life Insurance Company of Canada. Lawyer: Richard Startek. The plaintiff claims:

- Damages in the amount of $200,000 for non payment under a policy of life insurance.
- Pre-judgment and post-judgment interest.
- Costs of the action.
- Such further and other relief as this honorable court may permit.
- The plaintiff has duly requested that the death benefits be paid to him by the defendants. The plaintiff filed a claim under the contract of insurance on or about July 23, 1996. The plaintiff has not received any payment under the above policy of insurance. The defendants have refused and/or neglected to pay the plaintiff the aforesaid amounts, without just cause.

Warren Korol had asked insurance companies to watch for and report any claim on the life of Ranjit Khela. A lawyer at the Ottawa firm faxed a copy of the statement of claim to him. Korol picked up the fax and grinned. Dhillon. The son of a bitch was suing. Perfect. He would love to see Dhillon argue the claim in civil court.

* * *

On Wednesday, June 4, Korol and Dhinsa made the short drive from Central Station to the Crown attorney's office in the old Hamilton court building on Main Street. They met with assistant Crown attorney Brent Bentham. Korol knew their window of opportunity was shrinking. Strychnine could leach out of the body completely in as little as two years. Dhillon's boys had been dead 18 months. From Bentham's office, Korol spoke on the phone with Jim Cairns.

"I have to tell you, detective, I have concerns about an exhumation in India," Cairns said.

He went through his list. It takes a small dose of strychnine to kill an infant, and those twins had been in the ground all this time—it's an open question whether, if there ever had been poison in the babies, it would still be in the tissue.

Moreover, you have to identify the remains. If the graves were unmarked, you would need to match DNA from the remains with a parent to confirm the lineage. If Dr. Smith assisted, he would need to bring the bodies back to Canada to test them here, and the cooperation of the Indian authorities would be needed to do that. Cairns considered the endeavor a long shot. Korol handed his cellphone to Bentham.

"Brent, you should hear what Dr. Cairns has to say as well."

Bentham listened, his mind processing each part of the equation before him. An exhumation is a huge undertaking, even in Ontario. There are approvals to obtain. There's the cost involved. It's a big gamble. Even more so in India. Did they ever do exhumations at all there? Would they allow Canadians to come in and do it? Bentham was a careful man. Would he put the brakes on the enterprise?

"Hey, Brent, if you don't shoot you don't score." Korol grinned at Bentham, a hockey fan who played pickup each week.

The assistant Crown attorney was on board. They all were. Starting the legal machinery of treaty assistance with India and returning to India to continue the investigation would be expensive and time-consuming. But they were chasing a serial killer and had gone too far to back off now. Time was running out on the decomposing remains of the twins. The only thing they knew for certain was that they would never really know whether the bodies contained strychnine if they didn't examine them.

* * *

In June, Korol began regular communications with Sarvjit, Dhillon's niece who was now 22 years old. She told Korol she had once asked Dhillon if he thought a man could kill his wife. Dhillon did not reply. Sarvjit cooperated with Korol. She began listening to her uncle's telephone conversations and told Korol what was said. On

June 24, Korol received a page from Sarvjit. He called her back. She said that a friend of Dhillon's in Toronto had advised him he should call Kevin Dhinsa's home from a phone booth and say, "Dhinsa is dead."

On June 23, Korol opened a letter from Dr. Michael McGuigan, the poison expert in Toronto. Korol had submitted copies of the witness statements gathered in India. "The description of Kushpreet's death provides strong support for the implication of strychnine as the cause of death," Dr. McGuigan's letter read. As for the twins, "some aspects are consistent with strychnine deaths (i.e. crying, convulsions, stiffening or rigidity) while others are not (time course, vomiting). However, in the literature there are no reports of infants being poisoned by strychnine, so there are no reliable yardsticks for comparison. Based on the witness statements, strychnine poisoning is unlikely but it may well be worth disinterring the bodies."

Korol forwarded the report on to Danielle Beaulne, a paralegal in Ottawa working on the documents for the exhumation. On June 30, Korol returned a call from Beaulne.

"Detective Korol," Beaulne began, "Barb Kothe, the senior counsel here, is working on the Mutual Legal Assistance document. But she wants to know if, in light of the report from Dr. Michael McGuigan, you still want to travel to India?"

Korol didn't blink.

"Actually, Danielle, Dr. McGuigan's report is all the more reason to find out the cause of death of the children," he said. "We know for a fact—and this is in a book we obtained in India—that milk, when ingested, can slow down the effects of strychnine poisoning, and witnesses said that people tried to give the children milk when they were ill. And some of the physical actions of the children were, in fact, consistent with strychnine poisoning. Tell Barb that Detective Dhinsa, Brent Bentham, and I all believe the babies should be exhumed."

On July 2, Beaulne phoned Dhinsa. She was sending the finished treaty document to Pierre Carrier. Once the babies' remains arrived in Ontario, she said, the investigators would need to deal with the proper officials here, which would mean obtaining a

coroner's warrant to examine the remains. On July 29, Korol and
Dhinsa drove to a hardware store and bought two plastic bins
with lids. They were to carry the remains of Dhillon's sons. Then
they had two lockable aluminum boxes made, each big enough
to hold one of the plastic bins. Dhinsa obtained ground-penetrating radar equipment. The equipment was state of the art. But not
quite ready for India.

CHAPTER 17 ~ EXHUMATION

The jet touched down in New Delhi after four in the afternoon on Wednesday, August 13. Pierre Carrier spotted Dhinsa and Dr. Charles Smith lugging radar apparatus and the two containers. They all climbed into a High Commission van and left the airport. Carrier handed Dhinsa the signed Mutual Legal Assistance document—the license for him to investigate and dig up the remains in India. The next morning, a driver took them to Chandigarh, where Dhinsa once again shook the hand of Inspector Subhash Kundu.

The next morning Dhinsa, Smith, and Kundu left the hotel before dawn, drove four hours to Panj Grain. To Dhinsa, every hour now seemed precious. He had the documents issued by officials in New Delhi, but needed local approval to begin exhuming the bodies. So first they headed to the district administrative center, Faridkot, and visited the local magistrate, Som Prakesh. He sent them to a district prosecutor named Verma. An assistant led them into Verma's office, which was dominated by an enormous desk—a status symbol in India. Verma entered the room and sat grandly behind the desk.

"First, we have tea," he said.

Dhinsa continued in Punjabi.

"I need a warrant to proceed with the exhumation."

"You're a police officer, just do it," Verma said.

"I can't. I'm not a police officer in India."

Verma pointed at Kundu.

"He is. He can do it."

"No," Dhinsa said, "we need judicial authority."

"Well, you show me where the authority is and I'll give you the warrant."

Dhinsa sat in disbelief. You're the district prosecutor. I'm a visiting police officer from Canada, and you want me to show you the authority? Verma's assistant checked a reference book and said the authority for the warrant comes from the magistrate. Verma called Som Prakesh at home.

"Yes. I will give the authority," Prakesh said. "Come back and see me tomorrow for the documents."

Frustrated, they climbed back into their van and drove four hours back to Chandigarh. The next day, near Panj Grain, the magistrate presented them with a form to fill out so they could proceed with the exhumation. Finally, progress. "Complete this and bring it back tomorrow," he added. No one was on hand to process the document the next day. It was August 15, the fiftieth anniversary of Indian independence. A national holiday. More red tape. Tomorrow, tomorrow. Dhinsa burned.

Before returning to Chandigarh, they stopped at Panj Grain. Smith wanted to see the graves. They parked at the cemetery gates, walked up the narrow path at the edge of the village to the burial ground. Smith looked beyond the walls, noticed the fields. He had been told they were wheat fields. But these were rice paddies. Soaked in water. Moist soil. The remains of the infants might well have decomposed to nothing! Smith turned to Dhinsa, ranting.

"We need dry sandy soil to preserve the remains. These are rice paddies! There will be nothing there."

The van pulled up to the cemetery entrance. Smith and Dhinsa unloaded the ground-penetrating radar. Smith dragged a sensor along the dirt, searching for disturbances under the surface near the spot where witnesses said the babies were buried. He found one. A good sign.

The next day at 3 a.m. they were ready to return to the cemetery. In the rush to beat the traffic, with a long day's work ahead, Dhinsa and Smith forgot to take their sandwiches and bottled water from the hotel kitchen. They arrived in Faridkot and picked up the warrant from the magistrate's office then drove on to the cemetery. The magistrate sent a subordinate named D.S. Grewal and assigned two elders from the village to observe the operation. Smith and Dhinsa got out of their van in Panj Grain. It was only 7 a.m. but already the wall of heat and wet air were oppressive. It was the middle of summer, monsoon season. The heat and humidity was extraordinary; the sun's rays beat on the men like a hammer.

Dhinsa and Smith unloaded the radar as a crowd gathered. Soon as there were more than a hundred, mostly children, encircling the cemetery, standing on the brick wall in bare feet, watching. Two police guards armed with rifles stood nearby. The

Punjabi police had sent them to protect the Canadians. There was also a handsome Sikh man in uniform, four stars gleaming on his epaulettes. He had studied at Cambridge, spoke English with a British accent.

"The newspapers are aware that you are here. You are at risk," he told Smith. Some weren't pleased that Indian authorities had allowed the Canadians to chase Dhillon into his own back yard. Smith wiped the sweat from his forehead. Threats. The crowd. Clock ticking away on the remains. Unknown number of dead buried here. Rice paddies! Had he ever felt so much pressure?

* * *

Sarabjit's uncles, Bikhar Singh (left) and Biten Singh, in the cemetary

Exhumations, like autopsies, are a shock to those who do not know what to expect. The decayed human body is a sobering sight. The condition of a disinterred body varies, depending on time, the type of soil, and the climate. First the corpse turns gray and becomes shriveled. The flesh rots. In some instances, though, if the soil is moist, adipocere may form —a wax-like substance from body fats, that can delay putrefaction, so the features of the deceased are eerily preserved. Smith turned on the radar. It worked. And then stopped. It was the heat; by mid-morning it was so intense the machine couldn't function. Once again it was up to family members who had been at the babies' funerals almost two years earlier to point out the plots. Sarabjit's father, the babies' grandfather, walked to the spot at the far end of the rectangular cemetery, shuffled this way and that, and pointed at the ground.

"Here."

Smith produced small tools that resembled dentist's instruments. Villagers fetched shovels and picks. Smith started digging. Older farmers tried to take the tool from his hand.

"It's okay, I am trained for this," Smith said.

"We must help," replied a farmer in Punjabi. "This happened in our village. It is our duty."

As morning turned to afternoon, Smith and Dhinsa worked alongside the villagers, cutting through the fine layers of soil, each one a different color. Then they hit some brittle branches and thorns. An elder had put them there during the burials to keep wild dogs from digging up the bodies. Dhinsa took notes and videotaped the process. Warren Korol and Brent Bentham had stressed it: the exhumation and transportation of the remains had to be done with painstaking attention to detail, all of it documented. Smith and Dhinsa were kneeling on the ground now, scraping at the dirt with their bare hands, drenched in sweat, no water and no shade. Sixty-four centimeters down, they saw him. It was Gurwinder.

The baby had not been buried in a coffin. Only a skeleton remained, wrapped in blankets made of something similar to wool which was decaying, crumbling, now a grayish brown. They saw bits of blue and red—the boy's pajamas. The nylon material had not broken down. Dhinsa and Smith peered at what was left of the tiny body. There wasn't much. The skeleton was intact but the flesh had mostly vanished; discolored brownish bones were packed with earth. To Smith's chagrin there was no sign of any tissue from organs, no bits of liver or brain where poison would be most easily detected. Those organs break down the fastest.

Smith slid the remains onto the lid of the large plastic container they had brought from Canada. The doctor took a closer look and spotted a bit of black, sinewy tissue hanging from the hip bone. Perhaps it might offer something. He then placed the body and some samples of dirt that had surrounded it into a plastic bag and sealed them in the blue container. He labeled the container "twin A."

Smith and Dhinsa moved six feet to one side and started digging for the other baby. Again they reached a layer of branches and thorns, some shards of brick and, at 76 centimeters, the body.

Gurmeet. Blue and red pajamas. The second skeleton resembled the first. It was sealed in the green container and labeled "twin B." It was 6 o'clock and the sky was the color of polished ivory, the sun fighting to cut through the curtain of haze. Smith and Dhinsa placed the plastic containers in the lockable aluminum boxes, and the samples and equipment were loaded onto the van. The villagers offered them a drink. Dhinsa declined. He knew the rule. You don't drink water in India unless it's bottled.

"How about beer, then?" a villager asked.

Well, he thought, at least the beer will be in a sealed bottle.

"Yes, thank you."

The man told another to run and fetch the beer. He returned a few minutes later, the beer sloshing in an open bucket. Dhinsa rolled his eyes. Manners and a massive thirst made him dip a glass into the bucket and drink. Politeness also forced him that evening to sit down and eat a meal of eggs and homemade bread in the courtyard of Sarabjit's tiny home. Dhinsa knew his stomach would pay for accepting. And sure enough, he was sick later. Sarabjit, the boys' mother, had stayed at home during the dig. She cried whenever she thought about her boys. Smith asked her for a blood sample so he could establish the remains were those of her sons. She agreed.

Dhinsa awoke the next morning in Chandigarh and it dawned on him—he needed another warrant, this time to get the babies' bodies across state lines, from Punjab to New Delhi. Dhinsa and Smith visited the local coroner, an erudite Sikh man who sat behind a hulking desk eating chicken with his fingers. "You ... need," he said between bites, "papers ... Yes ... In Faridkot." They used up another day, driving four hours to the city to get a written order from the magistrate there. The next day Dhinsa was ready to take the remains to New Delhi but Subhash Kundu felt they needed authority from his supervisor, who was out of town.

"Enough already," Dhinsa said. "I want to go home. Let's get this done."

Dhinsa phoned Pierre Carrier, who made some calls. Dhinsa, Kundu, and Smith were off to the capital within hours. They arrived at the heavily guarded CBI building in New Delhi on Friday afternoon to transfer custody of the bodies. Now there was another hurdle. They met Carrier in the office of CBI superintendent H.C. Singh, a gray metal fan rattling on a table, an air conditioner humming in the window.

"Tea?" asked Singh's assistant.

Singh spoke in formal English.

"The Ministry of Home Affairs must give authority to release the exhibits, including the videotapes, documents, and remains," he said.

"I have no problem delaying the videotapes," Dhinsa said, "but we need to expedite moving the remains. I'm concerned about the condition of them."

"We will meet tomorrow with the minister to obtain his approval," Singh said.

Carrier took temporary possession of the remains. That night he drove them home in the back of his white Trooper. They sat in the back of the vehicle overnight, watched by the guard who always manned a post at Carrier's home. The next morning, Saturday, Carrier drove to the CBI office and met with Dhinsa, Smith, Kundu, and Singh. H.C. Singh looked at Dhinsa. "The minister of home affairs, Shiv Basant, is not available to facilitate the transfer at this time," Singh said flatly.

"What?"

"Yesterday was Raksha Bandan. An Indian national holiday. The minister is out of the city today."

"Why not just leave the bodies here," Singh continued, "and we'll take care of it on Monday."

"Look," Dhinsa said, "we must preserve the integrity of the remains. Pierre?"

Carrier knew the dance well. At the best of times, the Indian bureaucracy was glacial.

"The bodies aren't keeping and if this evidence is lost, the Indian government will be held directly responsible," Carrier said.

Singh said he would do what he could, but needed more time. The Canadians left. Carrier phoned the deputy minister of home affairs at home.

"I must tell you," Carrier pressed, "that the whole case will be lost if the remains are not moved quickly."

"I'll call you back in 10 minutes," the minister said.

Carrier waited. The phone rang.

"You have the okay."

"That's it, we can load the remains on the plane?"

"If you have any problems, just phone me from the airport."

As the clock struck midnight, Dhinsa and Smith arrived at Indira Gandhi Airport with the two aluminum boxes holding the remains. Dhinsa felt like kissing the woman behind the Air Canada counter beside the sign that said Flight 863, London-Toronto. Dhinsa watched the boxes loaded on board. The plane took off at 2 a.m. Indian time. They arrived six hours later in London, at 2:30 in the morning local time. At Heathrow Airport, Dhinsa observed on the tarmac as the remains were transported between planes for the flight to Toronto. Korol met them at the airport when they touched down back home.

Containers holding the twins' remains being loaded on the flight to Toronto

* * *

In Hamilton, Korol needed to shore up the case against Dhillon in the Ranjit Khela homicide before he could move forward on arresting. The key witness was Lakhwinder Sekhon, Ranjit's widow. He learned that she was now living in a women's shelter, having been ostracized by the Khela family. Korol knew that, in court, the family might well point the finger directly at Lakhwinder as the one who killed Ranjit. Korol and Dhinsa drove to the Khelas' home on Gainsborough Road. They talked strategy in the car. Just tell the Khelas they are still investigating, ask them if they know anything more about Ranjit's death. And then ask them if they know where Lakhwinder is. If the family passed up the chance to implicate her now, any later attempt to do so in court will lack credibility. At the house, Dhinsa spoke with Makhan Khela, Ranjit's father. Makhan had no new information. He said nothing more about Lakhwinder.

The next day, Monday, August 25, Korol and Dhinsa picked up Lakhwinder at the shelter and took her to the police station to obtain a new statement on videotape. She had given two previous interviews under oath, but had not told everything she knew. She feared reprisals from the family, feared she would lose her son Ranjoda, who was living with the Khelas at that time. The family wouldn't let her see him. Korol told her he just wanted the truth. And this was her last chance.

A Punjabi interpreter was on hand this time. Dhinsa spoke the language, but it was important that this translation be done by somebody clearly independent of the police. The questions began. She gave a long introductory statement. Then she dropped the bomb. "I know this much about Ranjit," she said in Punjabi. "He didn't die. He was killed."

Korol kept his expression flat. Just let her go.

"Ranjit received a tablet from Dhillon," she continued. "Dhillon had two pills, and Ranjit was told to take one, it will make him feel so good, will make him fly. Ranjit told me that Dhillon gave him the pill."

Finally, Korol thought, the truth. He let out a sigh of relief. The case was far from over, but they needed this break. She talked for several more minutes, then Korol interjected.

"What did Ranjit say to you exactly?"

"He was crying and I asked what happened and at first he said nothing. Then he told me that he had taken a pill that he had got from Dhillon and that something was happening to him."

"Was that the first time Ranjit told you about this pill?"

"When he got sick, that's when he told me, and I told the family and they didn't believe me."

She described the mistrust between herself and Ranjit's family. They wouldn't eat food she prepared, and she refused to eat theirs, too.

"People I talk to here and there, they tell me the other pill is for me," Lakhwinder said.

Korol knew that Lakhwinder was not the perfect star witness. But she was the one person who could, under oath, put the murder weapon directly in Dhillon's hand. That, in turn, would help link him to the circumstantial evidence surrounding the death of Parvesh Dhillon. That evidence, he hoped, together with Lakhwinder's testimony, could be presented in the context of evidence of Dhillon's murderous reign of terror in India.

The next day, Korol and Detective Gary Bishop, the officer in charge of witness relocation, met the director of the women's shelter. They talked about the threat to Lakhwinder, and her desire to be with her son.

"If Dhillon and the Khelas learn that she has told police about who gave Ranjit a pill, she is in danger," Korol said. "That fact cannot get back to them."

Two days later three police officers with the family crisis unit escorted Lakhwinder to the Khela home to take Ranjoda back. Ranjit's grandparents seemed confused when Lakhwinder and the police arrived. Their confusion turned to hostility. Lakhwinder searched the house for documents such as Ranjoda's birth certificate and her passport. Family members stepped in her way. Police told them to let her pass. Then Lakhwinder took her boy by the hand.

"You can't do this," said one of the grandparents. "You watch, we'll get him back through court. You'll never have him. We'll get him back."

It was a chaotic scene: people shouting in Punjabi and broken English, a police interpreter trying to translate what was being said to the other officers. One of the family sneered at Lakhwinder.

"You have made a big mistake in how you went about this."

"Don't worry," said another. "We'll tell the judge that she killed her husband."

Scott Gardner

Lakhwinder, Ranjit Khela's widow

The police led Lakhwinder and Ranjoda out of the house.

"Mom," Ranjoda said to Lakhwinder, "they told me you had left me and gone back to India."

The Khelas hired a lawyer to seek legal return of Ranjoda. The claim filed in family court said Lakhwinder was a suspect in the murder of Ranjit, that she had played no part in raising Ranjoda and over the past year had not cared for his needs, and that she had "mysteriously" abandoned the house.

While police helped Lakhwinder retrieve her son, Korol and Dhinsa attended the autopsy room at the Ontario coroner's office, along with Hamilton Police forensic detective Larry Penfold. Rarely had an autopsy drawn such an audience. Dr. Charles Smith and an assistant named Jeff Arnold were about to perform autopsies on Dhillon's two infant sons. Also in the room were Jim Cairns, Ontario chief coroner James Young, biologist John Newman, and toxicologist John Kertesz from the CFS. Korol approached the two aluminum boxes on the gurney. There was a sharp cracking noise as he cut the first padlock.

"We can check everything here, every item, the clothes, tissue, dirt, for strychnine," Kertesz said.

Newman said a major bone from each of the skeletons would be required to confirm through DNA that Sarabjit was their mother. Penfold catalogued every tissue sample held up and described by Smith, and took photos of them. The first autopsy finished, Korol cut the second lock and Smith began work on the body inside. There wasn't much to examine.

CHAPTER 18 ~ CHEMICAL COCKTAIL

Dhillon continued selling used cars at Aman Auto, with little regard for his situation. He hired a young woman to do clerical work at his dealership. Her name was Terri, 19 years old, blue eyes, blond hair. One day, he took Terri out for lunch to an Indian restaurant.

"My wife died two years ago," he told her quietly. "She had been sick for a long time.... You're a pretty girl," he said. "Very pretty." Terri told him she had a boyfriend. And then one day he handed her a videotape and said she and her boyfriend would enjoy it. Later she was with friends and popped the tape into the machine. It was pornography.

"Gee, Terri, nice boss," one of her friends cracked.

"Yeah, I know how to pick 'em."

Another time, Dhillon asked to take her to a "business meeting." She must dress conservatively, cover her head, show no skin but her face. Terri declined. When she didn't respond to his advances, Dhillon asked her to fix him up with her friends. Dhillon wasn't paying her on time, and then not at all. She told Dhillon she was going to call the cops. Dhillon paid her right away. Then she quit in September. A month later, she watched the news on TV about an arrest made by police. Terri was alone at the time, staring as the accused man's confused face flashed on the screen.

"Hey," Terri said aloud, to no one. "That's my old boss!"

It was Wednesday, October 22, 1997, when Korol and Dhinsa met in Brent Bentham's office. Once more they reviewed the case. Dhillon had motive and opportunity in the murders of Parvesh and Ranjit. Disposition? There was evidence that Dhillon was a liar, a fraud, a bigamist, a wife beater. They had forensic evidence that said Ranjit was poisoned, although they did not have that smoking gun for Parvesh's death. As for the evidence from India, they were still waiting on forensics, but witness statements strongly suggested Dhillon had poisoned his sons and his third wife, Kushpreet. The deaths in India could be used as "similar-fact" evidence that would create a mountain of probability pointing to Dhillon's guilt. Bentham did not leap into cases. He had to have a strong shot at conviction or he would turn down a case and have no second thoughts about it.

"You have more than reasonable grounds to arrest for these murders," Bentham said in his deep baritone. "And upon reviewing the evidence, as the Crown attorney, I would add that there is the likelihood of conviction."

Police had Dhillon under surveillance that morning. He was at his car dealership. At 9:30 a.m., the morning bright, crisp, and cool, Korol, Dhinsa, and Steve Hrab left Central Station. They made the 10-minute drive to Aman Auto. It had been almost two years and nine months since Parvesh collapsed. The unmarked white Crown Victoria pulled into the tiny parking lot and the detectives got out, knocked on the door. Dhillon walked out wearing a fall jacket over his long-sleeved shirt and dress pants. He was used to Korol and Dhinsa visiting him. But not at work. And not with Hrab, the one who had grilled him 10 months earlier. Dhinsa pulled the caution card out of his wallet and read it in Punjabi. "I am arresting you for the murder of Parvesh Dhillon and Ranjit Khela."

As Dhinsa spoke, Korol cuffed Dhillon. Click. Click. It felt good. Dhillon, Korol reflected, you are easy to hate. But he knew the fight was just beginning. Dhillon looked calm, even indifferent. He was confident it was a mere formality and he wouldn't be under arrest for long.

"You have the right to telephone, in private, any lawyer you wish. Do you understand?"

Dhillon nodded.

"I want to call a lawyer."

"Do you wish to say anything in answer to this charge?" Dhinsa asked. You are not obliged to say anything unless you wish to do so, but whatever you say may be given in evidence."

"What can I say—I didn't do anything," Dhillon said. "Don't worry about it. I know you're just doing your job."

At Central Station, just after 10 a.m., Korol searched him. Then Dhillon called his lawyer, Richard Startek. He asked if he could also call a friend.

"No," Dhinsa said.

The detectives escorted Dhillon to cell No. 4 on the second floor. Dhinsa worked the phones. He called the Khelas and spoke to Paviter Khela, Ranjit's uncle. "You must have something substantial on him to charge him," the uncle said.

At 11:30, Dhinsa opened the window looking in on the cell. Dhillon sat on the bench appearing nonchalant, his feet resting on a chair.

"Suspect looks well," Dhinsa wrote in his book. "Feet up on a chair."

At 1 p.m. Dhillon was permitted to phone his niece, Sarvjit. He asked about his daughters, Aman and Harpreet. He told Sarvjit to contact another friend and ask him to look after Dhillon's business at a car auction in Kitchener.

"Don't worry," he told Sarvjit. "I'll be back in two or three days. Everything will be fine. I didn't do anything. The police can do whatever they want, but I didn't do anything. Tell Harpreet I'll call her tonight."

He ate a sandwich of processed cheese on dry bread, drank a coffee. At 3 p.m., the detectives questioned him, first Dhinsa, then Korol, while others watched in the video room next door. A half-hour later, Korol booked Dhillon. At 5:43 p.m., Dhinsa phoned India to tell Sarabjit the news. It was the middle of the night there. He spoke to Sarabjit, and then her father, Gurjant. They were both relieved to hear the news.

The next morning Dhillon was loaded into a paddy wagon with several other men and taken to court downtown for a bail hearing. He was remanded in custody. His next stop was Barton Street jail. He was escorted through the back entrance, the sound of metal clanking against metal echoing off the concrete walls and along the corridors, and into his cell. His world, which had once stretched from Hamilton to the Punjab, was now just five paces long and three paces wide, with a toilet behind the door.

* * *

"Mein bekasoor haaan. Mein kujh vee galat naheen keeta."
"I'm innocent," Dhillon said. "I didn't do anything wrong."

He phoned friends and family from jail. He spoke frequently with his niece Sarvjit. "Whatever people are saying, they are all lies," he told her. "I don't know who is spreading them. People are spreading a lot of rumors and the rumors came to the police."

His behavior in India? He had been under pressure—such pressure!—when he had gone to Punjab. All those parents calling for him to take their daughters. Please marry her! Please! He could have married any of them. It went on like this, Dhillon maintaining his innocence, trying to implicate others. It was not his fault, any of it. He told anyone who would listen that he had been framed by rivals jealous of his success as a businessman. And Kevin Dhinsa was out to get him.

"Dhinsa, *teri ma noo. Jidan mein bahar aa gia, udan mein os mader chod ... Dhinsa nu kutnaa hey, Usdeeaan lataan torneeaan ney.*"(One day, when he gets out of jail, I will beat on Dhinsa, that motherf—er, break both his legs.)

One more thing, Dhillon assured Sarvjit:

"*Chintaa dee koee gal naheen. Ik din taan mein bahar aa hee jaana hey, lokaan nu pher sach pataa lag hee jaaegaa.*" ("Don't worry. I'll be out one day. And then people will know the truth.")

* * *

The spring of 1998 was the hottest in 50 years in Hamilton. The weather seemed to skip from the dead of winter to summer heat and rain in May, jerking white and purple lilacs prematurely to life. Then the rain stopped, leaving the blooms hung out to dry. The preliminary hearing into the murder charges against Sukhwinder Dhillon started on May 5, 1998, in an old courthouse at 140 Hunter St. E. downtown. A judge would decide whether the evidence warranted proceeding to a full trial. High-profile criminal lawyer Dean Paquette had replaced Richard Startek as Dhillon's counsel.

Parvesh Dhillon's cause of death was still conjecture, based purely on the symptoms she had exhibited. There was no question Ranjit Khela had been killed by strychnine. But who had given it to him? The evidence that Dhillon poisoned Ranjit was both the Crown's trump card and its Achilles heel. It relied on Lakhwinder. Paquette, a former Crown prosecutor himself, tore her credibility to pieces over the three days she was in the witness box. She was an easy target. Paquette pointed out to her that she had said nothing about Ranjit taking a pill when Korol and Dhinsa first interviewed her in September 1996. She also did not mention it in a second interview some time later. Only in her third interview with police did she offer her current version of the truth. What was the real truth? And what was her angle? She did not get along with Ranjit's family, and there was talk she was about to divorce him. She had served Ranjit his last meal not long before his death.

Hamilton Spectator archives

Defense lawyer Dean Paquette

Dhillon requested that he sit near the witness box, claiming that he could not hear what Lakhwinder was saying in Punjabi to the interpreter. He gleefully watched her struggle under cross-examination. Dhillon couldn't stand her, muttered epithets when she spoke.

The Crown's case had suffered a blow even before the hearing began. On April 22, Korol got a call from Joel Mayer at CFS. The test results from the remains of Gurwinder and Gurmeet showed the babies had likely been poisoned, but not necessarily by strychnine. The toxicology tests had found a cocktail of drugs in the bits of sinew hanging off their bones. Without a blood sample, it was impossible to tell how much they had ingested. At least six substances were detected:

- Harmine, a hallucinogenic drug, the key ingredient in a potent South American drink called *ayahuasca*, which is used among those of the Sao Daime faith in the Brazilian Amazon. The drug has no therapeutic use.

- Dicyclomine, an antispasmodic drug, a fine, white, crystalline powder with a bitter taste. Odourless and soluble in water.
- Diphenhydramine, an antihistamine, also used for gastrointestinal problems and for relieving spasms and cramps in the digestive system.
- Promethazine, an antinausea drug.
- Cotrimoxazole, an antibacterial drug commonly used in recent years in Third World countries to prevent secondary HIV infection.
- Doxylamine, a sleeping aid.

Korol grimaced. Strychnine was the essential link to Ranjit and Parvesh. The twins' deaths, which he and Dhinsa had worked so hard to chase down, now raised more questions than answers. He tried to stay positive. They still might be able to make their case. The chemical cocktail was surely lethal to newborns. And it doesn't just show up in the tissue for no reason. Someone had given it to them. And surely it was more than a coincidence that two healthy boys would both die within hours of a guy like Dhillon visiting them.

The preliminary hearing was the longest one anyone could remember, dragging through the summer and then into the fall of 1998. Dhillon remained confident he would get away with everything. The Crown had been calling witnesses from India, flying them over to testify, to repeat what they had told Korol and Dhinsa about Dhillon. That was fine with him. He had secretly arranged for one of the witnesses, Rai Singh Toor, father of Kushpreet, his dead third wife, to swear to an affidavit in India. In it, Rai said that he did not suspect Dhillon in Kushpreet's death. The Crown and detectives were not aware of the affidavit.

Dhillon saw Warren Korol sitting in court each day. Some days, before the judge entered the room, Dhillon turned around in the prisoner's box and smiled, mouthed curses at him, gave him the finger. Korol regularly met unsavory characters, but Dhillon was the worst: a liar, a coward, a killer to whom anyone was expendable, particularly those closest to him. In Korol's book, Dhillon crossed all the lines. Crooks, being crooks, lie and cheat. But there was still an etiquette, a mutual respect, he expected even from them. Korol had a job to do. It shouldn't get personal. He got in a suspect's face when the occasion warranted, but that was rare, and rising to Dhillon's taunts would just put the case in jeopardy.

Korol was certain Dhillon had people make crank phone calls to Kevin Dhinsa's home. The bastards would say something on the phone about Kevin's father, who had recently died. It was beyond the pale. You just don't do it. Korol assigned officers to keep an eye on Dhinsa's house. Korol felt his anger the strongest when Dhillon's niece, Sarvjit, was testifying. She had told the police so much about her uncle. And she had confided in Korol, poured her heart out to him. She called one day, sobbing, said her family had forced her to marry a "stupid man. I feel like a puppet."

"Why did they force the marriage on you?" Korol had asked.

"To get me permanent immigration status in Canada." She went on, "Whenever I am in front of Detective Dhinsa, I feel disgraced because I am not acting like an Indian woman should."

"Don't feel like that," Korol had told her.

Now, in the witness box under oath, Sarvjit denied everything she had said about Dhillon, even things for which there was already ample proof, even denying she herself had ever been married. Korol sat in astonishment. Dhillon. He put her up to this. The kid was terrified. Sarvjit stepped down from the stand. Dhillon, in the prisoner's box, glanced over his shoulder at Korol, looked him in the eye, and grinned. Korol felt the heat rise under his skin. He felt sick. He hated Sukhwinder Dhillon.

The case was not going well. Bentham, Korol, and Dhinsa felt deflated. All the evidence was amassed, but some witnesses altered their statements from what they had told the detectives— especially those brought over from India. Dhillon was intimidating witnesses by threatening their families back in Punjab. In Panj Grain, Sarabjit's brother received a warning over the phone: "Your family is giving evidence against Dhillon. You should know that you could be killed for it."

In Ludhiana, a cousin of Kushpreet's named Raju also got a call: "Get your parents to change their testimony. Or you're dead." His parents had been at Kushpreet's funeral, had spoken to Dhillon. One night in Ludhiana, Raju was attacked in an alley, hit over the head. He was sure it was Dhillon's friends.

Several times, Bentham had to invoke Section 9(1) and (2) of the Canada Evidence Act, asking the judge to allow him latitude to cross-examine his own witnesses on inconsistent statements. Only by using that hammer was Bentham able to get witnesses to talk, for example, about the symptoms seen in Kushpreet right before she died. The mood was not upbeat. Dhillon's confidence was not out of line, it seemed. On a positive note, a fresh face was about to join the Crown team and pump new life into the case.

* * *

Scott Gardner

Hamilton's chief Crown attorney, Dave Carr, called the young lawyer into his office. The two prosecutors on the Dhillon case were Brent Bentham and Linda Templeton. But in the middle of the preliminary hearing, Templeton was promoted to the bench. Bentham was in charge and he needed a second lawyer. Tony Leitch, a young prosecutor at just 33, had an inkling that he might at some point be put on the high-profile case.

Raju Mundi, Kushpreet's cousin, in Ludhiana

"Okay, Dave," he said. "What am I working on?"

Not all Crown attorneys, or lawyers, were built like Leitch. A football defensive end in college, he cut an imposing figure. He had big hands, size 15 ring finger, wore his hair cropped close. And his high-octane personality was a contrast to the understated Bentham. Tony Leitch loved a challenge, relished complex, demanding cases. Dhillon certainly qualified. He approached the job like a student on an all-night study session.

Warren Korol would slap a nickname on him during the trial. "Hey, who are you, the law-talkin' guy?" Korol said after Leitch mentioned an obscure legal point. The Law-Talkin' Guy stuck.

Leitch was not yet privy to all the evidence, but he was aware of the case and had already thought about it. It was too complicated to be a slam dunk, but he still thought it was a solid case for the Crown, notwithstanding the problems that had already cropped up. The key, he believed, was keeping all five deaths before the jury: Parvesh, Ranjit, Kushpreet, the twins. The issue of motive was important, but not as much as the improbability of coincidence: 1) Five people are poisoned. 2) The common denominator is Sukhwinder Dhillon. And in two of those deaths, he had a direct financial motive. A great case.

Growing up, Tony Leitch never felt pressure to succeed, not overt pressure, anyway. Fred Leitch, his dad, was an easygoing guy. Just do what you want to do, he told his son, and I'm sure you'll be good at it. But how many kids get invited into a judge's chamber at seven years old? The judge said to little Tony, "You know, your father is a very important man." And Tony burst out laughing.

Fred Leitch was a defense lawyer, and a well-known one at that. He always had legal papers strewn around the house, and Tony would hear the sound of his dad rustling about at four in the morning. At 13 years old, Tony looked out the window one day and saw the police guards. Fred was defending a murder case, and threats had been made against his family.

Tony knew the expectation was that he would succeed. Instead, he slapped success in the face. In 1984 he attended the University of Western Ontario, popular for its fraternities, sororities, and football, a school dubbed "The Country Club" for its well-heeled, party-loving student body. He wanted to play on the perennial powerhouse football Mustangs, party, and study—in that order. He spent much of his time either on the football field or on Richmond Street at the Ceeps, the cramped student pub where they served cheap but cold draught and bodies lurched to and fro in a hot crush until closing time, then poured out onto the street for Greek at Sammy's Souvlaki shack. As for football, Tony ended up sitting on the bench. And he almost failed first year. In second year, he failed all five of his courses.

Then something clicked. Tony married young, settled down, and got back into Western. He turned the energy he had previously burned on football and partying to his books and dominated the debates in political science classes, where his booming voice and articulate delivery overwhelmed all comers.

It all came together, his ability to think on his feet, to adjust to the situation, to instantly shift from one argument to another, recognize holes in his opponent's line of reasoning. He made the dean's honor list the next year. When it came time to apply to law school, he had to use his rhetorical skills to explain those two lost years at Western. If Leitch had unconsciously rebelled against his father's success, that was over now, except that, while Fred Leitch defended the accused, Tony prosecuted them.

If there was ever a case that could satiate his appetite for challenge, it was Dhillon's. Dave Carr, the head Crown attorney, assigned Leitch to help Brent Bentham prosecute. They complemented each other perfectly; one measured and taciturn, the other outgoing, energetic. They would need to marshal all their resources—and patience—for this one.

Scott Gardner

Assistant Crown attorneys Brent Bentham (left) and Tony Leitch

CHAPTER 19 ~ PARVESH'S SECRET

All things considered, opined the elderly man with the deep voice and thick Austrian accent, ricin is probably the most effective poison for murder. *Ricinus communis L.* It comes from the seeds of the castor bean plant. The victim becomes progressively ill—abdominal pain, vomiting, bloody diarrhea—but death is delayed three days or so. Amazing, really. Hamilton homicide detective Steve Hrab listened intently as Dr. Fredric Rieders spoke at the conference. It was October 1998, the preliminary hearing in the Dhillon case extending into its sixth month. Rieders had an international reputation as a toxicologist. Three years earlier, he had testified for the defense in the O.J. Simpson trial, helping lawyer Johnnie Cochran make the scientific case that Simpson was framed by the LAPD, that blood evidence found at the crime scene was tainted.

Born in Vienna, he was drafted to serve in the German army in 1939. But shortly before his papers arrived, the 17-year-old graduated from high school and as a gift from his family traveled to New York City to visit an uncle. War broke out in Europe, and when he did return, it was fighting for the Americans in the 20th Armored Division, his German language skills a big asset.

Hrab had come to Albany, N.Y., to attend a seminar for homicide investigators. At the end of the day, Hrab found himself sitting beside Rieders. Ricin's greatest advantage, he continued, is its short retention time: the speed with which it leaves the body. That's why it was a favorite weapon of the infamous Soviet KGB. They used it in the 1978 "umbrella assassination" of Bulgarian defector Georgi Markov.

Hrab engaged Rieders with more questions. The toxicologist talked about his laboratory in Pennsylvania, where he used equipment so sensitive it was capable of detecting toxins weighing as little as one picogram—a trillionth of a gram—in human tissue. That meant his equipment was far more sensitive than what the CFS in Toronto had to offer. Impressed, Hrab talked about the Dhillon case. Symptoms pointed to strychnine, but Parvesh's body tissues were two years old when they were tested and no poison was found in them.

Dr. Fredric Rieders, toxicologist

"Strychnine?" Rieders said. "The first strychnine poisoning case I had was when I was a lowly apprentice in New York in 1949. A pharmacist who had murdered his wife. It's not uncommon. You don't see it every day, but at the medical examiner's office in Philadelphia—I was there for what, 14 years—we'd get a case every year and a half or so."

"All we have are the block tissues left from the victim," Hrab said. "Could you look at those?"

"They are in paraffin wax blocks?"

"Yes."

"I've studied paraffin block tissue, although none involving alkaloids like strychnine. Mostly for metals and some other drugs," Rieders continued. "It would be a bit drawn out, and won't be exactly cheap. But it would be worth trying."

There was the issue of cost, which would be in the $30,000 range. But Steve Hrab could barely contain his excitement. In due course, Korol, Leitch, Bentham, and Joel Mayer from the CFS flew down to Pennsylvania to see Rieders. They were satisfied with what they saw. Rieders was hired to test 75 tissue samples from Parvesh Dhillon, one final chance to reveal her secret.

* * *

The preliminary hearing lasted 11 months and the Crown called 116 witnesses, among them CBI Inspector Subhash Kundu. Despite Dhillon's attempts to intimidate witnesses, he suffered a major setback when Rai Singh Toor, Kushpreet's father, took the stand. Dhillon expected Rai would help his defense, since the old man had signed the affidavit back home stating he did not suspect Dhillon was involved in his daughter's death. But on the stand under Bentham's questions, he now admitted that he had been intimidated into signing the affidavit.

The hearing ended 341 days after it began, on April 11, 1999. Provincial court Judge Morris Perozak ruled that there was sufficient evidence for Sukhwinder Dhillon to stand trial for murder in the deaths of Ranjit Khela and Parvesh Dhillon. As for Dhillon's lawyer, Dean Paquette, it is normal for the defense lawyer at a preliminary hearing to also represent his client at the trial. But Paquette told Dhillon he would not represent him further. Dhillon needed a new defender.

* * *

Warren Korol's white Lumina glided along Hamilton's dark wet streets. An unusually intense winter sun burned off the morning frost. The whole week had been freakishly warm. It was Friday, December 3, 1999. He thought of the case all the time, it had become a part of him. Dhillon's prelim hearing had ended eight months earlier. His trial for murder wouldn't begin for another nine months. The court system moved like a glacier. Such a long process. Korol had been 35 years old when the Dhillon file first landed on his desk. Hard to believe it, but 40 would be in view by the time the trial opened in the spring. Korol smirked. He remembered the day, at age 18, after he had passed the Hamilton police entry tests that could put him in the cadet program, that he mounted the stairs at Central Station for the interview.

"So how's Sally?"

The question was a reference to Korol's aunt, Mike Pauloski's widow. Korol heard back the next day from the police brass. He was hired. In other professions, start dates do not linger in memory. But cops are different. The day you put on the badge is like a birthday. Korol never forgot his first day: July 30, 1979. He loved the work. He enjoyed reminiscing about legendary officers from the past, men like John Petz, Kerry Eaton—and Kenny Knowles, the cop who once exposed corruption among vice officers who were keeping confiscated liquor. One judge called Knowles "the prince of the city." Knowles was a complicated man, however. He battled bouts of anxiety and depression and died very young, at age 44.

Like the Indians in Hamilton with whom he had spent so much time during this case, Korol's roots did not run very deep in Canadian soil. His grandparents had emigrated from Ukraine to a wheat farm in Saskatchewan. They lived hard lives and died young, his grandmother during childbirth and his grandfather after a horse pinned him against a barn wall, crushing him to death. His father, Maurice, was one of 10 kids. As a kid, Korol visited relatives out west. They all pitched in at harvest time, dad showing the kids how to operate the combine and milk the cows. Great memories. But his father had died young, in 1984, at just 60. Heart attack. Warren's mother, Lois, who had worked as a Bell telephone operator and was now retired, moved on, had to learn how to pay bills, drive the car. Rebuilt her life. Warren was proud of her.

His Lumina turned a corner. Korol's pager beeped. The number was familiar. It was Brent Bentham. Korol punched in the number on his cell.

"Hey Brent, what's up?"

Bentham, typically, hedged his remarks. All of the tests weren't finished yet, he said. But there was some news. Dr. Fredric Rieders had completed his testing. Korol's heart pounded. *And?*

"He found strychnine in Parvesh Dhillon's tissue."

Korol felt electricity coursing through him. Rieders's testing had found strychnine concentrations of 200 picograms in the tissue samples. On one level, the amount was so small it was mind-boggling. But Rieders pointed out that the presence of strychnine is confirmed when a one-gram tissue sample contains only 30 picograms of the poison. By that measure, Parvesh's tissue was soaked in strychnine. Later, the Crown arranged for a control test to be done at a lab in Montreal that boasted equipment similar to Rieders's. It, too, detected strychnine. Korol was pumped. This was the break. This was it! Parvesh had spoken from the grave.

* * *

Scott Gardner

Detective Warren Korol

Sukhwinder Dhillon's home in Barton Street jail had faded yellow-beige concrete walls, a tone so neutral, so devoid of emotion that it would not even qualify as a color. The cell contained two hard steel bunks with thin striped mattresses. If there was a third man in the cell, he slept on a mattress on the floor. There was a small white toilet, no lid, a miniature sink made of porcelain. Officials planned to substitute sinks made of stainless steel to prevent inmates from breaking off chunks that could be used as weapons.

In the corner of the room were books and magazines belonging to Dhillon's cellmate. Six of each, the maximum allowed. No posters were permitted on the walls. No graffiti, either. But following the rules isn't a strong suit for recidivists. So there were the crude pencil drawings of naked women. Opinion: "I hate this f—ing hell hole." Advice: "Don't commit crime." And: "I will boldly go where no man has gone before … so bend over bitch."

Beyond the confines of the cell was a common room with a TV where 30 men crowded for their allotted leisure time. Five metal tables were welded to the floor. No eating there, though. All meals were brought to the cells so inmates could not intimidate each other into handing over food. Inmates decided among themselves what to watch on TV each day. The rules say no "muscling" is allowed, that is, no intimidation to get your way. The prisoners were in their cells and lights out at 8 p.m. every evening. Each inmate is entitled to two visits a week, two people maximum per visit. After an extended stay or return engagements, life in jail becomes a "learned environment" for inmates, as prison officials put it. They learn to coexist, keep quiet at bedtime. They use the regimented meal routine to control their bodily functions, to go to the toilet only when a cellmate is not in the room.

The first time in jail for anyone is like a punch in the face. Life is suddenly flipped into another dimension. The new prisoner is trapped in small rooms of steel and concrete with strangers who may have maimed or raped or killed. He is surrounded by men with hard, pale faces, many possessing a vacant stare. There was at least one jailhouse incident involving Dhillon. Just before curfew one night in April 1998 he got into a fight with another inmate. Dhillon claimed he was stabbed. He was treated at Hamilton General Hospital and returned to his cell. His injuries were superficial. Police and jail officials were not able to establish what had happened.

Family members and a few old friends came to see Dhillon during visiting hours. They waited in line, single file, for their 15-minute visit. The waiting line outside the jail is a theater of the tragic. It is frequently made up entirely of females, often rough women with long hair framing leathery faces decorated with dark eyeliner and harsh blush. They wait to see their men, to sit on a round iron stool on the other side of a completely sealed window, able to talk only by telephone. The women wait their turn beneath a No Smoking sign, lit cigarets in hand.

"I found God a while back," one of them says. She hopes her guy in the House will find the Lord, too. "Patience and faith. Patience and faith. It's all about patience and faith," she adds, reciting her sermon in the smoky haze to the others.

"You can't expect God to deliver this week or the next. You have to wait. That's where strength comes from. You know? I pray for the little things. Yeah. They say you can't do that, no, but you can. I'll pray for a roll of toilet paper if I have to. I prayed my little girl would be potty-trained. Two days later, off came the diaper."

"*Next.*"

A voice drones over the outside intercom. The line shuffles forward.

Last time she visited Jimmy in jail she wore the miniskirt, platform shoes. Oh yeah. He was jealous. Big time! "You wonder if the guards read the letters, eh? I mean, I hope not. They'll think, f--k, that woman is crazy, one day she's writing all this religious shit, deeply religious, born again. The last letter, it was a steamy one, I mean hot."

"*Next.*"

She walks inside to the visitors' room and waits on a metal stool for Jim, who is then led into the room, on the other side of the glass. They smile and flirt over the phone. He talks bitterly about the guards. They are assholes, he says. He is not being treated right.

"I know, I know, sweetie," she says. "I know—look, you need to feel compassion for these people. Feel compassion for those who hate you. It's the way of Jesus."

A journalist with *The Hamilton Spectator* waited behind the glass, too. He visited Dhillon, unannounced. He was working on a series about the case. The jail-side door opened, and Dhillon appeared. He wore an orange jumpsuit and rubber-soled canvas loafers without laces. Without the square-shouldered suit he wore in court he looked rounder, less menacing, smaller. Dhillon spotted the writer and, not recognizing him, turned to the guard, a surprised look on his face. The guard shrugged. Dhillon took a step toward the window, then away from it, then toward it again, back and forth, looking like a frightened, confused, caged animal.

"No English!" he finally said, pointing to his head, his ears, as though he was also deaf and mute. He pulled a scrap of paper from his pocket and scribbled a phone number on it. "Brother. My brother."

"How are you?" asked the writer. "How are you feeling? That's all I want to know."

Dhillon pointed to his head again, shaking his head. "No. No English."

* * *

All lies and jest,
Still a man hears
What he wants to hear
and disregards the rest.
—Paul Simon, "The Boxer"

The Toronto defense lawyer with the close-cropped silver hair rose from his chair in the Hamilton courtroom, his physique trim and fit from the hours he spent swimming lengths. Dhillon had found a new defender.

Scott Gardner

Defense lawyer Russell Silverstein

"Respectfully, Your Honor, enough is enough," Russell Silverstein said. His client, Sukhwinder Dhillon, sat behind him in the prisoner's box. It was February 11, 2000. Pretrial motions in the Dhillon case were being heard before Ontario Court Justice C. Stephen Glithero. The Crown had previously recommended moving the entire trial to India to have access to witnesses without the cost of bringing them to Canada. But it had been seven months since the first overture was made to Indian officials, and there still had been no movement. It's time to give up and begin the trial—start it now, here in Hamilton, said Silverstein, who had taken on the task of convincing a jury that Sukhwinder Dhillon was innocent.

Nearly 20 years earlier, Russell Silverstein had worked behind a piano for a living out west. He was 25 then, had already graduated from the University of Toronto and taken two years off to live in France and teach skiing. After returning to Canada, he enrolled in law school at McGill University, then gone to Columbia University in New York and practiced law in Manhattan. He took another year off in 1980, as though trying to squeeze in a life before his career took over. He moved to Alberta, virtually lived on the slopes around Banff, paid his way by working as the piano man at a local bar. Then the music stopped and Russell Silverstein returned to the courtroom.

Now he was 45 years old and the après-ski crowd gathered by the piano had been replaced by a clientele that included drug dealers, wife-beaters and, now, a possible serial killer. He was still working the room. His eyes were dark, deep blue or perhaps gray, their exact color impossible to determine even up close. He was not tall, but appeared athletic and nimble, walked with an assertive air. Today he stood before Judge Glithero on the issue of when and where the trial would begin. He gestured toward assistant Crown attorney Brent Bentham.

"I do appreciate that my friend," he began with one lawyer's customary reference to another, "can bring any witness he wants from anywhere in the world—if he can pull it off."

Silverstein floated back to his seat in his black robe and white collar. He had got off another good line. In one quip he had pointed out the obvious—that Bentham was free to call his witnesses, while at the same time underscoring Bentham's home-field advantage. Bentham, a.k.a. the Crown, had a bottomless pot of money to fly in witnesses from India or anywhere else. It wasn't an option that he, Russell Silverstein, could possibly entertain.

Perhaps Judge Glithero, himself a former defense lawyer who certainly knew the disadvantages one faces when taking on the Crown, might consider Silverstein's inherent underdog status when considering other matters as well. Silverstein had also succeeded in making a point with "if he can pull it off." In other words, finding and bringing witnesses from India who would say what Bentham expected them to say, would be a chore indeed. Judge Glithero ruled that the trial would not go to India. It would begin in Hamilton, in September.

* * *

Seven months later, in September 2000, the trial of Sukhwinder Dhillon got under way at John Sopinka Courthouse in Hamilton

before a jury of seven men and five women. Russell Silverstein had
handled many tough cases in his career, but this one gave him little
room for optimism. The trial ahead would be a rat's nest, if the
interminable preliminary hearing had been any indication.

As for Dhillon, Silverstein would never talk to anyone about
any discussions with his client, but observers in court sensed a
level of exasperation in the lawyer. Dhillon brought newspaper
clippings to court for Silverstein to review, seemed to badger the
lawyer in their conversations. A defense lawyer must not present
evidence he or she knows to be false or allow a client to commit
perjury. But as a matter of ethics, the defender does not have to
believe a client is innocent. Did Silverstein believe the professed
innocence of his clients?

"I tend not to let myself disbelieve it."

Russell Silverstein had made a career out of defending some
nasty characters. That was okay. You don't have to become friends
with criminals, he would say. "You do your job." What he thought
of some of his clients did not matter. A year earlier, he had handled
the Hamilton trial of Mark Laliberte, an accused killer. Silverstein
won the case. When he heard he had been acquitted, Laliberte
turned to the lawyer and said—"hissed," said the story in *The
Hamilton Spectator*—"What's that mean? What's that mean?"
Silverstein hugged Laliberte. Laliberte burst into tears, yelling,
"Oh Russell, I love you!" as he and his girlfriend, according to the
Spectator, "whooped with joy."

Silverstein chuckled about the newspaper account later,
amused once again at the media's simplistic take on the trial. Not
that he was surprised. It's rare, he thought, for the press to nail
down the intricacies of a case.

Case after case, Silverstein saw the tears of victims' families,
heard the gasps of outrage in court as he defended his clients. He
watched a widow weep when he called the death of her husband
in a drug deal gone bad a "run-of-the-mill murder." He knew some
victims' families would be upset. It's sad. And it's understandable.
But emotion cannot deter a lawyer from doing what needs to be
done. He saw himself as an avenger, taking on the Crown to keep
it from treading upon the rights of others.

In Silverstein's mind, an innocent person might end up in prison despite his efforts. He could live with that. But he could never accept the burden of prosecuting someone who was not guilty. That would be the hardest thing to handle. When he looked into the dark eyes of Sukhwinder Dhillon, did he see a serial killer or a man wrongly accused? It didn't matter. It was not relevant. He was here to defend his client with all the legal skill he could muster. He had studied the evidence from every possible perspective. He knew all the facts of the case. The jury did not. But Silverstein also faced two top-drawer Crown lawyers. He was armed only with his understanding of law, his flair, and the assistance of a junior lawyer. Her name was Apple.

"Well, off to defend more criminals." That was how the 28-year-old lawyer with the unusual name spoke. Fresh out of law school, Apple Newton-Smith was still finishing her bar admissions when she was recruited to start at the Toronto firm of Pinkofsky, Lockyer. Shortly after that she was brought on board to assist Russell Silverstein with a client he was defending. They lost that one, but Silverstein asked if she would work with him on another case—Dhillon. They might even win this one, he said.

As for her name, over the years it became simply routine.

"What's your name?"

"Oh God, here we go again. Apple."

"Sorry, what's that? It sounded like you said your name was Apple."

"I did. And did I mention my sister's name is Rain?"

Apple Newton-Smith's father had studied philosophy; her mother was a writer and teacher. While living in England they had two daughters and divorced in 1981 when Apple was nine. Apple returned to Toronto with her mom. Her name was—"apparently"—owing to a connection with Sir Isaac Newton. He was a distant relation, her father said. Another story had it that, while her mother was nine months pregnant, she read Ibsen's *Peer Gynt* to the class she was teaching. There's a line in it that says the soul should not be like an onion where you peel back layers, but like an apple, with a core. One of the students said the teacher should call her new baby Apple.

Apple eventually majored in English and philosophy at McGill. And she started doing legal work with young offenders. Defending those charged with breaking the law seemed a practical application of philosophy, arguing about rights. Defending the wrongly accused—even better. What she thought of Dhillon, the wife-beater, bigamist, and alleged serial killer was irrelevant. He is the client. You prepare him for trial.

"It's not as if you have coffee with the guy. You do your job."

Chapter 20 ~ Lies All Around

It had been in April 1999 when Superior Court Justice C. Stephen Glithero took the phone call in his Kitchener office. The regional senior justice had a new assignment for him. A double-murder jury trial, accused named Dhillon, Sukhwinder Singh. The prelim alone had been nearly a year.

"It's going to be a long trial," he predicted.

Glithero's disdain for routine cases was well known. He did not shrink from challenges, he welcomed them. It had been back in 1967, September, the first day of the semester, when 21-year-old Steve Glithero stood in the doorway of the law school dean at the University of Western Ontario in London. Steve had applied to get into law school there and had been rejected. He had received letters of acceptance from three other law schools, but Western was where he wanted to go. His wife had a job in London and he liked the city. So he asked the receptionist if he could meet the dean.

"I don't think you understand," the dean said. "You didn't get in. We have refused your application. Good luck to you."

Steve Glithero left. The dean's rejection was merely the opening argument. He went back to the office the next day.

"You really don't get it, do you?" the dean said. "You were not accepted. Now please, I have work to do."

Two days later, he made his pitch once more. Perhaps the dean would simply get sick of him and give in, he reflected. Or call the police.

"Oh, all right," the dean finally said, capitulating. "Just get in class."

Fast-forward 25 years to a late July day. Steve Glithero is a crack defense lawyer in Cambridge and Kitchener, but on this day he is gliding in his boat on Georgian Bay, wind filling the sail. He was alone on the boat, as always. There was no phone, no fax machine. He was gloriously out of touch. He rounded a point and saw a friend waving frantically at him. What was going on? Someone back at the office had called the friend. If you see Steve, get him to a phone. This was important. He docked and went to the cottage. Then he returned the phone call to federal Justice Minister Kim

Campbell in Ottawa. He was no longer Steve Glithero. He was C. Stephen Glithero. Judge.

Superior Court Justice C. Stephen Glithero

* * *

Pretrial motions in the Dhillon double-murder trial began in the fall and ended early in 2000. To bolster their case, assistant Crown attorney Brent Bentham wanted to show the jury evidence of Dhillon's marriage to Sarabjit within weeks of the death of his wife Parvesh, and then of the subsequent death of the newborns, and also evidence pertaining to Dhillon's third wife, Kushpreet. On January 28, 2000, Glithero announced his decision. Ruling No. 1 said he would allow details of Kushpreet's death as "similar-fact evidence." That meant it could be used in prosecuting murder counts 1 (Parvesh) and 2 (Ranjit).

"In my opinion," Glithero wrote, "the Crown has led sufficient evidence to establish the improbability of it being pure coincidence that three people close to the accused died over a relatively short period, in different parts of the world, and in a manner involving symptoms of a fairly rare cause of death." But he added a caveat. "If the evidentiary foundation for this ruling is undermined" as a result of new evidence from India, he would reconsider his decision. The judge decided against allowing evidence of the twins' deaths, at least for now. The Crown would need a stronger link between Dhillon and those deaths. Still, for the Crown, the ruling was a big victory. They could proceed to round up witnesses in India to bring them once again to Canada.

Warren Korol was relieved. With the trial a few months away, all the work they had done, the legwork in India, had paid off. But the depth of their investigation also meant that the case was complex, spread over two continents, involving witness statements gathered from people in two languages. The mountain of evidence seemed the trump card. Korol had no way of knowing that the evidence connecting Dhillon to the death of Kushpreet was a lead weight that was about to sink their ship.

* * *

Chandigarh, India
Central Bureau of Investigation
March 2000

At his desk in the concrete bunker-like office, CBI Inspector Subhash Kundu read the fax passed to him by his supervisor. It came via Interpol and the Canadian High Commission in New Delhi. Kundu's services were required again. He carefully read the letter. Kundu enjoyed brushing up on his English. His lips pursed, the brown eyes sparkled. He was proud to once again help the Canadians.

Kundu was asked to contact 19 witnesses to inform them they were required to come to Canada in September to testify against Dhillon. They would enter Canada on special visa permits.

One group of witnesses was from Panj Grain, Sarabjit's home. The other group was from Tibba, including Kushpreet's family. But for the Kushpreet witnesses, Kundu was told they needed more than just Kushpreet's father, mother, and cousin, who had appeared at Dhillon's preliminary hearing. This time they wanted Kundu to find two additional eye witnesses: the village mayor and the medical helper. Their names were Ajmer Singh and Budram

Singh. The more evidence the better. A CBI driver took Kundu to Ludhiana to meet the prospective witnesses, who had been told to gather there. Kundu checked his list. Rai Singh Toor, Kushpreet's father and clearly the leader of the group, had brought everybody except witnesses number 16 and 17.

"Bring them to the next meeting," Kundu told Rai Singh. The old man looked frail and thin, but his eyes blazed fiercely from beneath his turban. On July 17, Kundu met the missing witnesses. Rai Singh was accompanied by a police "gunman," as he was called, for protection from Dhillon's loyalists. Rai Singh introduced the two witnesses.

"Inspector Kundu, this is Dr. Budram Singh. And this is Ajmer Singh, the mayor of the village."

"Are you willing to go to Canada to testify?" Kundu asked.

"Yes," the two men said together.

"It was my car," volunteered Ajmer, "that transferred Kushpreet to the hospital."

Kundu paused. "Show me your ID," he said.

Neither man replied. Rai Singh spoke up. "They do not have it with them today. I'll make sure they get the documents. I'll manage the business with the passports."

The men each signed a document: "I am willing to attend court in Canada as a witness as and when called by the Canadian authorities, provided that all expenses toward the above said purpose…will be borne by the Canadian government."

Kundu wrote the final words in his own hand: "Presently I am not having passport."

Later, Rai Singh took the men to a police station to verify their identities and request passports. He vouched for both; they were "having good moral character." A police officer approved the application forms. Several weeks later, Kundu met again with the two men to confirm their identities. He drove to Tibba. Ajmer and Budram both had photo identification. Kundu returned to his stark office to write his report. The Dhillon trial was to begin soon in Hamilton. He reported 19 witnesses contacted as requested, 19 witnesses verified willing to testify in Canada.

Everything was under control.

* * *

Warren Korol strode into Courtroom 708 carrying a briefcase, his arms and shoulders pushing at the seams of his suit jacket, shoes clicking on the floor. In the four years since he had started the investigation, his dark hair had grayed gracefully in places, offering a tarnished silver appearance under fluorescent lights.

He always chatted with bailiffs and security officers, learning their first names and memorizing them. He brought them coffee and pastries on occasion.

"Hiya, Art," he said to the bailiff.

"Hey Warren, you're losing too much weight," the man chided Korol, who years earlier had carried extra bulk when playing on the line for the Hamilton Hurricanes football team.

The trial about to begin, Korol's case of a lifetime, he carried himself like a cop who knew he had his man dead to rights. He grinned, joked, blue eyes dancing. Sitting next to Korol in the front pew of the court, on his right hand, was Kevin Dhinsa. He always wore a crisp shirt and dark tailored suit, black shoes polished to a high sheen. On occasion he left court to chat with Punjabi witnesses in the hallway, or went to the Crown's temporary office to organize notes to help the prosecutors with their questions for witnesses.

As for Dhillon, the beard he had vainly painted pitch black was now completely gray. He still had the stocky, rounded build and thick face. He sat in the prisoner's box next to a female Punjabi interpreter, who had to put up with his strong body odor day after day. Dhillon wanted people to think of him as a simple *jat* man, a farmer, surely incapable of such a heinous crime. Can't read or write, not even his own name. Certainly didn't know any English. It wasn't true, but he requested an interpreter and got one. That kind of thing wasn't unheard of in Ontario courts. He might even be able to use it to his advantage in court, to slow down the process and try to draw sympathy from the jury.

The interpreter spoke quietly to him as witnesses answered questions from lawyers, Dhillon looking puzzled whenever English was spoken. Dhillon, Korol thought, the lying bastard.

Brent Bentham reconstructed Dhillon's story in his opening statement. The jury heard about the three deaths: Parvesh. Ranjit. Kushpreet. They heard about Dhillon's three weddings in India. Ideally, the Crown would have had evidence of the twins' deaths included. In the end, Bentham withdrew his motion to introduce it. Strychnine had not been found. They could argue the point further, but why bother? They already had an overwhelming case.

Wednesday, November 1 dawned with sunshine and a gentle breeze. As court began that morning, KLM Airlines Flight 691 was over top the Atlantic Ocean bound for Toronto. It had left New Delhi the night before. Among its passengers were three people who were to testify at Dhillon's trial about the circumstances of Kushpreet's death, the "similar-fact evidence" that would help convict Dhillon. Rai Singh sat between men who carried passports identifying them as the mayor of the village, Ajmer Singh, and the medical assistant, Budram Singh.

In the courthouse, Kushpreet's cousin, Pargat Jhajj, sat waiting for his turn to testify at the Dhillon trial. He was next. Pargat was the one who had carried Kushpreet in his arms to the car. Outside the courtroom, he agonized over what to do. Pargat knew the KLM flight was on its way and that Rai Singh was aboard. He also knew about the men with Rai Singh and was ashamed of what his relative was doing. He decided that he had to tell what he knew, do the honorable thing. Truth may be relative in the justice system back home but this was Canada, and Pargat, for one, was taking it all seriously. He stood and approached Kevin Dhinsa, the detective he held in awe. Could Kevin spare a moment?

Pargat told Dhinsa that two of the witnesses on their way to Canada were not the men they claimed to be.

"What?"

Impostors. Two of the men were impostors. The words took Dhinsa's breath away. He walked into the courtroom, leaned over, and quietly relayed the news to Korol.

As Dhinsa spoke, Korol's expression was flat, then his face drained of color. He felt sick to his stomach. He nodded in the direction of Bentham. Tell him. Dhinsa whispered into Bentham's ear as well. We need to talk. Right now. Bentham interrupted his colleague

Pargat Jhajj, Kushpreet's cousin, at home in Tibba

Tony Leitch, who was questioning a witness, and asked the judge for a short recess. Outside the courtroom Dhinsa told the prosecutors what had happened. When court resumed, Bentham apologized to the judge for the abruptness of his request and asked for another recess. He would be making a submission to the court and needed time to prepare it. The jury was sent home for the day.

Korol and Dhinsa marched out of the courthouse. Neither spoke. They had a plane to meet in Toronto. Dhinsa told Korol the whole story, as relayed to him by Pargat. The scam had been Rai Singh's. He had found two replacements for the village mayor and medical assistant as witnesses. He would later say he was simply trying to make sure the Canadians had all the witnesses they needed.

Dhinsa never believed that. What he heard was that Rai Singh met with two men, Amarjit Singh Gill and Bhopinder Singh Grewal. Bhopinder owned a bar in a nearby village. Rai Singh was no stranger there. He owed Bhopinder money. Now Rai Singh had a proposition. He spelled it out over shots of whisky. If Amarjit and Bhopinder pretended to be the two witnesses, they would get a free trip to Canada. Once there, they could all seek refugee status—the impostors, Rai Singh, and his family. In exchange, Rai Singh's debts would be forgiven. The men accepted.

Korol was furious. Either Rai Singh was evil, thought Korol, or stupid—so f—ing stupid! Korol and Dhinsa checked out a 15-seat van from the police car pool and headed for Toronto. With Korol at the wheel, Dhinsa phoned a contact in Immigration.

"Jackie? Kevin Dhinsa. Long story, but we're expecting witnesses to arrive on KLM Flight 691. Can you help organize a party to meet them and take them through immigration? I'll be there to point them out to you. You'll need to contact the pilot, as well."

Korol phoned the RCMP at the airport and filled them in, asked them to be ready to meet the plane as well. The rest of the drive passed in silence. The partners said nothing, staring ahead at the long ribbon of blacktop. All the work, interviews, research, travel, preparation. It was all at risk.

* * *

In India, the assistant lifted the perspiring chrome water pitcher and refilled the glass for Mr. Rupin Sharma. Sharma had helped expedite the process of sending witnesses to Canada for Dhillon's trial. Things were rushed a bit, but everything seemed to go smoothly. He was deputy director for Interpol's New Delhi office, located in the salmon-colored CBI building, Block 4, ground floor. The phone rang and Sharma's assistant answered. It was the Canadian High Commission. Pierre Carrier had retired as RCMP liaison officer. Dan Ouellette, who had succeeded him, was on the phone. Ouellette had just spoken to Warren Korol. Korol was livid.

The assistant handed Sharma the receiver. He frequently spoke with Ouellette. This time, the easygoing Ouellette's voice was on edge. Rupin, everyone is getting burned on this one. How could it happen? Who was behind the ruse? Was it Subhash Kundu, the CBI inspector who helped arrange for the witnesses to go to Canada? No, it couldn't have been. Kundu is clean.

Sharma could barely believe what he was hearing. His English was serviceable, but was he misunderstanding? Impostors? The witnesses sent to Canada were impostors? Ajmer Singh? Budram Singh? How? What about the trial? Sweat beading on his forehead, Rupin Sharma took a long drink of water. The air conditioner rattled as it labored in the window, a metal fan whirred on a table, both fighting a losing battle against the heat.

* * *

The captain's voice came across the intercom aboard the KLM jet. "Your attention please, ladies and gentlemen. Upon arrival would all passengers please stay in your seats for a few moments? There is an immigration matter to tend to. Thank you."

The jet landed and taxied to a stop at the gate. The door opened. Four Canadian immigration officials came along, accompanied by two large men in suits—Korol and Dhinsa.

"There, there, and there," said Dhinsa, pointing out Rai Singh, his wife, and his daughter to the immigration officers. And those two, sitting on either side of Rai Singh, those must be the others we're looking for, he added.

Rai Singh smiled and waved when he recognized Korol and Dhinsa. He remembered them from the interview in India. They were here to welcome him, just as they had when he had come to testify at the preliminary hearing. The detectives escorted Rai Singh and the others to a secure area at the airport. Korol received a call from Tony Leitch. He updated Korol on what was happening. Bentham had told the judge about Pargat's claim. Pargat had then repeated his story under oath, that the two men with Rai Singh were impostors and that it was all Rai Singh's idea. Korol's pulse raced. He approached an immigration officer named Michael Youngson.

"I'm Detective Sergeant Warren Korol, Hamilton Police. There are two impostors coming through. I have confirmation now. Sworn testimony in court today. Go ahead and arrest them."

It wasn't Youngson's job to arrest. He would interview the men with the help of a Punjabi interpreter, then the RCMP could make an arrest. Youngson questioned one of the impostors. Now it was the other's turn. See whether their stories matched. The man sat in front of Youngson. He had no idea that the attention he was receiving was out of the ordinary.

"What is your name?" Youngson asked.

"Ajmer Singh."

"Your last name?"

"Singh."

Youngson repeated the question: "Your last name?"

"Jhajj," the man said. It was a common last name.

"Why are you here?" was the officer's next question.

"As a witness."

The man wasn't ready for the next question.

"How old are you?"

How old? Think. The year was…yes, 1962. How old? Year 2000…1962. Simple arithmetic, but it was hot in the interview cubicle and he was pausing for a long time now and….

"How old are you?"

"I was born in 1962," said the man.

"How old are you?" Youngson repeated, his tone steady.

How old…Quick, think! Nineteen sixty-two, two thousand, that's thirty-eight years.

"Thirty-eight," he said, finally.

Youngson thought back to his interview of the other impostor, the one whose passport identified him as "Budram Singh." The immigration officer had asked the man how long he had known Ajmer Singh. All his life, he had replied.

Now Youngson asked Ajmer the same question.

"How long have you known Mr. Budram Singh?"

"Six or seven years," he replied.

"Only that long?"

"Yes."

"Do you have any children?"

"Two."

"What are their ages?"

Ages?

"I don't know their exact dates of birth," he said.

"Sir," Youngson intoned, "they are your children."

Say something. Anything.

"Nine and twelve."

"Sir," Youngson said, "I don't believe that you are the rightful holder of the documents you have presented."

"Fine," the man said.

Rai Singh, meanwhile, lay on a bank of chairs in the immigration waiting area, napping. Korol and Dhinsa arrived to question him.

"We have learned," Dhinsa began, "that the two men who have flown with you from India are not Budram Singh or Ajmer Singh. Why did you choose to do this?"

Rai Singh said the real witnesses didn't want to come. He thought the other two men could take their place.

"I knew that we needed everybody," he said. "I got passports made."

The detectives next interviewed the impostors. The men admitted it was all a ruse. Scenarios raced through Korol's mind. The judge might throw out the Kushpreet evidence. It was growing late. The RCMP arrested the impostors and placed them in detention. Korol and Dhinsa took custody of Rai Singh and his family and drove back to Hamilton in the van. They stopped at the Royal Connaught hotel a few blocks from central police station. It was midnight.

Pargat Jhajj and his family were asleep in their room in the hotel. The detectives knocked on the door, waking them. No time to change out of pajamas. We're going to the station. Now. Korol told Dhinsa to keep Rai Singh's family and Pargat's family apart on the short drive. Don't let them talk to each other. In Korol's office, the detectives were joined by Bentham and Leitch. They interviewed everyone separately, trying desperately to determine what they could salvage of the case. It was 4 a.m. when they finally went home to try to get some sleep.

In the courthouse the next day, Rai Singh sat in the hallway outside the courtroom, awaiting his turn before the judge. Dhinsa walked toward him. He hated even looking at Rai Singh. The old man said something. Dhinsa ignored it, then stopped and leaned toward him.

"You disgust me, Rai," he said.

Rai Singh and the two impostors were brought before Judge Glithero. Even now, they changed their stories repeatedly. Rai talked about the deal he brokered, the impostors said they never wanted to come to Canada, they were forced, had been threatened. An immigration agent in India had put them up to it. Warren Korol sat in court, eyes glazed in disbelief. Lies all around. He knew it was over.

Defense lawyer Russell Silverstein saw his opportunity. A criminal trial is a series of battles. Win enough of them, you just might win the war. First, apply to have all the evidence about Kushpreet thrown out. The impostors had cast doubt on all testimony regarding her death. Second, apply for a mistrial. The jury had already heard some of the Kushpreet testimony, the entire exercise was compromised. Third, seek another venue for the next trial. This trial had been going for two months and had been covered extensively in *The Hamilton Spectator*. The local jury pool had been polluted. Fourth—the biggest move of all—apply for severance; have Dhillon tried separately in the deaths of Parvesh Dhillon and Ranjit Khela. Silverstein could defend his client more effectively if the two charges were tried separately, with different juries, different bodies of evidence.

Justice C. Stephen Glithero had some very big decisions to make. Dhillon sat in court, assuming his look of wide-eyed innocence for the judge. He had a shot. He might even get off. Just as he had always predicted. As for Pargat, he learned the price of telling the truth. Down the road, when he returned to Tibba, the phone rang in his small house. Pargat answered. "You should know that after all you've done, I'm sending a man after you," the caller said. "He'll hunt you down. You won't know when it's coming."

Chapter 21 ~ Similar Facts

"Come on, guys, we're still in this thing!"

In the Crown team's meeting room, big Tony Leitch tried to boost the spirits of the others. As the Dhillon case went through its peaks and valleys, when some of the team was down, others would speak up. Korol or Leitch would throw out some choice locker-room language. We still have him, it's not over yet. Bentham's cool was such that he could say just a few optimistic words and everyone would feel better.

The two impostors posing as witnesses were a problem, but they still had a shot that similar-fact evidence about Kushpreet's death could remain part of the Dhillon case, or that the murders of Ranjit Khela and Parvesh Dhillon would not be severed. However stupid or fraudulent the heartless scheming of Rai Singh was, it didn't change the facts. Leitch pointed out that several witnesses saw Kushpreet die soon after Dhillon last visited her, with symptoms consistent with strychnine poisoning, and she had gasped, "Dhillon gave me a pill." The testimony was real. These people can't even read, thought Leitch, so how could they have made up the symptoms of strychnine death? "They would have had to study at the knee of a toxicologist to get their stories straight," he said. Why not just let the jury hear it all, the entire mess of it, the prosecutors reflected—the Kushpreet evidence, the story of the impostors, and allow jurors to make of it what they will?

On Monday, November 14, 2000, the Crown, defense lawyer Russell Silverstein, Dhillon, Korol, and Dhinsa sat in court as Judge Glithero delivered his decisions. It was the worst-case scenario for the prosecution. First, the question of similar-fact evidence involving Kushpreet's death. Could the jury still decide Dhillon's fate if they were told about the impostors? Could they, in the American parlance, "disregard" what they had already been told by other witnesses? Glithero wasn't taking that chance.

It is, he wrote in his judgment, "a troublesome area of the law, namely when and to what extent a trial judge may embark on an assessment of the probative value or weight of impugned evidence.

"However, in determining the admissibility of similar-fact evidence the trial judge must, to a certain extent, invade this province. Despite it being beyond my role to make findings of credibility, it would defy common sense not to brand the two impostors as dishonest liars.... All of the similar-fact witnesses either admit having lied under oath or admit to having lied in statements given to Canadian authorities or have given wildly inconsistent statements at various times. These all raise issues with respect to credibility of these witnesses. The similar-fact evidence is highly discreditable, involving as it does an allegation of an additional murder."

That was it. Glithero threw out the evidence of Kushpreet's death, and Dhillon's alleged role in it. After the Kushpreet evidence was ruled out of order, the other parts of the trial fell like dominoes.

"I am declaring a mistrial," Glithero said. "A new jury will have to be chosen and the trial will begin anew."

He ruled the new trial would move from Hamilton to Kitchener, in order to select an unprejudiced jury pool. Dhinsa stood up and walked out of the courtroom. He approached the thin man with the turban sitting on a bench in the hallway. It was 2:17 p.m.

"Rai Singh Toor, I am arresting you for conspiracy to obstruct justice. It is my duty to inform you that you have the right to retain and instruct counsel without delay."

Back at the central police station, Dhinsa interviewed Rai.

"It is 14 November 2000. I am Detective Kevin Dhinsa. I am a police officer. Do you know where you are?"

"In court?" Rai asked.

"No, you are in a police station."

"I don't have anything to do with this, I am not going to touch it."

"You knew that these wrong people were not Ajmer Singh and Budram Singh. What were you thinking—they would give false evidence and escape?"

"It was not in my mind. I thought they were joking. I want to go. No one else wants to go. I will go."

"How did they come with you?"

"God knows. What can I tell you?"

"What?"

"God knows."

Kushpreet's death was off the table, but the Crown still had the Parvesh and Ranjit murders together. Would that change, too? Judge Glithero faced, in mid-December, his biggest decision of all. He sat in his office at home in Cambridge. He had carefully considered arguments from the Crown and the defense. Bentham and Leitch had argued that the similar-fact nature of the deaths of Ranjit Khela and Parvesh Dhillon justified trying them together. Glithero had come to a decision. He cleared his throat. He often dictated his decisions on tape for his assistant to transcribe later.

Click.

The recorder started. Glithero, his voice grainy from years of failed attempts to quit smoking, spoke.

"Ruling number 6. Severance application. The applicant accused moves for an order severing the two-count indictment and directing separate trials on each count. Period."

Click. Stop.

Glithero glanced at notes on the legal pad on which he had scribbled when Russell Silverstein and the Crown lawyers made their cases before him.

There were quotes from the lawyers, thoughts of his own, reminders to check case law.

Click. Start.

"Section 591 (3) gives the court the discretion to order that the accused be tried separately on each count."

Click.

He looked at the direct reference.

Click.

"Where it is satisfied that the interests of justice so require, the onus is on the applicant to show on a balance of probabilities that the ends of justice require severance."

Click.

Glithero had consulted the case law on similar-fact evidence.

Click.

"In determining whether to admit similar-fact evidence, the basic and fundamental question that must be determined is whether the probative value of the evidence outweighs its prejudicial effect."

Click.

He read from paragraph 50 in *Regina v. Arp*.

Click.

"There may well be exceptions, but as a general rule if there is such a degree of similarity between the acts that it is likely that they were committed by the same person, then the similar-fact evidence will ordinarily have sufficient probative force to outweigh its prejudicial effect and may be admitted."

Click.

The big question for Glithero was, were the Ranjit and Parvesh killings similar enough to be kept together in one trial?

Click.

"The Crown submits that the evidence demonstrates a system or pattern of conduct such as to demonstrate that the accused is responsible for the two deaths."

Click.

Glithero agreed the manner and symptoms of the Parvesh and Ranjit deaths were similar. But when Kushpreet's similar death was removed from the equation, the link between the other two deaths was weakened.

Click.

"Now that I am dealing with two deaths, in the same city as the accused lived, and that the accused had routine association with the two victims, I am less impressed with the association of the accused with each victim as an item of similarity and consider it less relevant to the improbability of coincidence."

Click.

The judge felt that "mere opportunity" for Dhillon was not enough to link the deaths of Parvesh and Ranjit before a jury. In Parvesh's murder, Sukhwinder Dhillon had motive and opportunity. In Ranjit's murder, the only evidence of opportunity was from his widow, who claimed Ranjit told her Dhillon had given him a pill. She was a flawed witness, Glithero thought. He dug an old case out of his files, from 1952. *Harris v. D.P.P.* It said that "evidence of other occurrences which merely tend to deepen suspicion does not go to prove guilt." Time to sum up. Glithero turned on the recorder again.

Click

"In my opinion, the evidence of the similarities in the manner of commission of the two deaths (assuming that of Parvesh Dhillon is a homicide) is not such as to make it likely that both were committed by one person."

Click.

Sukhwinder Singh Dhillon was getting a lifeline.

Click.

"I would not admit the evidence on each count as similar-fact evidence on the trial of the other."

Later, after Glithero made revisions, the assistant transcribed the ruling. Fifty pages even. Glithero read it over once more before sending it to the lawyers. His conclusion would rock the case: "I am satisfied that the accused has demonstrated on a balance of probabilities that the interests of justice require that the accused be tried separately on each count of the indictment. I order that the counts be severed." Glithero's eyes went to the bottom of the last page. He filled in the date, December 19, 2000, and signed his name.

* * *

Everything had changed. Now Dhillon had a chance at acquittal, a good one. Russell Silverstein knew it was an entirely new situation. Two trials, two juries, two separate bodies of evidence heard in isolation from each other. The first trial would begin in March. For the Crown lawyers, losing the evidence about Kushpreet was tough enough to swallow. But severing Parvesh and Ranjit? Common sense said they belonged on the same ticket. Two healthy young adults living in the same neighborhood die from a rare poison, and one man has the motive of insurance money in each death. Warren Korol felt as if he had been punched in the face. If those deaths weren't "strikingly similar," in legal jargon, then what the hell was? How could the trials possibly be severed? Korol thought back to the impostors and Rai Singh. And now the severance. Dhillon suddenly had a helluva chance to win. How could a case that had as many as five deaths on the ticket, be reduced to—in terms of what any jury would hear—just one?

Lead Crown prosecutor Brent Bentham outwardly kept his even keel. Sure, he wanted to keep the deaths together. The Crown's best case was showing the improbability of coincidence of two strychnine deaths in Hamilton's east end with the accused the financial beneficiary of each. But Bentham was philosophical. You have to live by the rulings. You don't like it, but you do the best you can. He reminded the others they still had the two poisoning cases. The severance wasn't fatal to their case. And, regardless of Glithero's ruling, they could still attempt to bring the victims together again.

Over the course of the prosecution, Tony Leitch would argue before the judge to revisit the issue several times, raising it whenever he could. Leitch figured that if they lost and appealed, the severance and the Crown's protest of it would be on the record repeatedly. But even Leitch, with his confident, youthful manner, felt his optimism flag.

With the nexus between Parvesh and Ranjit gone, the Crown needed a stronger motive in the killing of Parvesh than just insurance money. Leitch thought about the case every spare moment. Driving to work or in the shower, he considered tactics. Financial motive? Dhillon's financial situation prior to Parvesh's death was not good. But it was not grave. It didn't justify murder. Silverstein would surely make hay with that. Motive? Two hundred thousand dollars? A substantial sum of money, granted, but is that enough of a motive to kill your wife? My client is no saint, Silverstein could say, but is that enough motive for this man to kill the woman he loved, the mother of two beautiful young girls?

Young girls. Yes. Leitch remembered the evidence stuffed in the cardboard boxes in the Crown's office. Men wield the power in Indian culture. Everyone wants male children. The Dhillons had wanted a boy. Parvesh had had one abortion, maybe more, after determining she was carrying a girl. Was that Parvesh's decision? Not likely.

Once the trial began, Korol, Dhinsa, Leitch, and Bentham drove to Kitchener each day in a van. They talked strategy. One day Leitch mentioned his theory of a new motive. "What about the male child?" he asked.

There was the time the Dhillons went to a lawyer to see about adopting a son in India. "So who really wanted to have a male child in that cultural circumstance?" Leitch wondered.

Think about it: Dhillon kills Parvesh for insurance money and as a bonus gets to arrange to marry a younger woman with whom he can have a male child. Presto: a double motive. Korol grinned. Chalk one up to the Law-Talkin' Guy.

* * *

Bentham and Leitch had a big decision to make. The new trial for Dhillon was scheduled to begin on Monday, March 19, 2001, in Kitchener. It was the Crown's prerogative which death was tried first. They wanted to lead with their strongest case. If they lost the first trial, Dhillon could be freed on bail, forcing them to appeal, slowing down the process, destroying any chance of linking the two deaths in future. Which case was stronger? Toxicology tests had proved strychnine killed both Parvesh and Ranjit—although the evidence was a little trickier for Parvesh with the four-year delay between her death and the discovery of the poison in her tissue.

Korol and Dhinsa thought Parvesh was a stronger case for a jury. Dhillon had opportunity, was the only adult with her the day she collapsed. And jurors understand that some men kill their spouses. Bentham and Leitch leaned toward Ranjit Khela's case: incontestable evidence of strychnine in the blood; the unusual arrangement where Dhillon was the life insurance beneficiary; Lakhwinder's testimony that Ranjit told her Dhillon gave him a pill. Yes, there were problems with Lakhwinder as a star witness, but still, it was direct evidence.

The prosecutors decided to start with Ranjit's murder. But as with all things involving the Dhillon case, nothing happened the way it was supposed to. On Friday, March 16, Bentham received word that eight witnesses from Ranjit's family—several of whom had been in the house the night he died—were no longer in Hamilton. They were in India, and there was no sign they would return in time to take the stand. Dhillon's curse had struck again. The case against him in Ranjit's murder was now in jeopardy. If the Crown led the case without the Khelas, what would the jury think? Perhaps they'd draw the conclusion that one of the Khelas killed Ranjit, not Dhillon. Why else would they all take off for India with a trial looming for the man who allegedly had murdered their beloved Ranjit?

On Monday, March 19, with the jury excused, Tony Leitch rose before Judge Glithero and requested arrest warrants for the eight witnesses. Russell Silverstein agreed to the application. The judge ruled the family members were in contempt of court and issued the warrants. Three days later, Glithero adjourned the trial until May. Dhinsa called the Khelas in India. They agreed to return earlier than they had planned. Their flight landed in Toronto a few days later. Waterloo Regional Police and Canada Customs officers boarded the plane and identified the eight family members. They were all taken to a secure area. Suddenly, Piara, Ranjit's grandfather, clutched his chest, suffering an apparent heart attack. Family members simply looked on, not rushing to his aid.

Eventually one of the women went to check on him. Leitch later heard the story and chuckled. "I guess they'd seen his Redd Foxx routine before, eh?" Piara was taken to hospital and released the next morning with a clean bill of health. He joined the other seven family members in custody. They were all shortly released on bail on condition they appear in court when required. The Khela affair meant they would be available as witnesses, but the controversy and delay prompted Bentham and Leitch to change strategy. They would try Parvesh's murder first.

* * *

The trial began on May 16 in Kitchener. Sukhwinder Dhillon was led into the courtroom, the clacking of metal shackles announcing his arrival, and was seated in the prisoner's box. Through the twin doors of Courtroom 1, the eight rows of pews for spectators were arranged as in an amphitheater, the wood trim dark brown like the inside of a church. Ten tall windows allowed in light on the left of the room. There was a cubicle for the accused, a table for the lawyers, and, off to the right, the jury box. At the front of the room, raised high above it all, was the judge's bench with Ontario's coat of arms on the wall behind.

Waterloo Region Record

Sukhwinder Dhillon being led into court in Kitchener, Ontario

Lawyers for both prosecution and defense were dressed in the traditional black robes with white collars. On the left side, Russell Silverstein with Apple Newton-Smith beside him. To their right Brent Bentham, the lead Crown, eyes buried in his papers. Beside him, big Tony Leitch leaned back in his chair, smiling pleasantly. Front pew, right-hand side of the courtroom sat Warren Korol and Kevin Dhinsa in custom-made suits Kundu had sent them from India. A bailiff stood and commanded those present to rise as Judge Glithero entered the room. "Her Majesty the Queen versus Sukhwinder Singh Dhillon. His Honor Justice C. Stephen Glithero presiding. You may be seated." The jury filed in to take their seats.

"*Gal iddan hey, eh case paiey pickey khoon daa hey.*"

The voice of Neeta Johar, the Punjabi court interpreter, could be heard faintly coming from the direction of Dhillon's seat. She translated Bentham's blunt opening statement to the jury: "This is a case about murder for money."

The Crown began calling its long list of witnesses to give their testimony. Silverstein cross-examined each in turn. When the Crown was finished he could present his own evidence, if he chose. But that would carry a price. Under Canadian law, the defense gets the last word, addresses the jury last, only if it calls no witnesses. If it does call witnesses, the Crown speaks last. Silverstein decided to call witnesses, but the vast majority of the 92 people to testify at this trial were called by the Crown.

The first witness called by Bentham was a Hamilton woman named Parminder Bassi. She had known Parvesh back in Ludhiana, and had worked with her at the Narroflex factory in Stoney Creek. Inconsistencies in testimony emerged immediately. Bassi told Bentham that Dhillon himself had told her he gave Parvesh a painkiller pill the day she died. Silverstein pounced in his cross-examination. She had never made that claim before, not to Korol and Dhinsa when they interviewed her, or in court previously.

"I'm going to suggest to you today that this morning is the first time you have ever said that Sukhwinder told you that he gave this medication to Parvesh to take."

"Yes," she replied. "But he did tell me that he is the one who gave it to her. Today I am telling you—under no pressure—that this is what he said and this is the truth."

Bassi's change in testimony helped the Crown's case, but other witnesses who changed their tune did not. Parvesh's two daughters offered contradictory accounts of their mother's death. The youngest, Aman, took her place in the witness box, her hair in a pony tail, wearing wire-rimmed glasses. She had been six and in Grade 1 when she watched her mother collapse. At the preliminary hearing, Aman had testified that her mother shook on the floor. And now one of Bentham's key witnesses changed her story.

"Aman, did any parts of your mom's body move when she lay on the floor?" Bentham asked. Dhillon, in his box, appeared to wipe a tear from his eye.

"I don't recall," Aman said. "I'm not sure. She looked normal. Like she was sleeping."

Leitch hurriedly dug out Aman's prelim testimony from the stack of papers on the desk and handed it to Bentham, who showed it to the girl.

"Please read this section very carefully," he said. "Does this help refresh your memory about your mother's appearance following her collapse?"

"No. My memory is better today, and now that I think about it, I can't remember her moving."

Aman left the witness box and walked past Dhillon's seat. She did not look at her father. It wasn't the last time in the trial a witness would go south on the Crown. On five occasions, Bentham would have to invoke Section 9 (1) and (2) of the Canada Evidence Act, asking Glithero to allow him latitude to cross-examine his own witnesses over inconsistent statements. It happened again on May 31. Bentham called a woman who had been one of several people who rushed to the Dhillon house when hearing of Parvesh's collapse. But the woman no longer recalled the vivid descriptions of Parvesh's condition she had offered in past statements in court. Bentham accused her of changing her story.

"How can I lie?" the witness countered through the interpreter. "She was like a daughter to me. How could I speak against her?"

The woman blamed Kevin Dhinsa for misinterpreting what she had told police—even though she herself had repeated her account in court at the preliminary hearing. The parade of Crown witnesses continued, neighbors, paramedics, physicians at Hamilton General Hospital, forensic pathologist Dr. David King, Parvesh's family doctor Khalid Khan, insurance investigator Cliff Elliot, strychnine expert Dr. Michael McGuigan. Korol and Dhinsa testified on how easily they had purchased strychnine in India and walked it past airport officials in Toronto.

Silverstein cross-examined each witness. On the strychnine evidence, his primary argument was that if indeed strychnine was found in Parvesh Dhillon's tissue samples long after her death, it wasn't put there by her husband—it was contamination from testing at either the hospital or the Centre of Forensic Sciences. Or, if not contamination after her death, then Parvesh had consumed the poison herself, by accident.

Tony Leitch handled the forensic evidence part of the Crown's case. He called six laboratory technicians from Hamilton General Hospital to prove contamination of Parvesh's tissue samples was not possible. He asked technician Nancy Kunkel: "To your knowledge, is there any strychnine used in your laboratory?"

"None at all," she replied.

Silverstein asked a CFS official if the tissue sample could have been contaminated by strychnine in his lab. Dr. Joel Mayer said no, not directly, and that cross-contamination of the samples by airborne particles was highly unlikely. He said evidence in the Dhillon case had been kept together but that the strychnine powder the police had brought from India was kept separate from the wax blocks of Parvesh's tissue. Silverstein pointed out that some of the strychnine had been in a simple bag, not an air-tight container.

Silverstein said that Parvesh may have taken a strychnine product for therapeutic reasons—diluted versions of the product were available as homeopathic remedies popular in the East Indian community. Mayer acknowledged they could not be sure how much strychnine Parvesh ingested before her death.

"So she could have had a therapeutic level in her system?" Silverstein asked.

"Yes," Mayer replied. "There's no way to tell."

CHAPTER 22 ~ WONDERFULLY DEFIANT

On Wednesday, June 20, a key Crown witness took the stand. It was Dr. Fredric Rieders. His resumé was impeccable. He was now 79 years old, silver-haired and with his style and his Austrian accent, he oozed *gravitas* in court. Warren Korol grinned as he studied the faces of the jurors. Rieders talking about toxicology was like having Moses up there giving his opinions on religion. His flair for explaining complicated scientific processes in ways the jurors could immediately understand made him the perfect expert witness. How would the doctor characterize the volume of strychnine found in Parvesh Dhillon?

"The tissue contained a heck of a lot of strychnine," Rieders said. Dhillon listened as the phrase was translated into Punjabi. *Ohdey tissue vichin kafi kuchila nikli hey.* Russell Silverstein would need all his skill to rattle Rieders. He took his shots.

"What, exactly, does 'a heck of a lot' mean?" Silverstein asked.

"It means it's scientifically significant. She would have had to ingest quite a few milligrams for the count to be as high as it was."

Silverstein proffered a medical counter theory to the doctor. If, he said, Parvesh was using small doses of strychnine for therapeutic purposes, is it not possible that when she fell into a coma, the body stopped breaking down toxins—and that could account for the strychnine levels in her tissues?

Possible, said Rieders. But unlikely. Coma patients tend to excrete a lot of urine which greatly helps to eliminate poison from the body.

Rieders sized up Silverstein. He is well-informed, the toxicologist thought. Intense, but not overbearing. Rieders had appeared many times as an expert witness in U.S. courts. Silverstein was more civil in his questioning than the lawyers he was accustomed to facing. Rieders knew well the American lawyer's motto: if the facts are on your side, pound the facts; if the law is on your side, pound the law; if neither is on your side, pound the witness. Rieders had experienced the pounding first-hand over the years, the personal attacks, a hostile lawyer cornering him on the stand: "Doctor Rieders,

Scott Gardner

Jndr. Rieders, Ph.D.
Founder

Dr. Fredric Rieders took the stand.

let me ask you once again, did you in fact spike that sample?" It got pretty raw sometimes, but then the toxicologist and lawyer who had battled in the courtroom went out for lunch together.

What else could Silverstein have done with the Crown's star witness? He had heard something about Rieders running into difficulty over a lab calculation in a case in the U.S. not long before the Dhillon trial, but did not know the details. The problem had resulted in Rieders being dropped as a witness in that case. Silverstein knew that none of that mattered here, however. Rieders's finding had been confirmed by a lab in Montreal.

Korol sat in one of the pews, laptop computer on his knees for taking notes. As Rieders stepped down from the stand and exited the courtroom, Korol leaned over. "Hey, thanks for coming, Dr. Rieders," Korol said quietly. "Take care." The toxicologist left the courtroom and headed back to Pennsylvania, to his lab, where samples of Parvesh Dhillon's tissue remained in storage.

* * *

Sarabjit made one wish after her babies had died and Dhillon had fled. Just one. Let me see him one more time, let him look me in the eye and see that I am strong, stronger than him—and that I am taking revenge. On Thursday, July 5, Sarabjit had her chance, and she braced herself to once again face Jodha. She had traveled from Panj Grain to appear on the stand. She had never recovered from the deaths of her sons, still wept when she thought of them. As she gathered herself together and walked into the courtroom, she was afraid. All the people, for one thing. And there was Dhillon.

What might he do? Was she safe? Was her family safe back home? But she decided she would not show fear. Instead she would convey her anger to Dhillon. She would hide it no more.

No, she was not going to show what she really felt, call him a bastard. But simply showing her face in court, on the stand, openly confronting Dhillon, was for her like revealing her heart to the world. It felt wonderfully defiant. Here she was, a young Indian woman who had been told whom to marry, who had been brought up in a culture where women follow the male lead. She was standing up to a man—not just any man, but her husband. Sarabjit stepped into the witness box. She looked directly at Dhillon. He saw her, but his face was an expressionless mask, his eyes revealing nothing, looking as though he had never seen his second wife and mother of his deceased newborn children before.

Courtesy of the author

Wedding portrait of Dhillon and Sarabjit

Sarabjit's actual testimony was brief. Judge Glithero had ruled the Crown could not mention the twins, so the jury got only a glimpse of Sarabjit's marriage to Dhillon. All Brent Bentham could do was show the jury an hour-long videotape of the wedding. In the video, Sarabjit looked radiant clad in traditional gold and red, but her expression was dour. On the stand, all she could talk about in her soft voice was how their arranged marriage came to be, and how they had wed shortly after Parvesh had died—a damning detail, but only a sliver of the whole ugly story. Still, Sarabjit felt triumphant. She had stood up to Jodha. She stepped down from the box, looked right at him, for the last time. Dhillon turned away from her stare.

* * *

Russell Silverstein needed to hammer home the notion that Parvesh could have killed herself by accident, using homeopathic medicine. He had to sow doubt in the minds of the jurors. Murder in a Canadian court must be proven "beyond a reasonable doubt," a high threshold. Brent Bentham knew that homeopathics would be a powerful suggestion. He needed to use Dhillon's own statements to counter it. Bentham's key argument was that, in several exchanges with police prior to his arrest, Dhillon himself had never mentioned homeopathic treatments—what he called "*desi* medicine." In fact, Kevin Dhinsa had directly asked Dhillon on several occasions whether Parvesh ever took homeopathic medicine, and he had denied it. The question was, could the Crown get Dhillon's statements to police before the jury? The jury was dismissed on July 6 and the trial paused for a week while the lawyers argued the point.

The Crown tried to enter as evidence statements Dhillon made during four interviews: on November 17, 1996, at the first aborted polygraph interview; December 15 at his official polygraph test; March 17, 1997, in a conversation between Dhillon and Dhinsa; October 22, 1997, the day he was arrested. But in the end, nearly all of Dhillon's statements were declared inadmissible. Glithero did allow them to use statements Dhillon made to Dhinsa in a brief conversation on March 17, 1997, outside Dhillon's home as it was being searched. Dhillon had not mentioned homeopathics, or *desi* medicine, to Dhinsa—but then Dhinsa had not asked him about it directly, either. The judge ruled the detectives had overstepped their bounds or violated Dhillon's rights in a variety of ways to obtain the other statements. Dhillon's arrest-day statements were out of order, because police pressured Dhillon into speaking after the accused had said he had nothing more to say. The judge suggested that Dhinsa had erred in reminding Dhillon that he had once said Dhinsa was like his own brother, since they were from India. Dhinsa, Glithero opined, had tried to "undermine the resolve of the accused by appealing to their common ancestry and relationship." Further, Glithero said Dhillon was very likely intimidated on the day of his arrest by the presence of Detective Sergeant Steve Hrab, whom Dhillon had last seen at the heated interrogation 10 months earlier.

The judge did not stop there. He made a point of singling out
Hrab for his interrogation methods. The detective had never hurt
Dhillon physically, nor did he threaten the suspect. But Glithero
took Hrab to the woodshed in his ruling. "The interview conducted
by Officer Hrab," he wrote, "is in my opinion appalling and beyond
anything I have seen in 30 years of close involvement with criminal
litigation. I thought his performance to be disgusting and embar-
rassing to our system." Hrab was not in court for the ruling, but
later was unfazed by the verbal undressing, did not feel he had
crossed the line with Dhillon. Glithero also excluded statements
Dhillon made at the November 17, 1996, interview, because Korol
and Dhinsa had not re-read Dhillon his rights when they started
questioning him on both murders.

Korol shook his head. He knew the exclusion of Dhillon's
statements was a huge blow to the case. Dhillon could now say that
Parvesh consumed unknown quantities of mystery homeopathic
medicine, and the Crown had little to counter it.

The trial neared its conclusion. By mid-July, after some 90
witnesses had testified, the buzz among spectators in court was
that Sukhwinder Dhillon stood an excellent chance of walking free.
Family and friends of Parvesh who had witnessed her death had
been inconsistent or hostile to the Crown. As for Dhillon's motive,
yes, he had a financial benefit to kill Parvesh, but no more than
any husband would have to kill his wife for an insurance payout.
Moreover, had Parvesh actually been murdered? The presence of
strychnine in her tissues was not absolute proof that she had been
murdered with it, or even that it was in her body at the time she
died. To this point in the trial, as far as the jury knew, Parvesh
regularly took strange homeopathic remedies. The tissue samples
were more than four years old. In theory, they could have been
contaminated in storage. Police never found a trace of strychnine
in his house. Most of all, there was no smoking gun. No one saw
Dhillon give Parvesh a pill.

The biggest weakness in the Crown's case was that jurors
didn't know the real Dhillon. They were not permitted to hear the
extent of his abuse of Parvesh and her family, that he engaged in
insurance fraud, married three women in India, allegedly killed

one of them, as well as his newborn twins. All the jury needed was "reasonable doubt" to acquit him. There seemed plenty of it in late July 2001 in that Kitchener courtroom. Still, Warren Korol refused to believe Dhillon would get off. The system had given their case body blows but, paradoxically, Korol's faith in the system remained. Dhillon had to be convicted. Had to.

Russell Silverstein still had a crucial decision to make, his biggest of the trial. Should he put his client on the stand? The defense lawyer's ethic says you put your client in the witness box if the client wants to speak—and Dhillon wanted to. At the same time, the lawyer is obligated to provide the best defense possible—and if that means the client should not testify, lobby hard against it. There was risk in letting Dhillon testify. He was unpredictable. But perhaps the risk of not putting him on was too great, Silverstein thought. He weighed the pros and cons. In a circumstantial murder case, the lawyer's rule of thumb is you put the accused on the stand or else the jury will not believe his claim to innocence. The juror wants the accused to be able to get up there and say without blinking, "I could never kill my beloved wife, and I did not do it."

On the other hand, Silverstein could have made an argument to the jury that his client, while innocent, would not testify because of his problems with the English language, and his emotion over the case. O.J. Simpson had been kept from the stand by his lawyers, even though he reportedly wanted to address the jury to proclaim his innocence. Silverstein felt the odds favored putting the accused man on the stand. Dhillon would testify.

On Wednesday, July 18, Dhillon entered the witness box and swore to tell the truth.

"Mr. Dhillon," Silverstein began, "how old are you, sir?" ("*Tu-haadi umar kinnie hey?*")

"Nineteen fifty-nine."

"You were born in 1959?"

"Yes."

"And you were born in India?"

"Yes."

Silverstein walked Dhillon through his arrival in Canada in 1981, the early years with Parvesh. Dhillon testified that the money

paid out for her life insurance went to his daughters and to the
local Sikh temple. As a matter of necessity—because the Crown
might bring it up—Silverstein promptly introduced Dhillon's one
criminal conviction.

"I understand, sir, that in November of 1992 you were convicted of assault and received a fine of $300?"

"Yes."

The details of the conviction—his assault on Parvesh—were
ruled inadmissible. Silverstein did not let his mention of it hang in
the air. Assault? Against whom? The jury would have no time to
think about it. But it wasn't the end of the issue. Tony Leitch saw an
opening. With the jury out of the room, he asked Judge Glithero to
allow the Crown to tell the jury about the assault. The defense had
introduced the issue of Dhillon's character, Leitch argued, when citing
the accused's good deeds with Parvesh's life insurance money. It was
fair game for the Crown to respond. Let the Crown introduce the
assault on Parvesh to disabuse the jury of the notion that Dhillon
has redeemable qualities. Glithero denied the request. It would
be prejudicial to Dhillon, he ruled, to allow the jury to know that
Dhillon beat the woman he was accused of killing.

The trial resumed before the jury.

"What were your and Parvesh's plans with respect to having
more children?" Silverstein asked, leading Dhillon to the theory
of accidental poisoning.

"She wanted a boy."

"How about you? How did you feel?"

"It's always with hers and my consent. Yes, I wanted too."

"Okay. Well, first of all, did you want to have more children?
You personally?"

"Yes. But she wanted a boy."

"Okay. But did you have a preference as between having a boy
or having another girl? You personally?"

"To me, girl and a boy, it's God's gift."

"How did Parvesh feel?"

"She was saying, 'If I am carrying a girl, I'll go for an abortion.'"

They went through Parvesh's reproductive history. Harpreet
was born. Then Parvesh had a miscarriage or abortion. Then Aman

was born. Then Parvesh had an abortion in India. Dhillon said his wife took prescription medication to help with headaches. And in order to conceive a boy, she prayed and fasted.

"Now, Mr. Dhillon," Silverstein continued, "did you ever see Parvesh eat anything with a view to having a boy?"

"Yes. Once or twice, I saw her eating *desi* medication."

"What does *desi* medication mean?"

"I don't know. There was some plants, and I don't believe in that stuff. It's some herbal stuff."

"Did you ask her why she was taking it?"

"Yeah. And then she said, 'It's female stuff.' Women know all about the female stuff."

"Did you ask her where she was getting it?"

"Yes, she said: 'It is none of your business. It's female stuff.' She has a container and she has something, grinder—a grinder thing in that, and she used to take that teaspoon with hot water."

"And what was she using to grind this material, whatever it was?"

"We have a marble mortar and pestle. She was using that."

In his usual seat, front right, Warren Korol felt his stomach churn. Just like that, the jury now had reason to believe that Parvesh accidentally poisoned herself using homeopathics. It wasn't fair; Dhillon had never mentioned homeopathics or "*desi* medicine." He was lying. But the Crown could not use Dhillon's contradictory statements on the issue because the judge had declared large portions of the evidence from police questioning out of order. Korol was furious. He felt an urge to stand up in court and blurt out the truth. But maybe there was another way. He thought back to the interview Dhillon did with Ben Chin with Toronto's CityTV; Korol had urged Chin to ask Dhillon about homeopathics, get him denying it on the record. He resolved to review the tape and edit the relevant portion for the Crown.

Silverstein continued with the homeopathic line of questions. "Did you tell the doctors or nurses at the hospital anything about the herbal medicine that you had seen Parvesh take beginning some time in December?"

"No."

"And why not?"

"I thought people take that and it's not harmful. I didn't think it was important. I thought it was just an herb."

To further bolster his theory, Silverstein later called an expert in Punjabi culture to testify that women commonly take homeopathics in order to conceive a male. There are ads in Punjabi newspapers advertising remedies that will give parents a boy. And strychnine, in minute quantities, is used in some of those homeopathics. The expert said it was not uncommon for Sikh women to be secretive and superstitious when it comes to their desire for a male child. The Crown countered with testimony from Dundas naturopath Paul Saunders, who said minute levels of strychnine are sometimes recommended for complaints of impotence, constipation, urinary incontinence, and hangovers, but that strychnine is never used in connection with female fertility.

Silverstein took Dhillon through the day Parvesh died. Grocery shopping, lunch in the house, just the two of them. The girls came home after school, Parvesh prepared a snack. She needed to lie down, she had a splitting headache, felt dizzy. And then, said Dhillon, the next thing he knew she was on the floor.

"She was saying: 'My heart is going. My heart is going. I'm dying. I'm dying.' I tried to give her mouth-to-mouth resuscitation." In the witness box, Dhillon rubbed one eye as though wiping a tear, and took a drink of water. "She started to shake," he continued. "I can show you."

Dhillon climbed down from the witness box and walked back across the courtroom to the accused's cubicle. He lay down and stretched his legs across the length of a bench. He pretended his body was rigid, and started to shake, and arched his back, and said: "I'm dying! I'm dying!"

Earlier witnesses had given confusing and contradictory testimony as to the symptoms Parvesh had exhibited. Now Dhillon, the man accused of killing her, was making things clear. His graphic—and accurate—portrayal of the symptoms of death by strychnine was helping the case against him. Silverstein took just under five hours to question Dhillon. Now it was Brent Bentham's turn to cross-examine. If Dhillon hoped Bentham would be short with him, he was dead wrong. Bentham, as he did with all witnesses, moved methodically, deliberately, authoritatively. It was as though Bentham wanted to give the jury time to get to know Dhillon. Trap the accused on the stand as long as possible, keep him there like a fish flopping in the open air, leave him there to dry and rot. Bentham kept him on the stand for two and a half days.

CHAPTER 23 ~ CROCODILE TEARS

Brent Bentham broke the mold in several ways. Conventional wisdom says lawyers love to talk. But Bentham had a taciturn nature, rarely chatted with reporters, and even friends and colleagues were kept at arm's length about his personal life. To those who did not know him, he came across as serious, introverted. In private, he had a keen, though gentlemanly, sense of humor.

While Bentham never offered theories on the matter, perhaps his demeanor was a reaction to the figure cut by his father, a man Brent deeply admired. "Dynamic" was the word he used to describe his dad. John Bentham was an RCMP investigator and, toward the end of his career, a spokesman for the Mounties. Brent moved around Alberta as his father shuttled between field offices before finally settling in Ottawa in the 1970s. He wanted to follow in his father's footsteps. As a student he worked a summer in the Yukon, assisting investigators. It was probably the most enjoyable job he ever had. But full-time jobs in the RCMP were hard to come by. So he pursued the study of law.

Bentham pursued his calling relentlessly. There was no other conclusion to draw than he loved his work. He certainly was ambitious, but not in the conventional way: his wasn't an ambition to gain fame; it was an ambition to win, lock criminals away, do his job. Journalists tried in vain to pry information from him. He couldn't see what speaking with a reporter would accomplish in terms of winning the case.

As for personal acclaim, Bentham seemed to have not a kernel of ego. Money didn't concern him, either. A lawyer who has been in the Crown attorney's office for several years can apply for Level 3 status, which carries with it a substantial increase in pay. All the lawyer has to do is fill out the form. Bentham could never be bothered. He laughed at the notion of vying for a spot on the bench as a judge. He would be eminently qualified. But he liked his plain Crown attorney's black robe just fine. All that mattered was his work and his family. Three children. He coached minor hockey and soccer, was a Scout leader. He was unabashedly devoted to his kids, a point that Tony Leitch delighted in making to courtroom staff the day after the Grey Cup, the championship game in Canadian pro football.

"Okay, get this," Leitch announced. "Yesterday was the Grey Cup. And, while that was on TV, Mr. Bentham was at the theater watching *Harry Potter*." He turned to Bentham. "What were you *thinking*?"

The staffers chuckled. Bentham bowed his head, forcing a grin. It all made him sound like a saint. Nobody is, of course. But, whatever Bentham's weaknesses were, he never revealed them. He accepted cases without question, never complaining that one was less interesting than another. He rarely said a bad word about anyone. He had one other passion. Hockey. He played late-night games at Eastwood Arena with guys from all walks of life. The others probably didn't even know what he did for a living. One could imagine Bentham glorying in the anonymity of the rink, two teams, no individuals.

Bentham had been at his best in the winter of 2001, the day the first Dhillon trial crumbled into a mistrial. The impostor witnesses, everything unraveling, the detectives furious. Kevin Dhinsa had watched Bentham react with scholarly detachment. The prosecutor's mind silently processing the options, then providing directions to the detectives. A double murder case was suddenly at risk and Bentham, the lead Crown, talked with the same urgency as if they were discussing lunch plans. Incredible, Dhinsa thought. The detective was a movie buff. He assigned Bentham a role in the imaginary movie of the Dhillon story. Henceforth, the detective decided, the prosecutor would be known as "Cool Hand Bentham."

* * *

In the wood-trimmed Kitchener courtroom, Bentham rose from his seat and approached Sukhwinder Dhillon. He would not play with Dhillon. His personality would not allow it. He would not show the jury any wink or nod, would not give Dhillon the chance to come up for air. From his first question, in his deep, studious baritone, Bentham attacked Dhillon's character, subtly but powerfully.

"When did you marry Parvesh?" he asked. The translator repeated the question to Dhillon, "*Tuhaada Parvesh naal vihah kadon hoia see?*"

"1983," Dhillon answered in English.

"What date?" Bentham replied.

"I don't remember the date. It was second month, fifth, or I don't know."

"You don't remember the date that you got married?"

"Not…I…I can't read Punjabi. I can't read English."

"I'm not asking you to read. I'm asking you to remember the date that you got married."

"No."

"No, you don't know?"

"No…We got married second month in 1983. You can count."

"Well, do you agree with me that you were married 12 years?"

"Yes."

"Is it fair to say Parvesh worked pretty hard all her life?"

"We all do that. Indian people, Punjabi people, we all do that."

"And … and you're putting yourself in that category as a person who has worked hard all his life?"

"Yes. Yes. I work hard, too."

"She did those difficult jobs because she cared about the family?"

"Yes. It's in our culture that husband and wife, they both work hard."

"And again, you're putting yourself in that category as a person who works hard?"

"Yes."

So many cards showing Dhillon's dark character had been taken away from Bentham. He needed to play around the edges as much as possible, let the jurors read between the lines. The next day, Thursday, he poked holes in Dhillon's claim that he continued to suffer pain from a 1991 factory accident that left him on worker's compensation.

"You just tell us when you're having some difficulty standing," Bentham said.

"Yes. Even now I'm standing, I have pain. I cannot stand for very long."

"For the record, you've been standing up to this point in the day giving your evidence, haven't you?"

"Yes."

"And in fact, you put on a demonstration for the jury where you were able to lie across the bench in the prisoner's box with your head resting on the one edge, weren't you?"

"Yes, I did."

"And you got back up and you walked back up into the witness box?"

"Yes."

"I didn't see any pain on your face."

Dhillon had grossed more than $38,000 in 1994–95 from his fledgling used-car dealership according to his accountant, Bentham, noted. Yet he had reported zero income on his tax form that year and failed to tell the Workers' Compensation Board, which was paying him benefits for being unable to work, about his income.

"I was just starting out selling cars and I didn't know if I was making any money or not," Dhillon replied. "I can't remember. I must have forgot to report it."

"I'm going to suggest that money is more important to you than truth and honesty," Bentham said.

Next, Bentham focused on Dhillon's behavior following the death of Parvesh. He accused Dhillon of crying crocodile tears but of feeling no real grief.

"You went to India, you would have us believe, because you were devastated by the death of your wife. And yet, within three weeks of your arrival, you were engaged to a 21-year-old woman."

"Yes, they were forcing me, saying: 'You have to get married right away. You need somebody to take care of your girls. Who will look after the children?'"

"You picked her, first of all, because she was young and you thought she could bear you a son, something Parvesh had been unable to do."

"That was in God's hands," Dhillon said.

"And you had sex with Sarabjit Brar?"

"Yes. You do that. She was my wife, and after marriage, yes."

"Right. And at the time, obviously, you had sex with her more than once up until the time that you left India on May 9?"

"Must have. Yes."

"An attractive, 21-year-old woman?"

"People were ready to give me 18- and 16-year-olds, too. It's not a sin."

"And so you had the pick of anybody you wanted?"

"I'm telling you that I didn't get married because of sex. I got married because of my girls."

"And when you had sex with Sarabjit, were you able to take your mind off the tragedy of the death of Parvesh that had happened a mere two months earlier?"

"How can I forget that? Even today, I didn't—"

"Right."

"I didn't forget. You get married. You can't forget."

"Even though within two months, you're having sex with a 21-year-old woman after the death of your wife of 12 years?"

Dhillon said that some people in his culture get married the same day as a spouse's funeral. His message was clear: it's a different world; you don't understand. But Bentham would not let this cultural relativism pass, scolding Dhillon as though he were a rebellious teen. "I'm not asking about some people. I'm asking about you—was your wedding day a happy day for you?"

"Yes. Above the surface, yes."

"We saw, at length, the videotape. Are you telling us that you were able to hide your true emotions at the wedding?"

"Yes. Even now, it's hidden. You don't know—nobody knows what's inside me."

"I'll agree with that," Bentham said.

"Yeah. When someone looks at me, they say, 'Yeah, you look fine.' But they don't know whether I have hurt inside or not."

"Right. I'm going to suggest to you that you did a very good job in that wedding video of masking your supposed devastation at the tragic loss of your wife."

"Yes."

Bentham closed his questioning of Dhillon by tackling the homeopathic medication theory head-on. He had to deflate the notion that Parvesh took homeopathics and perhaps poisoned herself by accident. He asked Dhillon about his conversation with Dhinsa on March 17, 1997, as his house was being searched.

"Did Detective Dhinsa ask you to tell him where the *kuchila* was in your house? Did he ask you that?"

"I don't remember. I've never heard the word *kuchila* from him."

"I'm suggesting to you that he asked you where they could find *kuchila* in your home."

"Maybe he asked. He was writing. I wasn't writing."

"I'm not asking you about what he was writing. I'm asking what he asked you."

"I don't remember whether he asked me or not. I've never heard about *kuchila*."

"Your Honor," Bentham said to Glithero, "at this point I would like to address a matter with you. Perhaps it would be beneficial if we were to take an early lunch."

With the jury absent, Bentham asked Glithero to allow him to use a statement from Dhillon in his first interview with Korol and Dhinsa in October 1996. At that time, the detectives had specifically asked Dhillon about *kuchila*. Silverstein objected to introducing the statement. But Glithero sided with Bentham. With the jury back, Bentham confronted Dhillon with his lie.

"Detective Dhinsa told you that *kuchila* is a name for strychnine back on October 8, 1996?"

"Yes. I heard that from him."

"And I'm going to suggest to you that on March 17, 1997, you knew the police were searching your home for poison."

"Yes."

"And you understood that they suspected you at that time, March 17, 1997, of poisoning Parvesh?"

"I didn't give anything to Parvesh."

"But police thought you did."

"Police?"

"Yes."

"Yes."

"And you mentioned nothing to Detective Dhinsa about your wife taking *desi* medicine?"

"It was not in my mind, so I didn't say anything."

Bentham's message to the jury was clear: Dhillon knew he was suspected of poisoning his wife. If Parvesh really had taken homeopathics, he likely would have told Dhinsa about it. And then Bentham produced the ace card, the videotape that Warren Korol had brought him, the relevant portions spliced together. It was the TV interview with Ben Chin. Silverstein objected to playing the tapes for the jury. The judge sided with Bentham. Korol grinned.

"I don't know his name," Dhillon said in the witness box. "He was a Chinese guy."

"You talked to Mr. Chin for about 45 minutes in total."

"Yes."

"And you knew you were being filmed at the time."

"Yes. They told me they were making some movie."

Bentham played two tapes of interviews with Chin. Dhillon said nothing on tape about Parvesh taking homeopathic medicine.

"There was an opportunity for you to tell Mr. Chin that your wife, Parvesh, was taking *desi* medication. An opportunity to tell the public, not a police officer, that your wife had been taking *desi* medication."

"Didn't come through my mind."

Bentham said that strychnine was detected in Parvesh's tissue in November 1999.

"You knew that?" he asked.

"Yeah, last year they told me," Dhillon replied.

"That's something you learned in November of 1999. Correct? And it's since then you've come up with this story about Parvesh taking *desi* medication?"

"I didn't make up the story. She told me. I don't know what's in there. I've never seen strychnine. I've never seen *kuchila*."

"But you told no one about this *desi* medication until they found strychnine in her tissue samples?"

"I haven't seen anything like strychnine."

"But you told no one about this until strychnine was detected in her tissue samples?"

"It was never in my mind."

"And you told no one before you learned that strychnine was detected in Parvesh's tissue samples?"

"Maybe I did mention it," Dhillon said, "to somebody that, that ladies, Indian ladies take herbal medicine. I forgot. I don't know."

"Who did you mention it to?"

"I don't know."

"Names. Who?"

"I don't know. It's been four years I've been inside."

"You told no one about *desi* medicine until after you learned Parvesh's tissue samples had strychnine in them."

"In 2000 I was in jail and only then I found out. You think I, I was going to tell that to white people in jail?"

Bentham paused. "Those are my questions, Your Honor."

"They don't understand me, I don't understand them," Dhillon said.

* * *

The closing addresses began on Wednesday, July 25. Silverstein had to go first. Sukhwinder Dhillon was, Silverstein conceded, a flawed man. Not the best husband. Not the brightest man. But he did not kill his wife. And that's all that matters. Silverstein acknowledged his client lied in order to receive an inflated GST claim. He lied to the Workers' Compensation Board. That didn't make him a killer.

"It would be tempting to conclude that because Mr. Dhillon has a history of dishonesty, his testimony is all false and when he says he didn't kill his wife, it means he must have. Please don't say, 'Well, he lied to the WCB, so he is a big fat liar. He tells us he didn't kill his wife. Well, because he's a liar, we don't believe that.' Not everybody who cheats WCB, who has done some dishonest things, is a killer." Making such a leap, he said, "is a most specious and improper way to approach this case."

The financial motive? Not strong enough. Dhillon was not in desperate need of cash. He stood to gain from her death, the lawyer continued, "and I suppose we all stand to gain from the death of anyone for whom there is life insurance where we're the beneficiary. But not everybody who has insurance on one another runs around killing each other. Sure. Sure. He was $200,000 better off after her death. But that's it. That's the extent of the evidence of motive in this case. And when he got the money, he didn't go to Hawaii or buy a fast car. He deposited it in accounts for his daughters."

Parvesh may not have even died from strychnine poisoning, Silverstein told the jury. She had a troubled neurological history and might have died from a brain hemorrhage. Parvesh also took homeopathic remedies. She might have accidentally killed herself. Contamination: Parvesh's tissue had been stored at the CFS on a shelf beside the samples of strychnine police had brought back from India. He held up the clear plastic bag holding the strychnine samples.

"It sat beside the tissue blocks in a refrigerator. And a technician opened the bag and then leaves it in the fridge, unsealed. And there it sits for two years, that's 27 months this sample of *kuchila* is in the same toxicology section as the Parvesh Dhillon samples.... Only a fool would suggest that the laboratory findings wouldn't have an effect on your thinking. But the findings are not reliable. There's no doubt that strychnine was found in Parvesh's tissue samples. The issue, however, ladies and gentlemen, is how did it get there?"

He paused. Silverstein always tried to engage the jury in a closing statement, to avoid the legalese, to speak to them in a way anybody could understand.

"Contamination is a funny thing. It's like trying to prove a negative. I mean, it's very difficult to do. If I could prove contamination, well, wouldn't that be wonderful? What I want to show you is how unreliable this finding is.... This is not the *Exxon Valdez* oil spill or dropping a quart of milk on the kitchen floor. We are talking about a trillionth of a gram of strychnine."

He turned his attention to Dhillon's reaction to his wife's death. Bentham had portrayed the behavior as callous.

"There's a claim by Mr. Bentham that Mr. Dhillon ran off to India so he could—let's see if I understand this correctly—so that he could have sex, could find a young girl to have sex with. Well, does it make sense to spend money on three return airline tickets to India just to have sex? You don't have to fly to India to have sex. Not if you live in Hamilton."

Silverstein was almost finished. Had he planted doubt in the minds of the jurors? He appealed to their curiosity, their sense of the possible. Do not decide with emotion, based on a marriage videotape, or Dhillon's fraudulent finances. Play "medical detective," he said, to come to your own conclusions about contamination of the samples. Dispassionately consider the differences between Sikh and Western culture when it comes to marriage. Do not impose your own Western values and emotions.

"You know, the Crown would have a better chance of trying to prove beyond a reasonable doubt that she killed herself. I mean, that's the more likely scenario. Oh, Mr. Bentham will say, 'Ignore all the doubts, the holes in the case. Look at Mr. Dhillon. He is a tax evader! Mr. Dhillon, he filed a false claim to the WCB!' Yeah. Killed his wife because he had insurance on her. Beyond a reasonable doubt. Ladies and gentlemen, you are all immensely more intelligent than that, and your common sense must scream out that that's just not so. And then factor in the whole question of whether she even died of strychnine poisoning. You see, you have to worry about that, too. And you've got all this medical evidence and all these doctors saying, 'No, it could have been this and it could have been that,' and you have the tests with all their attendant problems. Ladies and gentlemen, you've heard it all. You've heard the evidence. Mr. Dhillon didn't kill Parvesh Dhillon. Thank you."

CHAPTER 24 ~ SECRET HANDSHAKE

Brent Bentham and Tony Leitch had long before started crafting the closing address, building the portrait of Dhillon they wanted the jury to see. The night before his close, Bentham huddled with Leitch in a hotel down the road from the courthouse. Leitch wrote out portions of the address, touching on medical and forensic evidence. Later that evening, Bentham sat at a desk in the hotel room, alone with his thoughts. So much about Dhillon had been left unsaid. The jury knew so little about the evil he had done. He had to hit the right notes to linger in the jurors' minds. He worked late, writing out his thoughts, dressed in a T-shirt and boxer shorts. Bentham had Leitch's typed passages in front of him. He wrote out his sections in pen, in point form.

There had been precious few witnesses who took the stand and spoke on behalf of Parvesh, who could talk about her life. Her parents, Hardial and Hardev, had passed away in the years following their daughter's death, but before Dhillon's trial. The truth. The truth. It came to him. The clock showed 2 a.m. He turned out the light and turned in, eight hours before he was to rise in court to try to put Sukhwinder Dhillon in jail for life.

On Wednesday, May 16, the jury entered the room and took their seats. Judge Glithero spoke.

"Mr. Bentham?"

"Thank you," he said, rising from his chair in his black robe and moving to the lectern. "Good morning, members of the jury."

"Good morning," several replied in concert.

First, he built the entire case against Dhillon once more, brick by brick: the medical evidence, the motive, the circumstances. Russell Silverstein had been the performer in court, working the floor, making his points with intonation and hand gestures, ad-libbing, making conversation. Bentham stood behind the lectern like a professor, his serious voice intoning on issues of law and fact. But he also personalized the case. Five minutes into his address, Bentham reintroduced the jurors to Parvesh Dhillon— her life, her work, who she was. He urged them to examine the wedding portrait of Dhillon and Sarabjit, the young woman he had arranged to marry in India within a few weeks of Parvesh's death and an innocent victim of his schemes.

"Ask yourselves," he said, "does he appear to be a crushed spirit devastated by the death of his wife?" He reminded the jurors that within minutes of Parvesh collapsing in convulsions, and before the ambulance had arrived, Dhillon had phoned two people and lamented that he was "ruined," and that his children would no longer have a mother.

"In my submission, ladies and gentlemen, these are the words of Parvesh Dhillon's killer who, being fully aware of the lethal properties of the poison he has tricked her into taking, is now prematurely pronouncing her death."

Bentham attacked the theory that Parvesh had accidentally poisoned herself with homeopathic remedies. That suggestion was an "eleventh-hour smoke screen" put up by Dhillon, who had never mentioned the remedies to anyone until after strychnine was found in Parvesh's tissue samples almost five years after her death. Bentham used Leitch's words to attack Silverstein's suggestion that the tissue samples had been contaminated in the CFS laboratory. Rather than quickly dismissing the notion, he hammered on it, trying to overwhelm any doubt. Bentham said the precautions taken to prevent contamination of the samples were like "a wall." His assault on the contamination argument was not unlike the "magic bullet" theory in the assassination of John F. Kennedy as he ridiculed Silverstein's argument.

"You must ask yourself, members of the jury, in assessing the likelihood of contamination, how the strychnine products escaped the interior drug lab, then the exterior Ziploc bag, made their way to a separate part of the refrigerator, through the box and through the plastic bag that contained Parvesh Dhillon's tissue samples. Ask yourself how, if this unlikely event did occur, the ethanol sprays used to remove surface contamination failed, how the fresh gloves used to handle the samples failed, how the clean bench failed, how the clean scalpel used to cut the tissues failed."

It was "the product of someone's imagination" to suggest trained scientists were spreading contaminants around a fridge.

Sukhwinder Dhillon, he said, has "lied to you repeatedly throughout his testimony." He returned to Dhillon's relationship with Parvesh, and countered the notion that Dhillon's actions were explainable in terms of Indian traditions when it comes to marriage after a spouse dies. Culture, Bentham said, is not the point. "Regardless of what culture you are from, I am going to ask you to judge the accused's conduct based on your own common sense and common human decency."

Bentham mentioned Dhillon's double motive, his yearning to have a son and another, younger wife. He spoke of Sarabjit. The defense had argued that Dhillon didn't need to fly to India just to find sex, that he could have found it in Hamilton.

"I'm going to ask you to assess the likelihood of the accused finding an attractive 21-year-old woman in Hamilton willing to have a relationship with him and, in my submission, his chances were slim to none."

Bentham had laid out his arguments. Now was the time to shine a light on the path he hoped the jurors would follow. "Let me summarize in the following fashion, members of the jury." Bentham, the quiet intellectual, now made the leap from rational argument to the emotional, opening his own heart, "Cool Hand Bentham" catching the jury and spectators off guard.

"One of the best measures of any society is the value it places upon human life," he began. "That is what distinguishes Canada from other countries where life is cheap. In our society, we believe that life is precious. Trials like this one protect our society and preserve those cherished values." *Unspoken message: This case is about more than a sudden death in Hamilton. Do not shrink from the larger philosophical issue, juror. This is about life—our way of life. Yours, mine, our families.*

Bentham looked at his point-form final notes scribbled in pen and stepped out from behind the lectern, facing the jury, as though embracing them. *See me. Hear what I have to say to you.* "I ask you, members of the jury, who carries the torch for Parvesh Dhillon?" *Torch: sudden, active, hot imagery. A gentle, beautiful woman, destroyed. Who picks up the flame for her? What is your answer, juror?*

Emotion welled inside Bentham but he kept it at bay. The words went through his head: keep it even. Even but forceful. He was in the moment, with no sense of himself. There was only focus. Bentham posed the question to the jury again. "Who speaks for Parvesh Dhillon, about her life, and about her final moments?" *For she cannot speak. She was silenced when her face froze in the death grin.* "It is not her parents. They are dead. It is certainly not the accused. And sadly, it is not even her two children, who seem to have had their memories of their mother dimmed." Bentham's voice was still serious and articulate but jurors, accustomed to his ice-cool manner, could hear the passion in his tone. He paused.

"The answer to the question, members of the jury, is that the truth speaks for Parvesh Dhillon." *The truth, the truth. The truth speaks for Parvesh Dhillon. That is your answer. You, members of the jury, you speak for her. You are the truth. Tell it.*

In his front-row seat behind the Crown's table, Warren Korol had sat stoically, the blue eyes narrowed with intensity, watching the case of his life being wrapped up in one speech. He was nervous, as if watching his own son give a valedictory address. And now the homicide detective swallowed hard. His eyes became moist. A shiver ran down his back. The truth speaks for Parvesh Dhillon: the line got to Korol, hit right in his soul. He would feel the same emotion years later, whenever he recalled the words. Brent had him with that line. Always would. And now Bentham had the jurors. One of them wiped a tear from her cheek.

"And the truth is that she was a hard-working, quiet, industrious person dedicated to her two children whom she cared for deeply. The truth is that she was coldly murdered by the accused who administered her a fatal dose of strychnine poison. And the truth is that in contrast to the 12 years of her life that she gave the accused, she was murdered by the accused for nothing more than to satisfy his insatiable greed. And therefore, you should find him guilty of the planned and deliberate murder of Parvesh Dhillon. I thank you for your attention."

* * *

Judge Glithero addressed the jury one last time, asked them to
retire and render a verdict. The jury of seven women and five men
deliberated eight hours but couldn't reach a decision. They were
sequestered overnight at a Kitchener hotel. Bentham, Leitch, Korol,
and Dhinsa went for dinner, then gathered in Leitch's hotel room
to watch a movie. There was little to say to one another about the
case. They were numb from the trial, tired of speculating what
might happen. The game was over. They watched *Enemy at the
Gates*, which depicted the bloody battle of Stalingrad. They had
grown so close through the journey, they felt like part of a hockey
team that had experienced all the ups and downs.

Before turning out the light that night, Korol lay in bed
reading.

*The road to Darkley passes through the border lands of County
Armagh, where the gray stone bridges and disused factory chimneys
add a further touch of desolation to the landscape in winter.*

He flipped the page. Korol was reading a book called *INLA:
Deadly Divisions*, an account of terrorism in Ireland. He was taking courses at McMaster University, working toward a bachelor
of arts degree. It would be the first university degree in his family.
Pursuing higher education later in life gave Korol an appetite for
more. Going to school, one night a week in winter, two nights a
week in summer, became Korol's night out, his passion. But on
the evening before a possible verdict, he was reading to distract
himself. There was so much the jury didn't know. The jurors will
be furious when they learn the whole truth, he reflected. Parvesh,
Ranjit, Kushpreet, the twins.

*The area is full of epitaphs of one kind or another. A few miles from
Darkley in a shabby little bus shelter is written: There are two solutions
in Northern Ireland. One is to get down on both knees and pray. The
other is to get down on both knees and shoot the other man.*

The case had taken so much from him there was nothing
left to feel. The anger, the sick feeling in his stomach as Dhillon

lied on the stand, the what-ifs in his head. Dhillon wasn't just a criminal, wasn't just cruel and a liar. He was an evil man. Would the jury see the same thing he did? They would need to feel it, to have an instinct for it, because they didn't know the whole story, not as he did. How could they truly see Dhillon, if they didn't have the whole picture?

Focus on the page.

Revolutionaries are dead men on leave.

It was the epitaph written for a pair of Irishmen murdered in a hotel. Korol grinned. A good line. He turned out the light.

* * *

The next morning, Justice C. Stephen Glithero drove 25 minutes from his home in Cambridge to Kitchener. He passed picturesque Galt Country Club, the golf course along the river where he played, drove through the old village of Blair. The sun labored to burn off the early morning mist that drifted over the Grand River. As they had for 10 weeks, Russell Silverstein and his junior counsel Apple Newton-Smith battled traffic on the highway out of Toronto. Korol, Dhinsa, Bentham, and Leitch walked from the Kitchener Sheraton Hotel to court. Glithero entered the courtroom. Everyone rose. The lawyers and clerks bowed. The judge took his seat; everyone in the room followed his lead.

The jury entered. Glithero welcomed them. Once jurors begin deliberation, they only return to court if they have a question or need a clarification. The jurors wanted one more look at a court transcript that focused on the symptoms of Parvesh's collapse. They wanted to review testimony given by Gurbachan Dhaliwal and her son, Darshan. Both had come to the house and had seen Parvesh in agony. But during the trial, when the Dhaliwals were called as Crown witnesses, both turned hostile on the stand, recanting their recollection of Parvesh Dhillon's symptoms after her collapse. Tony Leitch had cross-examined them, bringing into evidence their previous statements under oath that pointed to the strychnine poisoning symptoms Parvesh suffered. Transcripts in hand, the jurors went back to their deliberations.

The four lawyers pushed out from their tables, all trying to resist the temptation to guess what the jury was thinking. Why had they asked that particular question? What could it mean? Bentham, Leitch, Korol, and Dhinsa returned to the hotel to wait. It was all they could do. Wait. The sky was now an expanse of deep blue, the heat climbing by noon. Silverstein and Newton-Smith sat outside the courthouse playing Scrabble on a board laid in front of them on the front steps, shaded by trees, like two kids killing time at recess. They often played Scrabble at times like this, sorting through the jumble of letters to find combinations that made sense. Silverstein usually won. Newton-Smith consoled herself that it didn't necessarily mean he was a better player. How long has the jury been out now? Is the next minute going to be a good minute, or a bad minute? Hope for the best, she thought. Not guilty. That would be music to her ears. Guilty? It could happen. Be prepared for it.

Back at the Sheraton, Bentham, Leitch, Dhinsa, and Korol played the jury game, too. They knew it was nerve-racking, but they couldn't help it. They sat in the room, the lawyers in their black vests and matching pants. Korol and Dhinsa's suit jackets lay neatly folded on the bed. What was the jury thinking? Surely all 12 of them saw through Dhillon. The jury had deliberated for eight hours the day before. They were still at it. It could mean at least one juror is unsure of Dhillon's guilt. All it takes is one of the 12 to waver. The stakes had been so high and the emotions so pitched that, mid-trial, Bentham's wife, Rebecca, had given each of them a copy of Rudyard Kipling's poem "If": "If you can meet with Triumph and Disaster/And treat those two impostors just the same ..." She had intended it as inspiration, but the poem is about handling defeat like a man, standing tall no matter what others say. The Dhillon verdict was in such doubt, the poem now seemed useful advice.

Outside the courthouse, Apple Newton-Smith's cellphone rang.

"Yes?"

"Hello, Miss Newton-Smith," said the caller. "You are requested back at court, please."

"Is it a verdict or a question?"

"Verdict."

Her heart raced. She found Silverstein. The two of them hurried back into the building to their office and retrieved their gowns. Leitch's cellphone rang, too, the sound instantly putting an end to any conversation in the hotel room. He cradled the phone in his big hand. He said nothing at first. Then he turned to the others.

"It's in."

Two words, the last to be spoken among the group for what would seem an eternity. The four men walked briskly out of the room and rode the elevator in silence, said nothing on the way down, then emerged into the heat and sunshine. It was 2 p.m., the middle of the workday in downtown Kitchener, but it seemed as if there was not one car on the street, not one person on the sidewalk. They were oblivious to their surroundings. The sidewalk gleamed white. They all wore dark sunglasses as they marched, two in front, two behind, polished dark shoes clicking on the concrete. They continued the march, briefly along Benton Street and up Frederick Street, past King, Duke, toward Weber. The spire of Trinity United Church poked into the sky in the distance. It was just a five-minute walk but it seemed to take an eternity. The court building came into view. They marched quietly up the hill. Hill? There is a very slight incline along Frederick Street, but for the four men it was now a symbol, the last mountain to climb. The Dhillon case loomed so large in their lives, it occupied their collective psyche. They would all think about it often in years to come, the silent march up the hill. They passed through the yawning courthouse entrance, up the stairs, click-click-click, went through the dark wooden doors, down to the amphitheater floor of the courtroom.

* * *

Sukhwinder Dhillon was brought into the courtroom, wearing the used blue sports coat Korol and Dhinsa had provided him in an effort to remedy his odor the interpreter had complained about throughout the trial. He sat in the prisoner's box. Judge Glithero entered. Stand, bow, sit, straighten ties, deep breath. The jury came in and was seated.

Korol and Dhinsa sat in the front row, staring straight ahead, their arms crossed in expectation. Dhillon stood. It was 4 p.m. Every day of the trial, the jury foreman had worn blue jeans and a T-shirt, looking like a guy on summer holiday. But on this day, he wore a suit. He stood up in the jury box, with nothing in his hands.

"Have your reached a verdict?" Glithero asked.

"Yes, Your Honor," the foreman said. "We find the defendant—guilty, of first degree murder."

Murder. Guilty. *Kasoorvar.* The words rippled through the courtroom like an electric charge. Dhillon's face assumed the look he often wore, a mixture of confusion and surprise, eyes wide but with no tears, no emotion. He instinctively looked for an out. Dhillon knew that one man cannot convict him.

"They can't do that," Dhillon said to his interpreter. "It takes more than one guy." Silverstein asked the judge to canvass the jury. Dhillon waited for one voice to speak out for him.

"Guilty."
"Guilty."
"Guilty."
"Guilty."
"Guilty."
"Guilty."
"Guilty."
"Guilty."
"Guilty."
"Guilty."
"Guilty."
"Guilty."

Judge Glithero pronounced the automatic sentence: life in prison without a chance for parole for 25 years. Korol and Dhinsa still sat with their arms crossed. Stay cool. Korol felt his throat tighten with joy. The previous summer, with the trial still a long way off, Korol and Dhinsa had been told they were being given officers-of-the-month awards for their work on the case. Screw that, Korol had thought at the time. The true test of an investigation is a finding of guilt. Nothing less. Sitting now in court, Dhinsa felt a hand slip covertly under his elbow. It was Korol's. Dhinsa took the warm, thick hand and squeezed it tight. A secret handshake. Korol whispered out of the corner of his mouth.

"Now we can accept that award, partner."

Bentham, Leitch, Korol, and Dhinsa gathered a few minutes later in a small office in the courthouse. Away from the eyes of the public, the bear hugs began. Korol felt his jaw tighten, his eyes dampen, and the tears fall. Proving Dhillon's guilt had been the biggest victory of any of their careers, but he had taken his pound of flesh from all of them. The emotion of the moment hit Brent Bentham with special force. He had suffered his own loss during the meandering course of the trial of his life. His father, RCMP man John Bentham, had been in poor health for some time and died young in Ottawa, at 67. His father would never know that his son gave a stirring closing address that brought jurors to tears and very likely turned the key on Dhillon's fate. It was all too much now. In the little room, with just his friends and no one from the outside to see him, Bentham was the most emotional of them all. Cool Hand Bentham broke down.

CHAPTER 25 ~ MURDER FOR MONEY

Now she got her daddy's car
And she cruised through the hamburger stand now
Seems she forgot about the library
Like she told her old man now

Driving through the streets of Kitchener in Korol's police pool van, the four men sang along to Beach Boys hits, the hymns of summer with universal lyrics that took each back to places and faces of the past. The van windows were down and the hot summer breeze messed their hair as they sang, their voices happily straining to reach falsetto notes.

And with the radio blasting
Goes cruising just as fast as she can now
And she'll have fun-fun-fun
Till her daddy takes the T-bird away
And she'll have fun-fun-fun
Till her daddy takes the T-bird away
Woo-oo! woo-ooo-ooo-ooo-oo!

The afternoon was cloudy, hazy, and hot. The staid Crowns and intense cops wore shorts and T-shirts for the victory celebration. Not far from the exit onto the 401, Korol pulled into a place called Moose Winnooski's, a northern-lodge-themed roadhouse decorated with worn dark wood, Muskoka chairs, screen doors that evoked sounds of a summer cottage when they rattled shut, and signs pointing the directions to northern locales. They soaked up every bit of the over-the-top ambience. It was perfect. Bentham and Leitch gave Korol and Dhinsa a box of cigars each. They opened them right there and smoked the entire box that night, all 25 stogies, indulging themselves. Bentham was the only one of the four who didn't enjoy an occasional cigar. But now, in victory, he surrendered and joined the others in lighting up. They laughed, teased, tossed their money around, their faces glowing with emotion, like giddy college kids celebrating the end of exams, sore from smiling and numbed by the cold beer and shots of liquor they consumed. A few other lawyers drove up from Hamilton, a couple of other cops, too, and joined them on the patio in the still warmth of the evening. The sun sank, vanishing and reappearing between layers of cloud, a perfect burning sphere of gold sandwiched between the darkening purple above, and the hazy sky above the horizon shaded pink, pale blue, and tangerine.

From left: Warren Korol, Brent Bentham, Tony Leitch, Kevin Dhinsa

* * *

The guilty verdict was a conclusion, but not an end. There never seemed to be any end with Dhillon. When Brent Bentham was first assigned to the Dhillon case he was 38 years old. One week after the verdict, he turned 44. There was one more trial to go, for the murder of Ranjit Khela. And were there other skeletons, literally, in Sukhwinder Dhillon's closet?

Pretrial motions in the Ranjit Khela case started November 26, 2001, in Hamilton, with Judge Glithero presiding. It had now been four years since Dhillon had been arrested. He was slimmer, his hair was now silver-gray. It helped soften his look but, in court, his eyes seemed as big as saucers, still possessing a wicked light. He rocked in his seat anxiously, rubbing his beard, looking side to side, behind him, to see who was in the courtroom.

Russell Silverstein and Dhillon wanted to change tactics for round two. They requested a trial by Judge Glithero only, no jury. But the Crown holds the option. Silverstein duly asked the Crown if they would agree. Bentham and Leitch refused.

"There's nothing I can do," he told Dhillon in court.

Dhillon repeated his demand.

"There's nothing more I can do—we'll talk about it later," Silverstein said in a stern whisper.

Leitch, who was acting as the lead prosecutor in Ranjit's murder, rose and launched into the Crown's submissions. Leitch and Bentham weren't about to let the issue of similar-fact evidence die. They wanted to bring the deaths of Ranjit and Parvesh together again, tell the jury that Dhillon had been convicted of killing his wife with strychnine. If Leitch won this argument, Silverstein knew, his client was doomed, again. Leitch was going for broke, trying to get Glithero to break new legal ground. Confession of guilt is accepted as similar-fact evidence. But Dhillon hadn't confessed to killing Parvesh.

"I realize, Your Honor," Leitch said, "that what I'm asking for hasn't been granted in the past." But he noted that Silverstein had "conceded that the cause of death for Mr. Khela is strychnine poisoning. And so, to prove that the accused had access to the murder weapon, the past murder conviction will go toward showing he had that access."

If Glithero allowed the conviction as evidence, it would almost certainly guarantee victory for the Crown. Or would it? Leitch continued: "There is a danger for us, Your Honor. The Parvesh conviction is under appeal by the accused. If he is successful and is acquitted, then a conviction in the Ranjit Khela case, resting on the Parvesh conviction, would mean a new trial. But we are prepared to take that risk because the evidence is strong enough."

Silverstein rose and argued that to allow the conviction as evidence was prejudicial to his client. Moreover, His Honor had already ruled long ago that the two deaths did not belong together. "The death of Parvesh Dhillon remains a distraction," Silverstein said. "Now, it may seem an affront to common sense, to the person on the street who can't believe I would say, 'So what?' regarding Parvesh's death. But what is the meaning of a jury verdict? Legally, it's the opinion of 12 jurors." There was not, he said, "a scintilla of law" to support Leitch.

Court retired for the day. As he had attempted to do in the first Dhillon trial, Silverstein would need to convince jurors it was possible that Khela could have accidentally poisoned himself. Or, if the death was indeed a murder, he wanted to point to other suspects, primarily Lakhwinder Sekhon, Ranjit's wife, the one who had served Ranjit his last meal. She had motive, too. Lakhwinder could collect life insurance benefits. Moreover, their marriage had been stormy. Silverstein planned to enter evidence suggesting that Lakhwinder had reason to hate her late husband, while Dhillon and Ranjit Khela were the closest of friends.

Lakhwinder had plenty to be bitter about, Silverstein would argue. Ranjit had tricked her into signing divorce papers that gave him custody of their son. He had told her that the divorce would be on paper only so that she could marry and sponsor another of his brothers still living in India. Ranjit committed adultery soon after their 1992 marriage. He hit his wife and left her deaf in one ear. Another time, he cut her hair off in a rage. He forced Lakhwinder to have two abortions, the last one just weeks before his death. Silverstein also wanted to argue that other people in the Khela home on Gainsborough Road in east Hamilton had opportunity that June night in 1996 when Ranjit collapsed in strychnine's death grip. Access to the murder weapon? Silverstein would use the Crown's own globe-trotting research against it. The Hamilton police detectives had purchased strychnine in Punjab easily and had brought it into Canada. Well then, in point of fact anyone could do the same. Anyone.

Glithero asked if it was fair to leave the jury with the impression that members of Ranjit's family had special access to strychnine but Dhillon—a convicted strychnine murderer—did not. The judge released his decisions on December 7, 2001. First, the trial would be held in St. Catharines, a city 45 minutes east of Hamilton, because the pools of potential jurors in Hamilton and Kitchener had been contaminated by media coverage. Second, Silverstein would not be permitted to point to an indefinite number of suspects in Ranjit's death. He could use just one alternative suspect: Lakhwinder. As for Tony Leitch's attempt to once again link Parvesh and Ranjit in the trial, Glithero was not persuaded. As at Dhillon's most recent trial, the two deaths would remain separate. The new jury in the Ranjit Khela case would know nothing of Parvesh or the fact that Dhillon had poisoned her.

* * *

On Tuesday, September 24, 2002, less than a week before the trial, Korol, Dhinsa, Leitch, and Bentham met for lunch in downtown Hamilton. They had become friends. And the game was on again. It was Korol's day off. The afternoon was warm and sunny, he wore casual tan pants and a patterned beige short-sleeved shirt that hugged his arms and shoulders. He reached into a kit bag, pulled out a piece of dark plastic, then slid it onto the table. It was a hospital X-ray of what looked like a skull. And that thing wedged in the back?

"Yeah, it's an arrow," Korol said. "The guy took it right in the back of the head." And? "He survived, actually. Doctor said it wedged exactly along the line that he would normally cut if he was performing brain surgery. Any other spot, and the guy's dead. As it is, the doctor just removed it and sewed him up. No problem."

Korol had worked on the case. The victim had been sleeping and his buddy, horsing around with a crossbow, had aimed at him. Whap, right in the head. The buddy fled the scene. It didn't take Korol long to find him. Again he picked up the X-ray. "I thought I'd mount it, put a light behind or something," he said, grinning, as though talking of decorating with a potted plant. "Make a nice conversation piece."

Jury selection began the following week in St. Catharines. About 80 people were in the room before the judge. He told them that in addition to the usual reasons a potential juror might be excused from serving, he wanted anyone who knew details of the Dhillon case through the media to identify themselves. One man said he had read about the case in the papers.

"Will it impact your ability to be impartial?" Glithero said.

"It might, yes," said the man.

"You are excused."

In the age of the Internet, it seemed a naive exercise. Any potential juror could discover the facts about Dhillon simply by typing his name online. All it would take was for a juror to walk one block from the courthouse, sit down at one of seven computer terminals on the second floor of the St. Catharines Public Library—no membership card necessary—type "Sukhwinder Dhillon" into the Google search engine and learn in seconds that Dhillon had been convicted of poisoning his wife last July. The Crown lawyers and the detectives knew how easy that would be. Warren Korol, wearing an emerald-green sport coat he had made to order by Raymond's of India, watched the lawyers pick the jurors.

"We're leaning toward picking anyone that has Internet access," he cracked.

Before the murder trial began, the man whose actions had led to the mistrial had his own day in court. Rai Singh Toor, Kushpreet's father, had been charged with obstruction of justice. Rai entered court, his narrow face ridged with creases. He wore slippers the color of tarnished gold. He kept his bony hands folded over his chest, as though soothing a burning heart. He looked frail, but the black and gray tangle of his beard, black turban, and dark, deep-set eyes gave him an angry, intense aura. The impostors from the mistrial fiasco had been tried and found guilty under the Immigration Act of using false or improperly obtained documents to enter Canada, and of obstructing justice. They had been sentenced to two years in jail and ordered deported to India on their release.

The case against Rai Singh seemed open and shut. John Abrams, a tall, lean defense lawyer, was calling no witnesses. But then nothing to do with Rai Singh ever seemed certain. Korol sat in the gallery, reviewing his notes. A Crown named Toni Skarica prosecuted Rai. John Abrams knew he was in tough. During a break in the proceeding, Skarica noticed a stack of books on the desk in front of Abrams.

"What is that, a stack of Bibles for your client to swear on?" Skarica quipped.

"I fear it will take more than that," Adams shot back.

Rai Singh's trial lasted barely two and a half days. Abrams argued that Rai had not willfully obstructed justice. He was merely trying to make sure the prosecution had all the witnesses it needed. But Skarica said Rai's actions—and more important what resulted from them—were too much. "The accused caused a mistrial in the double murder trial after two and half months of evidence," Skarica said. "And as a direct result of his actions, the Crown lost significant, cogent, compelling evidence on the most serious crime in our justice system."

Justice David Crane rendered his verdict: guilty. Rai Singh's wife, Daljit, and his daughter were in the courtroom. Daljit moaned, then began crying. Rai Singh stared with intensity, but no sorrow.

A few weeks later, Rai Singh appeared again before the judge, this time for sentencing. "Mr. Toor's intention was to commit perjury and arrange others to commit perjury," Crane said. As he spoke, Rai Singh checked the time on the clock on the wall.

The judge sentenced him to three years in prison, after which he would be deported to India. It was the ultimate punishment for a man who so badly wanted to get into Canada. For a case in which coercion or intimidation were not factors, three years was the longest sentence for obstruction of justice in Canadian history. He was led away in shackles. Daljit rose, turned to leave court, and saw Kevin Dhinsa. She pressed the palms of her hands together in the traditional Indian sign of greeting and respect, and nodded her head. Dhinsa looked at her and said nothing.

* * *

Inside the Crown attorneys' temporary war room in the St. Catharines courthouse were the boxes of evidence in the five-year legal battle against Dhillon. They had labels like Ranjit Medical, CFS, Cause of Death, and Forensic Testing. They posted photos on the wall. There was a golf scorecard with a message in blue ink for Brent Bentham that said, "Good luck Brent v. Dhillon." Dhinsa taped a sign on the back of the door: "Brentdeep Singh Bentham/ Anthonywinder Singh Leitch." In contrast to the Crown's clubhouse, and as if to underscore his inherent disadvantage in this second campaign to convince a jury to acquit Dhillon, defense lawyer Russell Silverstein had a modestly proportioned office just outside the courtroom. Silverstein was acting alone, with no junior counsel. Apple Newton-Smith, who had assisted in Dhillon's first trial, had moved on to other cases.

Dhillon entered the courtroom in an olive-colored suit he would wear for the entire trial with a red and black square-patterned shirt underneath. His gray hair was shaved tight at the back and sides to reveal rolls of flesh on the back of his thick neck. It was Monday, October 7, 2002.

Korol, his laptop open, looked out over the top of his half glasses. In his suitcase was a book titled Great American Speeches. He was up to U.S. president Harry S. Truman's address after the dropping of the atomic bomb. At times during breaks in the trial, Dhinsa worked on a Tom Clancy novel or checked his PalmPilot, allowing himself the pleasure of glancing at the photos of his infant son he had saved on the screen.

Silverstein asked that Dhillon's shackles be removed for the trial. Judge Glithero agreed. A police guard unlocked the handcuffs and slid them off, then Dhillon bent forward so he could remove the ankle locks.

"Mr. Silverstein," intoned the court registrar. "Is that Mr. Sukhwinder Dhillon in the box?"

"It is."

"Mr. Sukhwinder Singh Dhillon is accused of committing murder in the first degree of Mr. Ranjit Singh Khela by poisoning. How do you plead?" Translator Neeta Johar started to repeat the question in Punjabi to Dhillon, but he understood.

"Not guilty," he said to her in English, and the translator repeated his plea.

In the prisoner's box, Dhillon rubbed his right thumb with his left, rocked in his seat, looked at the jury with no expression on his face, his eyes vacant. Glithero instructed the jurors. They must find a verdict based on the evidence. The accused, Mr. Dhillon, is presumed innocent until proven guilty. The Crown must prove his guilt beyond a reasonable doubt.

"That means Mr. Dhillon cannot be probably guilty, or likely guilty. Or guilty on a balance of probabilities. Absolute certainty is impossible," but the jury must be sure he committed the murder in order to convict him.

The unspoken issue of Dhillon's track record was the shaky foundation on which the trial rested. The accused was a convicted murderer, but the jurors could not find out about it. "Avoid all media," Glithero told the jury. "Discuss the case with no one." In the American justice system, the judge noted, jurors routinely hear information not germane to the case. The judge asks the jury to disregard this statement or that. "In our system, if there's something you ought not to hear, you won't hear it. Please do not do any research on your own or investigating on your own into this case."

Dhillon bristled as he watched Dhinsa walk to the front of the courtroom, sit at the desk, and aid the computer slide presentation from Tony Leitch. Intentional or not, Dhinsa's presence in front of the jury was a smart move by the Crown. Show the jurors that this is not a case of ganging up on an East Indian. Show that one of the investigators is himself of Indian background. Leitch went through his opening address, recounting Dhillon's dealings with Ranjit Khela and Ranjit's death. Leitch repeated the phrase Bentham had used in Kitchener.

"This is a case of murder for money."

Dhillon mumbled under his breath in Punjabi as Leitch spoke. "This is not an episode of *Law and Order*," continued Leitch, "but I ask that you pay attention as closely as possible."

Russell Silverstein sat back reflectively in his chair, left leg crossed over right, the tip of one arm of his glasses between his teeth. He knew he had a better shot this time. He could offer the jury another suspect. There had been no such alternative in the first trial. And he had a new tactic to convince the jury his client was innocent.

CHAPTER 26 ~ STAR WITNESS

Dhillon's conviction for the murder of Parvesh loomed over the trial every day. As the parade of Crown witnesses took the stand, everyone in the know in court was mindful of what might slip out. Judge Glithero seemed to lean in his seat in anticipation whenever a witness spoke. What if they uttered her name, just by accident? He worried about a mistrial. It could happen any time. Three times during the trial the interpreter asked Glithero to excuse the jury when a Punjabi-speaking witness was testifying. The witness had been speaking about Parvesh and Dhillon. So she did not repeat in English what was being said.

Silverstein, in turn, had to be cautious not to hint at any suspects other than Lakhwinder, or suggest that she had special access to strychnine that Dhillon did not. If he did, the Crown could pounce and introduce the Parvesh murder. Game over. "We need to ensure," Leitch said to Glithero, with the jury out of the room, "that the cat is not let out of the bag—at least not until Mr. Silverstein decides it should be let out."

In the absence of the jury, the debate over disclosing slices of Dhillon's past to the jury was an ongoing one among the lawyers. During a lunch break, Silverstein and Leitch argued about disclosing Dhillon's finances. Dhillon had received more than $200,000 in life insurance after Parvesh's death. Leitch wanted the jury to hear about the payoff, even though he couldn't say exactly where it came from. He wanted to say it was found money, insurance benefit money, cash that Dhillon wasted.

"I want to shine the light on that," Leitch said, "that he pissed this money away."

"I don't see the relevance," Silverstein said.

"I want the whole truth out there," Leitch replied.

Leitch took his case before Glithero.

"The jury should see his financial affairs fully. The bugaboo for us, Your Honor, is we can't say he got the $200,000 from the death of his wife. But it can be described as insurance proceeds, with no attribution. For all we know, the money was from a car accident benefit. The jury needs to see the money moving around, they need to see the greed, and that he had some level of sophistication. The jury needs to know it came from a source that wasn't his business."

The payment would go to prove motive: Dhillon handled money poorly and was desperate for more. So he had Ranjit take out a big life insurance policy, then killed him for it.

Judge Glithero sided with Leitch. The Crown, he said, seeks to paint a picture of Dhillon as an irresponsible, unorganized person who walked into some money and wasted it—"to show, in the vernacular, need and greed." To deny the jury at least some idea of where the money came from, he added, "doesn't paint an accurate picture."

* * *

Russell Silverstein did not question the cause of Ranjit Khela's death, but Tony Leitch called forensic evidence on the issue to show the jury how rare, and tortured, his death was. Poison expert Dr. Michael McGuigan took the stand. He was one of several witnesses in the trial who had also appeared at Dhillon's first murder trial. Leitch asked him how rare strychnine deaths were in his experience.

"How frequently have you encountered cases of strychnine poisoning?"

"In 20 years in Toronto, I saw maybe two or three cases," McGuigan answered.

Warren Korol stopped typing on his laptop and peeked over his reading glasses. He looked at Dhinsa and smirked. Two of those cases were Dhillon's victims. Korol shook his head. If only the jurors knew the truth.

* * *

The Crown's star witness bowed to Judge Glithero. It was Thursday, October 17, 2002. Lakhwinder Sekhon, who normally dressed in Western-style clothing—jeans, leather jacket—today wore a flowing Indian dress. Through the interpreter, Brent Bentham questioned her. He slowly led her through her personal story, the first arranged marriage she had never wanted, then her relationship with Ranjit. Bentham aired her past, painting her as a flawed and fearful woman who ultimately found the courage to tell the truth. The next day, Lakhwinder dropped the bomb, pointing at Dhillon as her husband's killer. And she said Ranjit's family had remained silent in exchange for some of the insurance money.

Lakhwinder testified about Ranjit's last words. Just before he went into convulsions, she told the jury, Ranjit told her Dhillon had given him a pill. The pill, Dhillon had told Ranjit, would help his back pain and improve his sex life. Dhillon "told him that it's a strong pill, once you take it, the pill will send you flying," Lakhwinder said.

Dhillon muttered to himself as Lakhwinder spoke. She talked about how Ranjit's family reacted when she woke them to tell them he was sick. She recounted that Ranjit's uncle, Paviter Khela, phoned Dhillon.

"And what did he say?" Bentham asked.

"Paviter was saying, 'What has happened to him? What did you give him?' And then, after Paviter listened to Dhillon, he said, 'Ranjit has told everything to his wife, so what is going to happen now?'"

Silverstein rose to cross-examine. His goal was to undermine the notion that Dhillon had given Ranjit any pill and, at the same time, to point the finger at Lakhwinder as the killer. Silverstein turned the heat up on her and did not let up.

"I'm going to suggest to you, Miss Sekhon, that Ranjit never told you anything of the sort. And you never told his family or anyone else anything like that."

Silverstein grilled her about her inconsistent statements, about lying under oath on a variety of matters, and in particular about the fact she did not tell police about Ranjit's final words until more than a year after his death. She had not mentioned any pill until August 1997. Why did she finally tell the police, he asked, after three interviews?

"I respected the police, they were like God," Lakhwinder replied.

Perhaps the meaning of her words was altered in the translation, but Silverstein pounced.

"Like God? Like God!" he said, voice booming in the courtroom, raising his hand in a heavenly gesture. "They were like God to you. And yet still you did not tell them the alleged truth until a year after Ranjit died?"

Silverstein focused on Lakhwinder's often stormy marriage to Ranjit. She had reason to dislike her husband, even hate him, Silverstein argued. The relationship was not merely bumpy, but horrific at times. The forced abortions, the abuse, the sham divorce. As he questioned her, Lakhwinder finally broke down, sobbing. Had Silverstein's line of questioning gone too far in the eyes of the jurors? Or had he unmasked a suspect?

"All I want," she said, tears rolling down her cheeks, "is for Ranjit to come back so he can tell you what happened. I am not making anything up. Whatever has happened, that is what I'm telling you."

At his desk, Tony Leitch made notes. Later that day, with the jury out, Leitch made another pitch to bring Parvesh into the trial. The defense had crossed the line, Leitch said. In assassinating Lakhwinder's character, Silverstein had painted her as the kind of person who could kill her husband—even as the jury could not know about Sukhwinder Dhillon's character. The defense had invested in Lakhwinder a disposition to murder, Leitch said. That wasn't fair, not when the jury didn't know about Dhillon's proven disposition to murder. He had done nothing of the sort, Silverstein countered. It was a tough debate: Leitch building his case point by point, citing case law, Silverstein using few notes and employing his best courtroom rhetoric, spiking his comments to Glithero with phrases such as "it is elementary." Silverstein won the battle. Glithero decided to keep Dhillon's conviction out of the mix. The defense, Glithero said, had done what defense lawyers do: vigorously cross-examined a star witness on the facts of her testimony. To allow Dhillon's conviction as evidence would prejudice his right to a fair trial. The fact is, Glithero said in his ruling, "there are warts on this witness."

Korol and Dhinsa looked on, grim-faced. Warts? Korol leaned forward, his elbows on his knees, and hung his head slightly.

"Wouldn't want the jury to know about Dhillon's past, though, eh?" he muttered. Korol understood the system. He knew that Glithero would never let the jury hear about Dhillon's past, not unless Silverstein made some big slip-up. On an intellectual level, Korol could accept that. But in his heart he knew it wasn't right, damn it. The jury should know the truth.

* * *

Silverstein chose not to cross-examine most of the Crown witnesses, or did so very briefly. It was as though he was willing to let the Crown tell the story, then let contradictory testimony and the alleged scheming of Ranjit's family create reasonable doubt. He did not want the jury thinking that police had paid any special attention to Dhillon following Ranjit's death.

On Friday, November 15, insurance investigator Cliff Elliot took the stand. Elliot had to be careful not to let slip any mention of having had any dealings with Dhillon prior to handling the claim on Ranjit. Before Elliot took the stand, with the jury out of the room, Silverstein objected to Bentham's intention to have Elliot say that he phoned police about Dhillon. Silverstein argued that mentioning police in the context of a routine insurance investigation was prejudicial to his client. It suggested that Elliot had reason to suspect Dhillon. "If a 90-year-old man dies, and the wife collects the life insurance claim, would the insurance investigator phone police? I would think not," Silverstein said.

Glithero ruled in favor of the Crown. Elliot could mention the phone call to police. "The jury won't hear the real reason for Mr. Elliot's suspicion," Glithero noted. Elliot took the stand. He told the jury of Dhillon's strange behavior, his lack of emotion, during the interview about the claim on Ranjit Khela.

"Those are my questions," Bentham concluded. Then, almost before he had uttered the last word, Silverstein stood up and sat down in one fluid motion, interjecting, "No questions, Your Honor." *Get the man off the stand.* The trial adjourned for lunch. Out in the hallway, Tony Leitch shook Elliot's hand. "I thought you handled the cross-examination quite well, Cliff," Leitch said with a broad smile.

The Crown had a third key witness, a man named Inderjit Singh Mangat. Mangat told the jury what he had told Dhinsa and Korol five years earlier, that when he went to the Khela home a few days after Ranjit's death to offer condolences, Lakhwinder had told him and a few other people that Dhillon had given her husband a pill before he died. Mangat said that Dhillon had overheard Lakhwinder, and then denied giving his young friend anything. With the Khela family contradicting Lakhwinder's story, Mangat was essential to the Crown's case.

Testimony from Ranjit's grandmother, Surjit, proved equally important. Surjit had contradicted Lakhwinder's account of the night her grandson died. Nothing had been said about Dhillon giving her grandson a pill, Surjit said. But now, on the stand in front of Bentham, Surjit seemed to support Lakhwinder's testimony that the family had in fact confronted Dhillon and asked him what he had given Ranjit. Then Surjit tried to back away from her concession. Dhillon was her "special boy," she said, because he was Ranjit's good friend. The only reason her family questioned him was because Dhillon had been with Ranjit all day and into the night. Why then, asked Bentham, did Uncle Paviter phone Dhillon that night?

"Because he had been with Ranjit." But so had another of Ranjit Khela's friends, and nobody had phoned him, Bentham pointed out. Why not?

"I don't know."

The damage was done. Surjit's testimony suggested that Lakhwinder had told the truth, and that the Khelas had, in fact, suspected Dhillon that night. It lent more credibility to Lakhwinder, while damaging that of the Khelas and, more importantly, Dhillon.

The Crown wrapped up its case by calling detectives Dhinsa and Korol. When Dhinsa entered the witness box, Dhillon grew restless. "Do you swear that the testimony you are about to give is the truth, the whole truth, and nothing but the truth?"

Dhillon grumbled at his seat. Warren Korol was the last witness. Like Dhinsa, he explained how easy it had been to buy strychnine in India and bring it back into Canada. With the Crown's case finished, Silverstein rose.

"No evidence, Your Honor."

He had reversed his strategy from the first trial. He would keep Dhillon off the stand, and hit cleanup with the jury, speak to them after the Crown in closing remarks. This time, he would get the last word.

At 5:30 a.m. Wednesday, November 27, Tony Leitch rose to continue polishing his closing words on his laptop. Leitch had worked late and slept poorly, thanks to the cold he was fighting. That morning, Leitch's wife, Joanne, drove down to St. Catharines to watch her husband in action in the courtroom for the first time. She was tired herself, having been up and down all night looking after their two young children, who also had colds.

Court was about to begin. The jury would be seated soon. Russell Silverstein walked past Korol and Dhinsa to speak with Dhillon, who was sitting in the prisoner's box. Both Silverstein and Dhillon appeared to have new haircuts.

"Hey, Russell," Korol said, "you guys get your hair cut at the same barber?"

Silverstein said nothing.

The jury quietly entered. They were dressed casually in sweaters, vests, flannel shirts, jeans; there was the petite woman with blond hair in the second row, the earnest woman who took notes on her clipboard each day, the young guy in front who always looked uninterested. Leitch fought through his cold and began his address at the podium. He was methodical going through the evidence, on occasion raising his voice, speaking faster and with more emotion than Bentham had in the first trial. The Crown doesn't need to prove motive, Leitch said, it must only prove that Dhillon was responsible for Ranjit's death by strychnine. But the motive was there in any event: "need and greed."

Dhillon needed money to expand his "shiny new car business. The accused took advantage of Ranjit Khela's trust." Then he showed the jury Ranjit's checkbook. It had been found in Dhillon's home when the police searched the place. Ranjit had paid for the insurance policy on his own life, perhaps from this very account. "Tragically, Ranjit was duped into signing his own death warrant,"

Leitch said. He spoke of the conspiracy of silence between the Khela family and Dhillon.

"Here is the conspiracy in black and white!" he said, voice rising as he held up the copy of the form enlisting the help of a lawyer. The sheet had the names of several members of the Khela family, and Dhillon's. Leitch was already into his address when Lakhwinder entered the courtroom. Did her presence in court to watch help her credibility with the jury? As Leitch recounted what had happened the night Ranjit died, Lakhwinder broke into tears and had to leave the room.

Leitch knew Silverstein would attack Lakhwinder in his closing address. So he praised her. She had acted strangely for a woman trying to pocket insurance money, he said. Ranjit's former employer even had to track her down to pay her his workplace life insurance. "That's odd behavior for a woman who killed her husband to get money," Leitch said. He paused. Did he have the jury's attention? He looked into their faces, saw the young guy in the front row who seemed uninterested. Don't worry about it, Leitch thought. The guy always looks like that. Leitch rattled off Dhillon's lies to Cliff Elliot. "Lie number 1…lie number 2…There they are, 13 proven lies."

Leitch had hit his stride. At the break, outwardly relaxed, he spoke with his wife and a friend, motioning as though working on his golf swing. "It looks like the jurors are actually interested in what you're saying," his wife said. Tony grinned. "You sound like someone who is surprised by that."

After the break, he continued, looking down at his typed notes. One section had the heading "Corroboration of the Pill." The evidence shows that neither Ranjit nor Lakhwinder had motive to falsely implicate Dhillon, he said. Neither had animosity against the accused. The next heading: "Lakhwinder not gilding the lily." If she was lying, if she wanted to frame Dhillon, she could have said that she actually saw Ranjit take the pill from him. It would have been easy to do. But she had not said that.

He took the jurors back to the night Ranjit died, and the confrontation between Dhillon and the Khela family, proving that they suspected him. The family had called Dhillon to the house.

"And they asked him, 'Did you give him the pill?'" Leitch raised his voice. "And Dhillon said, 'I didn't give him anything!'" The voice was booming now, filling the room.

Leitch closed by talking about evidence suggesting Dhillon was drinking the night of Ranjit's death, and the danger that it could result in a finding of manslaughter, not first-degree murder. There was no evidence Dhillon was drunk, said Leitch. And in any case, "if you find, and I submit you should, that the accused formed his intent to kill Ranjit Khela before they took out life insurance together, then the accused's intoxication on June 22, 1996, is completely irrelevant." Leitch once more defended Lakhwinder. There was no way she could have killed her husband. "She wept—over his dead body," he said, slowly. "She…told the truth…I ask you to return a verdict of first degree murder."

Court was adjourned until the next day, when Silverstein would address the jury.

* * *

Russell Silverstein did not typically type out his closing comments. He always wrote some points down, and ad-libbed the rest. Now, with the Crown address completed, Silverstein returned to his hotel room and reviewed notes he had made from Tony Leitch's address. He paced the room, thinking. *I fear Mr. Leitch may have left you, members of the jury—he may have left you with the wrong impression.* As well as having the advantage of speaking last, Silverstein had a stronger argument to make than in the first trial. He had an alternative suspect. Lakhwinder hated her husband; Dhillon was Ranjit's close friend.

Later that afternoon, Silverstein went for a swim in the pool. There had been a time when he swam laps for several kilometers every day, but he hadn't done that for some time now. How many lengths should he swim today? The question was meaningless, he reflected. Meaningless unless you know the dimensions of the pool. That afternoon, he swam about 1,500 meters. The pool was 12 meters long. That's 125 lengths. Even as his slim figure cut through the water, he reviewed tactics in his mind. Reasonable doubt. This case is *littered* with doubts. The standard to convict is that you must be sure. Well, what, members of the jury, can you be sure of? Back to the room, then dinner. Late evening, back at his desk, more notes. Counter the Crown's main points. Skip points that will only cause trouble. But above all, review the evidence in a way that connects with the jury. Tell a story. Weave in allusions to the evidence that fits the story. As usual, he would try to combine content with performance. He was in bed by 1 a.m.

At 9:30 the next morning, Silverstein paced the hallway outside the courtroom, alone. He had been alone the entire trial, facing off against the Crown team, the detectives. The defender, taking on the greater resources of the state. Outside the courtroom, during breaks, Leitch could chat with his wife or a friend, Bentham huddled with Korol and Dhinsa, reporters always seemed to be chatting with someone from the team, although never the tight-lipped Bentham. Silverstein was always off on his own, talking on his cell, or walking around, thinking. The defense lawyer needs an ego, a gunslinger's mentality. Silverstein had it. He passed Leitch in the hallway on his way into court. Leitch nodded in greeting.

"So, you thinking about all the things you should have said?" Russell asked, deadpan.

Leitch laughed, kept walking, appreciating the rib.

Outside the courtroom in a hospitality cubicle, Silverstein poured himself a cup of coffee.

"Hey Russell, why don't you get your client to make it for you?" Korol cracked. Dhillon, the poisoner, had once offered the detectives a drink when they questioned him at his home. They had declined. Silverstein started to smile, then stopped and glared.

"That's a cheap joke," he said, and returned to his seat.

"Some things just need to be said," Korol said with a grin.

CHAPTER 27 ~ "HAVE A NICE LIFE"

Silverstein launched into his address at 10 a.m.

"It is a pleasure to have the opportunity, finally, to stand before you and address you directly," he said to the jury. Finally. It was as though the Crown had prevented him from speaking to this point in the trial. And now the truth shall come out. He was in his element, performing, ad-libbing, talking to the jury, the stage his. He always tried to catch the jurors' eyes. He believed that if you speak to them extemporaneously—or, at least, appear to do so—they will be more interested. He had to be an entertainer. That was the word he used to describe his approach—entertain the jury, and you will get and keep their attention, connect with them.

"You are judging the fate of another human being," Silverstein said. "This case is not about insurance money, this is a criminal trial. The burden on you is to find guilt beyond a reasonable doubt. You don't have to be certain of guilt, but you must be sure of guilt. Not to an absolute certainty, but you must be *sure*." He said the word louder, with more emphasis, like a hard note on a piano. Are you *sure*?

"I fear Mr. Leitch may have left you with the wrong impression," he continued, and then challenged the Crown point for point, bringing the jurors inside his own head. Focus on the rational. Do not let emotion get the better of you. We are here to uphold the law. Do the right thing, the intelligent thing. Ranjit Khela died horribly, yes. Nobody denies that. But that's not what this trial is about. "Don't let the agony of his death infect your reasoning."

Silverstein drew back his left foot, balancing the toe of his shoe on the floor, both hands grasping the lectern. "There's no doubt Ranjit Khela died of strychnine poisoning, but in order to convict Sukhwinder Dhillon, you must be able to answer 'No' to these two questions: One, might Ranjit have died accidentally? And two, might his wife Lakhwinder have killed him? If you answer 'Yes' to either of those, you must acquit him."

Ranjit Khela could have killed himself accidentally, Silverstein argued. He had been disillusioned with Western medicine, he could have turned to Indian homeopathic remedies to help his back and impotence. Diluted strychnine could help both problems.

Or he could have been killed by his wife, Silverstein continued. Lakhwinder had better opportunity than Dhillon, had served
Ranjit his last meal, and had been alone with him just before he
went into convulsions. She had better motive, too. She stood to
gain financially from his death, from life insurance and getting
part of the house. And there was strife in their marriage. Ranjit
insulted her, called her fat, forced her to have two abortions, cut
her hair, abused her. She was angry that his parents were coming
to live with them.

"Motive of the heart and soul and animosity are greater [than
money]," Silverstein told the jurors. "Lakhwinder hated Ranjit's
guts. And yet, by all accounts Ranjit and Mr. Dhillon were the best
of friends." Lakhwinder longed for a better life, an escape. Moreover, it was a stretch, Silverstein argued, to assume that Dhillon,
in the insurance agent's office one day with Ranjit, suddenly, on
the spot, hatched a plan to have his friend take out a policy and
then kill him for the money. How on earth could Dhillon have
come up with that so quickly?

At his seat Warren Korol, typing on his laptop, peered over
the top of his glasses and smirked. Every day the full Dhillon story
was kept from the jury, he grew more irritated. "Dhillon had a
plan on the spot because he did it before when he killed his wife,"
Korol growled quietly to Dhinsa.

Silverstein now turned his attention to Dhillon's lies to Cliff
Elliot. Dhillon had lied to the insurance investigator, Silverstein
said, to hide the fact he was not Ranjit's uncle as he had claimed
on the insurance form. Just because he lied didn't mean he had
murdered one of his best friends. Defrauding an insurance company is wrong, there's no question of that. "But that doesn't make
him a killer."

And what about the manner of death? The Crown claimed
Ranjit consumed a large amount of strychnine, inconsistent with
accidental death or with eating it in his food, given the poison's
extreme bitterness. And yet, it had taken Ranjit two or three hours
to die. That suggested the dose was in fact quite small, didn't it?
Korol burned; strychnine deaths can be drawn-out affairs, and
Silverstein knew it. Parvesh's death had been just that.

Silverstein lanced Lakhwinder's credibility one more time. She is a liar. She lied to police, lied under oath, repeatedly. And now, all of a sudden, we should believe she is telling the truth? "It is impossible to accept a word she says about anything." He wrapped up. Echoing Bentham and Leitch, he said that, yes, we value life in Canada. "But there are other values in this country and other civilized countries, and one of those values is the enlightened system of justice that we have. And it says that before a person can be found guilty of any crime, you must be sure—*sure*, which is what 'beyond a reasonable doubt' means. You can't be sure of anything in this case. And you must acquit Mr. Dhillon."

Judge Glithero spent Monday explaining the rules to the jury, then sent them to deliberate. They hung charts on the wall, family trees, other documents, like students working on a group project. If the jury did not have a decision by 9 p.m., they would be seques- tered for the night in a hotel and barred from discussing anything about the case until they resumed deliberation together. At 8:30 p.m. Monday night, December 2, they arrived at a verdict. Ten minutes later the cellphones rang. The verdict was in. The lawyers, the judge, and Dhillon gathered in Courtroom 11. The jury was brought in and took their seats. The foreman stood up.

Guilty. Sukhwinder Dhillon was guilty of the first degree murder of Ranjit Khela. Silverstein asked that the jury be polled. Each juror spoke aloud.

"Agree."
"Agree."
"Agree."
"Agree."
"Agree."
"Agree."
"Agree."
"Agree."
"Agree."
"Agree."
"Agree."
"Agree."

Several jurors choked with emotion as they answered. One of the women cried as she spoke the final word. Korol knew that the pain the jurors felt sending a man to prison for life would have been mitigated if they knew everything Dhillon had done, his trail of murder and bigamy. For the jurors, the story had been incomplete. Glithero thanked the jury for their work. The six men and six women stood and filed out of the silent courtroom.

Dhillon had grumbled to his interpreter constantly over the course of the trial, but kept his anger within the confines of the prisoner's box. But now, a convicted murderer for the second time and no longer before the jury, Dhillon couldn't take it any longer. He stood up and began shouting in Punjabi at the judge: "No justice! No justice!"

Dhillon turned around. Warren Korol's face glowed with victory. Beside Korol was Dhinsa, a look of quiet satisfaction on his smooth, tanned face. Dhillon hated him most of all. "The Indian police officer got me," Dhillon cried. "I haven't done anything! Dhinsa—it was Dhinsa. Framed me! Told Lakhwinder what to say!"

"No justice!" Dhillon shouted in Punjabi in court.

With Dhillon waving his arms and shouting, Korol feared for the safety of the Punjabi interpreter. There was a court security guard, but Korol moved to the front of the courtroom and stood next to the box. If Dhillon wanted to take a swing, finally, at the cop who had hunted him from Hamilton to Ludhiana, this was his chance. Dhillon did nothing. Korol looked straight ahead and spoke. "Have a nice life, Dhillon."

* * *

Dhillon was already serving a life sentence for murdering Parvesh. In the United States, a killer like Dhillon—if he was convicted in a state that did not have the death penalty—would be serving two consecutive life sentences, perhaps 200 years, after being convicted for a second murder. But in Canada, sentences are concurrent. The fact that Dhillon was also guilty of killing Ranjit Khela did not change the term. He would still serve one sentence of life in prison. He would be eligible for parole after 25 years.

The main implication of the second conviction was on Dhillon's likelihood of success with the so-called faint hope clause in Canada's Criminal Code. The clause allows a prisoner to apply for early parole, under certain conditions, 15 years after conviction. The law was changed in 1997 so that multiple killers could not apply, but the change was grandfathered. Dhillon's crimes were committed in 1995 and 1996, so he would still be eligible. The Crown lawyers felt a double conviction would persuade any parole board to reject his application.

Many of those familiar with the Dhillon case wanted to see the killer deported to India, jailed there. Then again, in Indian bureaucracy the right price and influence can achieve anything. If Dhillon were deported, surely he'd find a way to get early release. On the other hand, given another tradition in the Punjab—revenge— perhaps justice more swift and brutal would await Dhillon once he got out of an Indian prison. It is unlikely Dhillon will ever be returned to India. He is not a new immigrant; he is a Canadian citizen and had been a Canadian for more than a decade at the time of his first murder conviction. He has all the rights of any other citizen—including the right to serve his sentence, likely to last the rest of his life, in Canada.

* * *

You couldn't see it on his face, not at all. But surely Justice C. Stephen Glithero felt relief, somewhere inside, when Dhillon was convicted for the second time. Glithero had labored to ensure Dhillon's right to a fair trial, and was forced to make difficult decisions. From one perspective, his rulings had been too much in favor of the defense, given everything that Dhillon had done or was suspected of doing. In denying the Crown's repeated attempts to enter evidence of Dhillon's other crimes, the judge forced the prosecutors to go the extra mile, work harder. Glithero had separated the two trials. He had ruled out of order several statements made by Dhillon because of what he believed were inappropriate police procedures. Glithero had trusted the jury to determine the truth without having access to all the information. They had convicted Dhillon based on the evidence they had been given. The system had worked the way it was supposed to. Had the juries in Kitchener and St. Catharines acquitted Dhillon, Glithero's rulings would probably have made headlines across the country: "What the jury didn't know." He would have been a very unpopular judge in some quarters.

But Glithero never cared about public opinion. He made his decisions based on what he felt was right, to guarantee justice for Dhillon. And two different juries decided that justice for Dhillon was life in prison. Soon after the second trial ended, a journalist called Glithero to talk about the case. Judges rarely speak to reporters. Glithero wasn't like other judges. What about the severance decision? Didn't it give Dhillon a shot at acquittal? "It was a difficult call and I came to the best decision I could," Glithero said. "It's there, if the Court of Appeal doesn't like it they can do something else with it. If these sorts of things were easy issues, then the lawyers wouldn't need a decision from me, would they?"

He returned to his St. Catharines hotel. It had been a long haul, with many nights away from his wife. During the trial he grew a thin mustache. And he fell yet again off the no-smoking wagon, just as he had done many times over the years. Fresh air awaited, however. Glithero had two weeks' vacation time coming to him in

February. Perhaps one week to hang around home in Cambridge. And the other week? There had been no time to talk it over with his wife. A trip south sounded nice. Maybe Florida or Arizona. Exactly where, he wasn't sure. Get some sun, play some golf. He loved the sport, played at Galt Country Club in Cambridge, a pretty course along the Grand River. No lumpy greens or modern man-made design touches that plagued other new courses. Galt is old school. What you see is what you get.

"So what's your handicap?" asked the journalist. Glithero waited. The former defense lawyer considered the question.

"Seventeen," he said. Then he paused. "You're not going to print that, are you?" he said. "Geez, what a mean son of a gun you are."

* * *

The prosecutors and detectives left the courthouse after it was over and walked two blocks in bitter cold to a restaurant and bar called The Honest Lawyer. Later, Russell Silverstein joined them for drinks. It's a lawyer's tradition to get together with your adversary once the battle is over. In fact, years ago, competing lawyers gathered for drinks as soon as the jury retired to deliberate. That doesn't happen much any more.

Silverstein lamented that he had been defeated, but was glad the trials finally were over. The case, and Sukhwinder Singh Dhillon, had consumed so much of his life. For Bentham and Leitch, Dhillon was the longest and most complicated case in their careers. It would not be long before Tony Leitch found himself arguing, again, before a different judge, that similar-fact evidence be allowed in a murder trial. The game did not change.

Bentham went back to work. The media exposure from the Dhillon trials had been considerable. But the experience had made the taciturn Crown attorney no more open with journalists. Near the end of the second trial, a reporter approached Bentham in the corridors of the courthouse. Was the journalist after some insight from Bentham into the case? No, he simply wanted to know where Bentham had attended law school. Well? Where was it? Bentham said nothing as he walked. Really, that's it, law school. Where did you go? Please. Bentham finally gave in.

"Osgoode," he muttered.

"There's my lead," joked the reporter in mock-scoop fashion. 'Brent Bentham went to Osgoode'!" Bentham grinned to himself and kept walking, saying nothing.

* * *

In the end, Silverstein had been surprised by the verdict. Court-room staff who watched him in action thought Silverstein had, in fact, convinced the jury to acquit his client. What happened? Silverstein had played his strongest hand. He was able to address the jury last. But going last is perhaps overrated, he reflected. The jurors had to have guessed something was up, thought Silverstein. They had watched the interpreter request adjournments from the judge when Punjabi witnesses were on the stand. Why was that? What was it that they shouldn't hear from the East Indian witnesses? They had heard evidence that Dhillon came into some insurance money prior to Ranjit's death. What was that all about? There was just too much swirling around Dhillon. But no one knew what the jurors had been thinking, or ever would. In the United States, jurors routinely talk once a verdict is rendered. It's against the law in Canada for jurors to speak about the nature of their deliberations.

At The Honest Lawyer, Korol spoke to Silverstein. "Hey Russell, where are you staying tonight?" Silverstein had checked out of his hotel and not made new arrangements. "Stay at our place," Korol said. "Plenty of room." That night, as Dhillon lay in his cell, the two Crown attorneys, two detectives, and the defense lawyer sat together in a room at the Four Points Sheraton, had a few beers, reflected on the case. The battle was over. The two sides had gone at it hard over two trials. It was never personal, they were all doing their jobs. It was time to blow off steam, rib each other about the case that had dominated their lives. They talked well past midnight, into the early hours, before turning in. Silverstein slept on a pullout couch in the room of his opposite number, Bentham, and Korol.

In the morning, as the others slept, Silverstein got up, dressed and left the hotel for court. His shoes crunched in the new snow. It was the coldest winter morning of the year, the air pricked exposed skin like frozen needles. Mist rose from Lake Ontario and hung in the air like pieces of cotton. By the time he arrived at the courthouse, the sun was shining brilliantly, causing snow that swirled in the harsh wind to glitter like silver confetti.

Silverstein was proud of his handling of the second Dhillon trial. He had won many of the small battles, the submissions before the judge. He had succeeded in keeping so much information about Dhillon away from two juries. Now he loaded boxes with legal documents and cleaned out his small office in order to return to Toronto. There was no break or vacation planned. In fact, Silverstein was to have handled a bail hearing in St. Catharines that very morning. The hearing had been postponed, though, so it was time to go. He carted the boxes out on a trolley, down the elevator, and out to his car. Then he walked back inside. He looked fit and had dressed casually in taupe corduroy pants, a sweater, and brown leather bomber jacket. On his last trip down the elevator, a court staffer asked if the trial was over.

"Yes, last night," he answered.

"And?"

"Convicted."

He didn't use the word "guilty." No doubt in his own mind he had proved that his client was not guilty beyond a reasonable doubt. But the jury had decided otherwise. They had chosen to convict. Before he headed back to Toronto, Russell Silverstein poured himself a coffee at the courthouse snack bar, stirred in cream, then walked briskly with his assertive stride down the long hallway, one hand in his pocket, head up, and exited out a side door, alone.

CHAPTER 28 ~ LIVING VICTIMS

It was two days before Christmas 2002, at Barton Street jail in Hamilton. Sukhwinder Dhillon sat behind the glass partition in the visitors' area, took the phone receiver in his hand. In 30 days the convicted double murderer would be moved east to Millhaven Federal Penitentiary near Kingston. He had filed appeals on both convictions. Russell Silverstein had declined to continue as his lawyer. The appeals, as well as all of Dhillon's court costs for more than five years, would be paid for by legal aid. A journalist sat on the other side of the glass accompanied by a Punjabi interpreter. In Punjabi, Dhillon said he would not speak to the reporter. "I'm appealing," he said. "I won't talk without my lawyer."

In his orange prisoner's jumpsuit and laceless sneakers, Dhillon looked smaller, rounder than in the suit he had worn in court. His hair and beard were even whiter now. He had continued to soften in jail.

"Tell Dhillon it's over," the journalist pressed, through the interpreter. "Tell him it's over, he was convicted, and now is his chance to give his side of the story."

"No," Dhillon replied, shaking his head. "It's under appeal. I won't talk."

"Ask him how he feels."

"I don't belong here. I'm innocent."

Dhillon hung up the receiver, stood, and walked back to his life behind bars.

In Dhillon's mind, he clung to the hope of getting off on appeal, or early parole. He had never confessed. And if he got out, what would he do for cash? The money he had from Parvesh's death was all but gone, and he never collected any money from Ranjit's life insurance. No one would ever get that money. The claim was void. But there might be other ways. Maybe he'd have the money from the lawsuit by the time he got out.

Lawsuit? In 1999, while Dhillon was in jail waiting for his trial to begin, he filed the lawsuit. It was over a slip and fall he claimed he suffered in a Hamilton apartment building lobby in April 1997. The statement of claim papers had been delivered to the head office of a building management company in St. Catharines. Dhillon claimed the lobby floor had been wet and slippery. The papers said that Sukhwinder Dhillon, the plaintiff, sought special damages from the fall of $200,000, plus $50,000 for pre- and post-judgment interest, and costs of his action. Co-plaintiff Gobind Dhillon, his mother, sought $25,000 plus "GST on costs." His daughters, the papers said, represented by their now-official guardian, Dhillon's niece Sarvjit, each claimed $25,000 and Sarvjit herself claimed $25,000.

The claim said that since the fall Dhillon's "enjoyment of life and basic amenities have been severely curtailed … he is unable to climb stairs. The plaintiff is in pain and taking medication, is unable to engage in social and recreational activities to which he was accustomed, and unable to carry gainful employment. [It has] caused inconvenience and discomfort, he is unable to do normal household chores to which he had been responsible." The injuries "caused great pain and shock to the plaintiff." As for the kids and Gobind, they had "sustained a lack of guidance and care and companionship that the plaintiffs might reasonably have expected from Sukhwinder Dhillon, if he had not been injured."

Guidance, care, and companionship.

In February 2003, six years after the "fall," Dhillon sat in his Millhaven cell serving a life sentence. The injury claim, according to a lawyer he hired in Hamilton, was "firmly open." There's a big "if," but if the claim ever goes before a judge and Dhillon is awarded damages, the money would be payable in

Dhillon filed a lawsuit while in prison.

due course. Prisoners have the right to vote. And win lawsuits. The lawyer said where the claim goes from here is up to his client. A nice deal, lawsuits.

* * *

Dhillon had been convicted twice, but there were still so many loose ends to the story. Kushpreet. The twins. Warren Korol would always be certain Dhillon killed them all. But Dhillon would never answer for those deaths. No charges were ever laid in India. It left Korol with an empty feeling. And then there was the third brother. Korol had found out about Darshan late in his investigation. But there was never enough evidence to consider entering it before the court. But it was there in Korol's investigation notebook.

Aug. 19, 1997

That was the date he typed, summarizing notes he made in a conversation with Sarvjit, Dhillon's 22-year-old niece. One day Sarvjit had paged Korol. She wanted to talk about her late father, Darshan. She told him events that happened one day back in January 1992, in Ludhiana. Korol wrote:

Sarvjit Kaur Dhillon told me that her father had died a short time ago while in India but there was no post-mortem done.

Sarvjit said that she had been there when her father died. The kids were told it was a heart attack. It did not seem like a heart attack. She was 17 at the time. As Darshan passed away, she saw recognition in his eyes for her. He clutched at his throat, tried to say something to her, but couldn't. His teeth were clenched tight together. There it is again, thought Korol. The death grin.

Sarvjit told me that her father cried and his body was rigid. She told me that her father became ill after he drank something. Sarvjit told me that Sukhwinder Singh Dhillon was in India at the time of Darshan's death. Sarvjit said she was disturbed that Sukhwinder

Singh Dhillon did not mourn his brother's death, he was not acting like a person who lost his brother, and he was drinking a lot.

Dhillon was there for the mourning that followed Darshan's sudden death, there for the reading of the *Kirtan Sohila*, sprinkling of the ashes in the sacred river. He stayed three months. Dhillon had watched Sarvjit, tears filling her eyes. He walked over to her. Don't cry, Dhillon said. Don't be sad. Your father was once a police officer. He surely had many enemies.

Sarvjit Kaur Dhillon told me that Sukhwinder Singh Dhillon suggested that maybe someone poisoned her father.

* * *

There were the dead in Dhillon's wake. There were also his living victims. The best that could be said about the fate of Dhillon's second wife, Sarabjit Kaur Brar, was that she lived to tell about the nightmare. But she carried a wound that would never heal— the loss of her babies. She thought about them every day, tried to remember the few healthy living days they had enjoyed before dying in her arms. Sarabjit could not even contemplate the hope that the boys' souls were with God. They had been too young, they had no souls. It brought tears to her eyes. As for the babies, the remains of Gurmeet and Gurwinder were buried again in accordance with Sarabjit's wishes.

Sarabjit found out about the guilty verdict in Parvesh's murder a couple of days after the fact in the late summer of 2001. She had awakened, alone, and seen the Punjabi-language newspaper on the kitchen table. Her brother had left it for her. No note, just open to a headline. Guilty. Jodha was found guilty. Sent to jail for life. He was getting the punishment he deserved. Her eyes lit up and she smiled. And she said it, quietly, but firmly. "*Hungi!*" Yes! It felt sweet. She read the news at her home—near Brampton, Ontario. In the days following the first Dhillon trial, she had filed papers claiming refugee status in Canada for herself and her parents. Through Dhillon, in a twisted way, she had indeed made it to Canada, and had a shot at staying.

Sarabjit found her life in Canada was not the paradise she had once imagined. She slept on a mattress on the floor of a basement her family rented, worked at the airport packing in-flight meals, while her parents toiled at a mushroom farm. She liked the summers, a nice change from the scorching Indian heat, but she hated the hard, gray winters, when the air seemed to rake your face. When she was a little girl, Sarabjit had talked about it with her friends. *Cane-a-da*. Land of beauty, wealth. She thought Canada would be everything, and in fact for her it was nothing. Everything is work, work, work. Up in the morning, home at night. Start all over again. Did she want to return home? No. In Panj Grain she would never be able to marry again, not after being divorced and having children. But here, in Canada, a more liberal culture, they don't care about that. For Sarabjit, that was the only saving grace of the Canadian dream.

As time wore on, Sarabjit earned more money, picked up a few more words of English. Her face, a sullen mask months before, seemed brighter, prone to break into easy smiles. She acquired a new confidence, could look men in the eye when she spoke to them, just like a Western woman does. She missed home terribly, the village, the weather, her friends. But she did not want to return to them.

Sarabjit was still living in Ontario in early 2003. In November 2002, she and her parents received the immigration papers in the mail. They must attend a deportation hearing. The ruling came early in the new year: they were ordered to leave Canada.

* * *

Many of the Punjabis subpoenaed to testify in the prosecution of Sukhwinder Dhillon used the opportunity to claim refugee status—17 of them in all. One who was unable to do so was Dhillon's fourth and final wife, Sukhwinder Kaur. She was never called over as a witness, and never made it to Canadian soil. She had married Dhillon to get into Canada. But that union was null and void when it came to light that he was already married at the time of the wedding. So she married another Indian man who lives in Canada—Vancouver, British Columbia—in the hope of making it overseas. In the summer of 2002, she sat in her taupe-colored house in the village of Dhandra, the room darkened to beat suffocating heat, fans churning to circulate the air. A journalist paid her a visit. Sitting on her bed, she began to cry. It's the visa. It's not fair. She was supposed to be granted one several years ago, and now her application was being held up again, even though she has a new husband in Canada. She looked like a broken woman, but she kept her focus on the goal. No photos, she told the journalist, and no comment on anything—unless they can get her a visa to Canada. Then she would deal. Talk to the lawyers, she said, the Hamilton detectives. Here is my passport. Look at it! They promised me a visa if I cooperated in the Dhillon case. She rose from the bed, left the room, a silhouette in the darkened hallway, then disappeared.

One young woman who did land in Canada, and did not leave—at least not back to India—was Nirmaljit, known as Pinky, the friend who had comforted Sarabjit on the day of her arranged marriage to Dhillon. Pinky had been called by the Crown at the first murder trial in Kitchener for her evidence as a witness to Sarabjit's wedding. After the trial, she applied for refugee status. By the fall of 2002 she had married an illegal immigrant from California and disappeared from the scene.

Then there was a man named Jaspal Singh. He came to Hamilton for the obstruction of justice trial of Rai Singh Toor. Jaspal was a Ludhiana police officer who inadvertently helped Rai Singh obtain false passports for the impostor witnesses. In September 2002 Jaspal arrived in Hamilton, along with Inspector Subhash Kundu of the Central Bureau of Investigation. Kundu testified, and so did Jaspal Singh. Jaspal was due to fly back to India with Kundu. Instead, he claimed refugee status. As was the case for Kundu, his visit to Hamilton in September 2002 was his second to testify in matters relating to the Dhillon case.

The night after his testimony, Subhash Kundu sat with a couple of Canadian friends on a restaurant patio on King Street, not far from the Royal Connaught where he was staying, the night air cool, nursing a Corona beer. He figured he'd stay in India. That was where he had status, respect, as an inspector with the CBI.

And in Canada? Who knows where he'd end up? But now that he was in Canada a second time, giving him another taste of the country, his English getting better all the time, even he, Subhash Kundu, felt himself dreaming, just a bit. After finishing the beer, he strolled back to the hotel with his friends. They all went up to his room, talked some more. He presented the Canadians with a gift, a bottle of Old Monk rum. What did his friends think? What should Kundu do? Should he try to immigrate? Could he find work here? He had his wife back in Chandigarh, the kids. The refugee route was not for him. Kundu decided he would return to India and think about it. Ice cubes clinked in glasses, then Kundu poured two fingers of rum in each.

"Cheers. To Canada."

CHAPTER 29 ~ ASHES

Dhillon hated Warren Korol and Kevin Dhinsa, and he despised Ranjit Khela's widow for fingering him to police. But if not for one man, the chain of events might never have begun, and Dhillon might never have ended up behind bars. In that sense he was brought down by a human lie detector, an unassuming man who ultimately sealed the killer's fate. The Velvet Hammer.

It was a morning in the late fall. Four men teed off on the eighth hole at Pineland Greens public golf club, in rural north Hamilton. The weather had been damp and gray but mild, and the ground was still in good enough shape to let them play. Pineland is a forgiving course, a nine-hole affair. They took the sand traps out a while back. It's a bit deceptive, though. You still have to get the ball in the hole, as the duffers put it. Most of all, it's a scenic place, a relaxing one. The four retirees played their weekly game there every Friday morning, 10 a.m. sharp.

That morning, it started as they hit on the second-last hole. A few flakes at first, then flurries, snow gathering on the ground. They should have packed it in there, on No. 8, walked in to the clubhouse. But Cliff Elliot and the other three couldn't do it, couldn't let it go. They squinted through the blowing snow, trying to locate their white golf balls flying through the air. When a ball rolled on the green, it gathered snow as it went, like a snow ball. Their pull-carts left zigzag tracks in their wake. They laughed, searching for their golf balls, then deciding, hell, leave 'em there until the spring thaw.

Cliff Elliot was no longer semi-retired. He had retired for good, finally, not long after he made the crucial call that started the ball rolling toward the conviction of Sukhwinder Dhillon. If Elliot had not taken extra steps in his investigation of the life insurance claims, drawn the connection between Parvesh, Ranjit, and Dhillon, the killer may well have remained free, perhaps murdered again.

A few days after the golf game in the snow, the temperatures plummeted. Cliff Elliot sat in the living room waiting for his wife, Amelia, to bring some coffee from the kitchen. Cold out

there today, not even golf weather. There was always the seniors'
center, other activities. Except it was hard to see Elliot as a senior.
He looked as if he should still be pounding the pavement, working the phones, unearthing another insurance cheat. But no, that
was all over with now, the thick black book of contacts didn't get
opened much any more. And the Dhillon affair was finally over,
or at least he thought it was.

Elliot had heard about all the refugee claimants, the witnesses who came to Canada to testify and wouldn't go home. All
of them had been caught in Dhillon's storm, too. Ah, but was it
Dhillon's storm, or Clifton Elliot's? The Velvet Hammer shook
his head and smiled at it all, feeling the coffee mug warm his
hands. Amelia brought in a plate of homemade chocolate-chip
cookies, fresh from the oven. Elliot was a modest man. But he
was Amelia's hero. Inside he knew, surely, that if not for him,
Dhillon would have gotten away with it. And, if not for Cliff
Elliot, the Punjabis who came to testify and then said they were
refugees would have had to find another way to live the golden
dream in Canada.

"You know," Elliot said in his British-flavored accent, "some
of those people, they should consider giving me a gift of some
kind." Cliff Elliot winked and chuckled, sipped his coffee. Amelia
beamed at him from across the room.

Cliff Elliot near his home

* * *

Warren Korol liked to think of his work in homicide as a sport. It was a healthy way to approach the job. Embrace the game, he believed, do your best, play it well. It's all you can do. The Dhillon case was a different one, though, uniquely frustrating. Korol never could fathom how so many witnesses could change their stories and lie, even some who were victims in the path of Dhillon's murderous greed. The lying, during interviews, in the witness box under oath—it was plain disheartening. He was used to people he encountered in his job lying to him. You show up at the doorstep and ask a guy where he was at the time his friend was bludgeoned with a hammer, the guy's memory might suddenly fail. But most of the time, even the nasty pieces of work he confronted could be forthright. "You don't have to talk to me" was Korol's standard line to suspects. "So don't say anything unless you tell the truth. I respect you if you tell the truth, and I respect you if you tell me to screw off. But don't lie."

Even the worst ones understood the ground rules. But not in the Dhillon case. Lies to police officers, perjury in front of judges. Even when confronted with evidence of an obvious untruth, some witnesses either denied the proof or merely reacted with a shrug. *Well, maybe that happened.* When the dust settled, though, Korol could look back on the Dhillon case with a competitive fondness, the entire mess bringing out the best in his game.

He wanted to teach some day. And with this case, there was so much he could pass on to other police officers, so much he had learned. Just before Dhillon was convicted of murder for the second time, Korol graduated with a bachelor of arts in anthropology from McMaster University. He would begin studies toward a master's degree. In January 2003, Korol reached another rung on the police career ladder he had started climbing at age 18. He was named an inspector, meaning he was now second in command of vice, drugs, intelligence, major crimes, sexual assault, child abuse, fraud, and domestic violence.

Six years after he received the Dhillon assignment as an inexperienced homicide detective, Warren Korol looked no worse for wear. He still walked with confidence, the playful smirk on his mouth, eyes with the metallic ring bordering a core of deep blue. There were scars, too, though they were hidden beneath his emotional armor where few ever saw them. As the Dhillon case wore on, Korol's family life suffered. At first it was little things, like the longing in the voice of his little guy on the phone when he called home from India. The boy couldn't understand why Dad was away for so long. Later Korol's marriage suffered. It was a tough time; it brought a tired gray film to the usually animated face. But Korol emerged from that, too, still seeing his three kids nearly every day, working in partnership with his wife, moving on.

Korol had always wanted to work homicide. In hindsight he was happy, without question, that he was handed the Dhillon file in the fall of 1996. It was the ultimate challenge. It doesn't get any better than that. It was Korol's ambition and enthusiasm for challenge that drove him deep into Dhillon's world and kept him there until that last day in court. All experiences connect in some way, completing the puzzle of a life. For the homicide detective, there is a cumulative price to pay for the constant exposure to human darkness, the bludgeoned skulls, rape victims, child autopsies, justice not done. Warren Korol perhaps spent little time wondering how it had shaped who he was. But it would always be there, all of it, a part of him. So would Sukhwinder Singh Dhillon.

The Dhillon case was the ultimate challenge for Warren Korol.

* * *

Korol had vowed to boycott the TV show. For a long time he stayed away from it. But here he was, relenting, sitting through an episode of *The Sopranos*, a series about the Mafia. He shouldn't have. In that night's show a few of the characters were on a golf course, casually talking about whacking people. Killing them. Korol smirked. Good for laughs, eh? Hollywood, he thought, makes heroes of these guys, warping the public's sense of the pain that bastards such as these bring upon others in real life, fuelling the self-image of thugs. Korol knew guys like that in the real world. He crossed paths with them out on the street, just as his uncle Mike Pauloski had done in the 60s, when Pauloski chased down Johnny (Pops) Papalia in The Hammer. Korol knew the truth. The kingpins weren't funny, or intriguing. They were nothing but pieces of shit—petty crooks and cowards. In the old days, those guys got their kicks making late-night crank calls to Uncle Mike's wife, Sally, harassing her nearly to the point of a breakdown.

Over time, Hamilton's reputation as a Mafia city became more quaint than anything else. Had it ever been like the stories? Did bootlegger Rocco Perri really exist? Did he lie encased in concrete at the bottom of the harbour? Or was that a *Sopranos* repeat? The line between good and bad blurred. Papalia, "The Enforcer"—who spent nearly one-quarter of his 73 years behind bars for possession of drugs, breaking and entering, assault, conspiracy to import narcotics—was, according to the media, "respected and feared, the last of the city's old-time godfathers." It burned Korol.

For a cop, in homicide, there are few opportunities for closure. One case leads to the next, and the unsolved cases linger in the consciousness like tiny pieces of broken glass that every so often bare their edges. There are occasions, though, when the story really does end and justice seems black and white, perhaps even poetic. For Warren Korol, there was that one spring afternoon not too long ago, a Saturday, a moment independent of time, when his life seemed to come full circle. He was at home, a day off. Morning drizzle and fog lifted to reveal layers of cloud. He worked on his new backyard deck, wrestling with a machine he had rented to burrow post holes in the soggy ground. His cellphone rang. It was Superintendent Bruce Elwood. Elwood got right to the point. There had been a shooting. A contract hit.

"Yeah?" Korol said curtly. "And?"

"And we need some help," Elwood said. "Can you come in?" They needed someone to get to the morgue to officially check in the victim's body.

"Bruce," Korol said, unimpressed, the news not yet sinking in, "I've got this thing on the go. Got a post-hole auger machine here and it's costing me money."

But Korol agreed to go in. The personal significance of the shooting settled in as he changed clothes and slid his Glock into the shoulder holster, then drove to Hamilton General Hospital. Korol parked, entered the ER, walked up a hallway to the gurney where the body lay covered with a sheet. A police guard stood alongside.

Korol escorted the attendant wheeling the gurney down to the morgue in the basement. The gurney stopped. He pulled back the sheet. The propane-flame-blue eyes looked at the cold, lifeless, wrinkled face. Korol stared for a moment, making sure it was the man Elwood said it was supposed to be. It was indeed Johnny Papalia. Pops. The Enforcer. The old man had been in poor health. A bullet in the head didn't help. The skin was bruised, the white sheets stained from the wound in the back of his head. A bullet of a particular caliber, when fired into the skull, actually moves around inside, striking the brain, until the energy of the projectile expires. And so the eyes were wide open, and black, as if dark marbles had replaced the irises.

The Mafia don had been shot execution-style in the left side of the head earlier that morning on Railway Street. Papalia had outlived many of the police officers who once pursued him—like Uncle Mike. Pops, the bad, and Pauloski, the good, were the focal point of the prized 1961 black and white photo that hung on the wall in Korol's office. Uncle Mike had died in a car accident at the hands of a drunk driver on Upper James in 1967, a full 30 years before Papalia would roll in a hearse past hundreds of onlookers, denied official funeral rites by the Roman Catholic Diocese of Hamilton for his sins.

In the morgue, satisfied that the victim was indeed Papalia, following protocol, Korol took a Polaroid photo, filled out a proof-of-death form. It was the final chapter in the godfather's life, a story in which his hero Uncle Mike wore a white hat 30 years earlier. The steel door opened, a sheet of cold air floated out. Korol pushed the gurney into the freezer, shut the door tight, taped it with an official seal. The routine over, it hit him. He was booking Pops into the morgue. The bastard who had tormented Uncle Mike, sent mock funeral wreaths to Aunt Sally, spread the word around town that Mike and Sally's son would be kidnapped. The son of a bitch who had his people phone Sally late at night, when Mike was out on the job, whispering that Mike Pauloski was in the morgue. Well, now Papalia was in the morgue. And Korol was doing the honors. He reached for his cell.

"Aunt Sally? It's Warren. How're you doin'?" He grinned broadly. "You'll never guess what I'm doing right now, Aunt Sally." She had always been a feisty woman, and still was. She could tell something was up, but said nothing. "I'm puttin' John Papalia in the morgue. I had to call. I bet Uncle Mike is looking down on me right now."

"I don't know what to say," Sally replied. "Other than it's about time."

Warren Korol walked out of the hospital. The day was gray. He walked under the ceiling of cloud that faintly glowed silver with diffused light, the smell of damp grass and earth coming to life. A warm, firm wind tousled his hair.

* * *

Dhillon was not a practicing Sikh. If he had ever embraced Sikhism's tenets, he had abandoned them early in his life. Born in northern India 500 years ago, the religion rejected the multiple gods and entrenched caste system of Hinduism. But both religions share a belief in reincarnation and karma. For Sikhs, the soul begins in God and the mission is for one's soul to return to be with Him, while at death the body returns to the earth. The souls of those who live a noble life, or strive for it, may return to

God. The souls of those who live a dishonorable life will instead plunge back into the cycle of existence, the true hell on earth, reincarnated in a form other than human. The souls of the most evil people will end up in a snake, perhaps, or worse, a nonliving form. The cycle will repeat many times over until one day the soul is given another chance within a human being. True believers know where Sukhwinder Dhillon's soul will go upon his death. The snake, certainly, or perhaps a stone, embedded in the cold earth, beyond light's reach.

As for the desired earthly destination for many Punjabi Sikhs, Canada remains coveted. That journey ended tragically for Parvesh Dhillon. But then the true believer knows her soul will take a much different route than her husband's. Parvesh's story on earth came to an end in the Punjab one day not long after her death, at Kiratpur Sahib on the warm, emerald-green waters of the Sutlej River. The Sutlej is where the last rites of the three Sikh gurus were once performed, and Kiratpur Sahib is, along with the Golden Temple in Amritsar, the holiest of places for Sikhs, the place where the ashes of their dead are brought. Sikhs reverently visit the white temple there, and the watery resting place for the ashes of their people. Parvesh's parents brought her ashes here. As it happened, both of them were less than two years from their own final trip to the river; their daughter's sudden death had sapped their life force.

Had Parvesh never left the Punjab, she might have lived to old age, her green-blue eyes watching her children grow, witnessing the tug of war between old customs and the modern world. And, had she lived and died in India, her body would have burned in a traditional funeral pyre, flames igniting the banyan and ashok logs stacked around her. The heat of the pyre would not have been nearly as intense as that of a modern crematory oven, and there would have been no mechanized pulverizing of the bones afterward.

After a traditional cremation, family members go to the Sutlej. The first bag, containing chunks of bone, is emptied into the water, splashing rudely. From the second bag come the charred ashes, coarse bunches of them. But Parvesh had made it to Canada, the land of the golden dream. She had the benefit of a Western cremation.

Scott Gardner

The Sutlej River at Kiratpur Sahib

And so, from the low bridge at Kiratpur Sahib, her father opened the bag, allowing fine, pale ash to float down, dotting the water like raindrops, or touching the surface with the gentleness of rose petals, then floating slowly downstream. If God truly wrote Parvesh's story, that wasn't the end, not quite. The tiniest particles paused in the thick air, then whisked into another dimension of time and space by tropical winds, east over Chandigarh. They floated up higher still, into the dry air and blue skies of the Himalayan foothills that ring her homeland, over the rolling green ridges and silver waterfalls near Simla, before finally descending again onto the trees below, to be stirred on occasion when the breeze blew strong.

Epilogue

March 2008
Hamilton, Ont.

Warren Korol strode along King Street downtown, trench coat collar turned against a cold wind. Years back as a young uniformed cop, Korol drank coffee all day, then one day, tired of the habit, ripped the lifeline out, quit cold turkey for years. Today he stepped into the Jet Café and ordered a cup.

He had been 35 years old when he started chasing Dhillon as a detective and was now 47, had marked his birthday a few weeks earlier. Even with 50 in his sights, he was far from the picture of a jaded, faded cop. The hair had grayed but was still full, Korol kept it tight on the sides, short on top. The blue eyes were framed by a smooth face that defied the years, and he had dropped several pounds to 215 since getting into serious running. Planned to enter his first 30-km Around the Bay road race in Hamilton, followed by a longer marathon in Ottawa.

"I'm still in the Clydesdale class," he said with a grin. "We're not breakin' any records or anything. But running has done a lot for me."

He is now Inspector Warren Korol, has held that title with Hamilton Police for five years. The last two he's worked as chief executive officer in the office of the chief. Korol has enjoyed the post, but misses investigative work, hoped to return to more of it in the spring when he was to be moved to a position as inspector with the downtown patrol branch. While his professional life moved ahead at a brisk clip after sending Dhillon to prison, his personal life has not always been tidy. But through it all his greatest source of pride remains maximizing time with his children, working together with ex-wife, Charlayne, to bring them up. The pair are often seen sitting together at their kids' ball games.

Korol took a sip of his coffee, thought more about the bond he and Charlayne share, and the kids—and this is the one thing that gets to him, the ice under his skin melting now, face flushing, eyes tearing. Anything to do with the kids, he can't help it, it chokes him up. He paused a long while, gathering his composure. "We continue to care about one another. Our number-one thought is raising our children."

The Dhillon investigation, and the media attention from his role in it, did little to hurt Warren Korol's rise in the police service. It was the case of a lifetime and, no matter what he does, the experience will always stand out in his career. It was also a high point for his old partner, Kevin Dhinsa. But for Dhinsa, the road after was not nearly as smooth.

Dhinsa was convicted of drunk driving in 2003 and was demoted. And then, later, 12 women—11 officers and one civilian employee—filed workplace harassment allegations against him. As of March 2008, he was suspended without pay because of that controversy. None of it, of course, alters what Dhinsa accomplished in the Dhillon investigation. When Dhillon's second and final murder conviction was announced in court, there was one name the killer took in vain: Dhinsa. He had played a crucial role in the case, and a difficult one. From the beginning, he was the one who couldn't dissociate himself from it entirely, leave it at work. As a member of Hamilton's Sikh community, dealing with witnesses, some of whom knew members of his own family, it was a difficult situation, especially early on. He received threatening phone calls. Dhinsa handled it all with courage and grace. So much happened while justice ran its course. His father and sister died, his wife gave birth to a son. But at the end of it all, Dhinsa took great pride in helping lock Dhillon up.

Another player involved in the Dhillon investigation who met with far more controversy was Dr. Charles Smith. The man who exhumed Dhillon's dead twin sons in India, a once-renowned pediatric forensic pathologist, had his reputation taken to the woodshed at a public enquiry, where it was learned that he had botched 20 death investigations, sometimes resulting in false convictions. As it happened, his work on the exhumation of the twins was not part of that inquiry, and Dhillon's alleged murder of those babies never made it to court. For Brent Bentham and Tony Leitch, the Crown attorneys who prosecuted Dhillon, that was probably a good thing. If the Crown had somehow hung part

of its case against Dhillon on the twins' murders—and therefore
Smith's work—his subsequent disgrace would have been fuel for
Dhillon's appeal.

Dhillon filed his appeal soon after his convictions, but as of
the spring of 2008, it had still not been heard at the Ontario Appeal Court in Toronto. He retained a stubborn belief that he would
somehow be found innocent in the end, but those familiar with the
case know that he does not have much ground on which to stand.
He was tried on the murders of Parvesh and Ranjit separately, the
presiding judge kept damning evidence about Dhillon's scheming
and murderous behavior from two juries, and yet they still convicted him. His convictions seem as appeal-proof as they come.

Tony Leitch, now 42, keeps a busy schedule prosecuting high-
profile murder cases, and his work of late includes a special assignment to work an ongoing, exhaustive case in Toronto in which
police corruption is the focus. He says he aspires to one day work
as a head Crown. And an appointment as a judge some day? He's
not going to jinx that by even talking about it. As for the Dhillon
case, he will never forget it, a young prosecutor having the opportunity to work the case of a lifetime, along with the team of
Korol, Dhinsa, and Bentham.

"No doubt I'll never do another strychnine poisoning case,"
he said. "It was an amazing case. And it remains the best cocktail
party story I have."

As for Bentham—"the best Crown in Hamilton," in Leitch's
words—the lead prosecutor in the case, true to form, says little.
Friends say he does not covet a judgeship or head Crown position.
It is not part of his wiring. He prefers mucking in the trenches,
putting offenders in jail, and saying little about it. For the taciturn
Bentham, one has to read between the lines when considering the
impact of the Dhillon case. The walls in his office downtown had
always remained bare, absolutely nothing hanging, no framed
citations, no newspaper clippings from one of the most storied
prosecution careers in Hamilton; no personal photos or art of any
kind. At work Bentham has never adorned, commemorated, or
celebrated, as though glancing at the past and savoring it even for
a moment would take the edge off his performance.

Today, there is one exception. One day, long after the Dhillon case had been put to bed, Tony Leitch walked into his colleague's office. Tony had mounted a full page from *The Hamilton Spectator*, a spread from the series on the case called "Poison" that had caused a big stir in the city during its five-week run in the newspaper. He had one made for Brent as well. But Bentham, true to form, ignored it, and the board sat on the floor in his office, leaning against a wall for the longest time. But eventually, somehow, it found its way onto a hook. To this day it's the only thing hanging on Brent Bentham's wall.

* * *

Warren Korol nurses his coffee. Does he still think about the case? It crosses his mind quite often, and that includes each time he pulls one of the custom-made suits he had ordered from the Punjab out of the closet, or grabs some Indian takeout at the restaurant on Main Street he frequents. He had never really eaten Indian cuisine before the big trip, but over there he developed a taste for the spices, samosas, curries. He'd love to make a return journey to India someday— under more relaxed circumstances this time. He still meets on occasion with Bentham and Leitch, to bounce ideas off them or just for a beer. They all became so close during the trials. The bond will always be there.

As for the appeal, Korol isn't concerned about it getting any- where. But if it does see the light of day, he's more than ready to get back in court again. In the end he never could fathom Sukhwinder Dhillon. Korol had always believed some people are simply funda- mentally good, and that Parvesh was one of those people. Dhillon? How could he have it in him to do the things he did, especially to his wife, a good and beautiful person like her? Korol was unable to answer his own question. All he could ever really conclude was that Dhillon was an evil man, pure and simple.

But in the days and months after Dhillon was shipped off to prison for life, while Korol took pride in a job well done, his thoughts focused not on the killer, but the kids, Parvesh's daugh- ters, Harpreet and Aman. It kept playing over and over again in his mind. The young girls had watched their mother die, were called to testify in the murder trial against their father, and then seen him locked away. And Korol was the one who put him there. It got to him. How could two young girls deal with that? He was not a religious guy, but Korol prayed for the girls. Ultimately, a few years down the road, he heard the best news of all. The girls had continued growing up in the house in east Hamilton, raised by a guardian, and Harpreet recently graduated from McMaster University, in nursing, and at the top of her class. She is now 23 and went overseas to do work, enrich her education. Aman, 20, the younger daughter, is still attending McMaster and doing very well also. Successful young women.

Out of all the ugliness, the death, the lies, Korol thought, came something good, a happy ending of sorts. He smiled. All the obstacles thrown their way, he reflected, it would have been easy for Parvesh's daughters to lose it all, to grow up bitter at the world, but they rose above it, became good people. The kids were going to be okay. It made him feel—settled. Yes. Warren Korol took a final sip of coffee, rose from the chair, buttoned his trench coat, and marched back to the police station.